D1595638

THE I TATTI
RENAISSANCE LIBRARY

James Hankins, General Editor

POLIZIANO

GREEK AND LATIN POETRY

ITRL 86

ANGELO POLIZIANO
◆ ◆ ◆
GREEK AND LATIN POETRY

EDITED AND TRANSLATED BY

PETER E. KNOX

THE I TATTI RENAISSANCE LIBRARY

HARVARD UNIVERSITY PRESS

CAMBRIDGE, MASSACHUSETTS

LONDON, ENGLAND

2018

Series design by Dean Bornstein

Library of Congress Cataloging-in-Publication Data

Names: Poliziano, Angelo, 1454–1494, author. | Knox, Peter E., editor,
translator.
Title: Greek and Latin poetry / edited and translated by Peter E. Knox.
Other titles: I Tatti Renaissance library ; 86.
Description: Cambridge, Massachusetts : Harvard University Press, 2019. |
Series: I Tatti Renaissance library ; 86 | Includes bibliographical references and
index. | Text in Greek or Latin with English translation on facing pages ;
introduction and notes in English.
Identifiers: LCCN 2017047330 | ISBN 9780674984578 (alk. paper)
Classification: LCC PQ4630.P5 A6 2018 | DDC 871/.04 — dc23
LC record available at https://lccn.loc.gov/2017047330

Contents

☙❧

Introduction   vii

GREEK AND LATIN POETRY

Introduction

꧁ ꧂

For a young man looking to make his way in the world of fifteenth-century Italy, one of the most promising paths to fame and, if not fortune, at least a comfortable life, was literature. That was the path pursued by Angelo Ambrogini, who was born in 1454 in Montepulciano, the city in Tuscany from which he would later take the name by which he became known to history, Poliziano, or in its latinized form, Politianus. His family was one of the most prominent of the city, but in 1464 when Poliziano was only ten, tragedy struck when his father, Benedetto Ambrogini, an eminent jurist, was murdered in a blood feud with another local family. The event clearly precipitated a critical turning point in the future poet's upbringing, but curiously it is one that he nowhere refers to in his surviving works. It is nonetheless clear from Poliziano's declarations of poverty in his early poetry that the family suffered financially as a consequence of his father's death, a situation that one would naturally infer in any case, given the circumstances of the times. And so it was that at some point in the following years, but certainly before 1469, Poliziano, the eldest of five children, was sent to Florence to live with a cousin, Cino di Matteo Ambrogini, there to complete his studies.[1]

During this time Poliziano's personal circumstances were modest, but he managed nonetheless to attend lectures in the Florentine Studio by the leading scholars of the day. He studied Greek with John Argyropoulos and Andronicus Callistus, both prominent members of the Byzantine diaspora that intensified after the fall of Constantinople in 1453.[2] Argyropoulos taught Greek in Florence until 1471, when he departed for Rome upon the elevation of Pope Sixtus IV, with whom he had become acquainted earlier during a stay in Padua. In Florence, Poliziano frequented his lectures on Aristotle, referring to the Byzantine later in his *Miscellanea* as *Argyropylus ille Byzantius, olim praeceptor in philosophia noster*. In 1473 Poliziano addressed two epigrams in Greek (*Epigr. Gr.* 11–12) to his teacher after he had decamped to Rome, one of them the earliest epigram of the Italian Renaissance composed in the Doric dialect, clearly a bravura display of technical expertise by the pupil for the benefit of his former teacher. Of greater consequence to Poliziano's early formation as a poet, however, was his attendance at lectures on the *Iliad* by Callistus, who succeeded Argyropoulos at the Florentine Studio in 1471.[3] In the *Elegy to Fonzio*, Poliziano recalls the courses that he attended on Aristotle, Homer, and Demosthenes (193–98):

> Rursus in Andronici doctum me confero ludum,
> Qui tumidi nodos laxat Aristotelis
> Smyrnaeique docet iucunda poemata vatis:
> Iam populat Graias Dardana flamma rates.
> Fulminei posthac aperit Demosthenis artem,
> Aequiparat nostri quem Ciceronis opus.

Again I go to the learned school of Andronicus, who unties the knots of Aristotle's obscurities, and instructs me in the sweet poems of Smyrna's bard: already he has reached part where the Trojans destroy the Greek ships with flame. Afterward he expounds upon the brilliant technique of Demosthenes, for whom the works of our very own Cicero are a match.

It is also likely that Callistus introduced him to the epigrams of the Greek Anthology compiled by the thirteenth-century Byzantine scholar Maximus Planudes.[4] Poliziano copied a selection of epigrams from a manuscript that Callistus brought with him from Padua when he relocated to Florence in 1471.[5] The impact of this collection on the impressionable mind of the still seventeen-year-old Poliziano cannot be overestimated. It was his studies in Greek poetry in general, and Homer in particular, that provided the stimulus to Poliziano's literary instincts, propelling him at a precocious age into the limelight of Florence's thriving intellectual scene.

It was in the years from about 1470 to the middle of the decade that the young poet began to attract the attention of powerful patrons with his compositions in Latin and Greek. His major project during this period was a translation of Homer's *Iliad* into Latin hexameters, the work that led Marsilio Ficino to refer to him as *homericum illum adolescentem* in a letter to Lorenzo de' Medici (*Epist.* 1.17). Poliziano consciously formulated his project as a continuation of the translation by Carlo Marsuppini (1398–1453), a noted humanist and Medici loyalist, later chancellor of Florence. He had been commissioned by Pope Nicholas V in 1452 to translate the *Iliad*, but at his death in 1453 had completed only Book 1. Probably from the first Poliziano conceived of the translation as the means to attract a patron, and in that respect it was a resounding success.

Homer's poem served as the vehicle to extol Lorenzo de' Medici's civic, artistic, and martial accomplishments, the last of which were on display in his victory in a ceremonial joust held in 1469 in the Piazza di Santa Croce. Poliziano highlights that event in the dedication that accompanied Book 2, written not long afterward, probably in 1470:

> O cui Tyrrheni florentia signa leonis
> Sullanamque urbem et sancti decreta senatus
> Commisere dei, Laurenti maxime, gentis
> Maeoniae, serpunt geminae cui tempora circum
> Aoniae laurus; nam seu tibi munera Martis
> Sint animo, effusis ageres sublimis habenis

Cornipedem toto cedentes aequore turmas
Impellens, meminit simulacra ingentia pugnae
Area magna Crucis, cum te, sublime volantem,
Fundentemque equites, et magno robore duras
Miscentem pugnas, clipeos galeasque ruentem,
Elato spectabat ovans Florentia vultu.

O magnificent Lorenzo, the gods of Homer's race have entrusted to you the flourishing standards of the Tuscan lion,
the city founded by Sulla, and the conduct of its sacred senate, and round your brow runs the Muses' laurel. For the
Piazza Santa Croce commemorates the mighty tournament,
when your thoughts turned to the works of Mars, as you
rode astride your stallion at full gallop, driving before you
the troops retreating over the entire plain. Florence cheered
with joy as she watched you flying on high, routing the other
knights, powerfully joining the harsh battles, smashing helmets and shields.

The success of his *Iliad* secured Poliziano employment as a secretary to Agnolo della Stufa, a prominent adherent of the Medici
faction in Florence. And by 1473, with the appearance of Book 3,
it earned him a place in Lorenzo's household, in the imposing
Medici palace on the Via Larga. Translations of Books 4 and 5
followed, but by 1475 Poliziano had abandoned the project, as his
adventurous poetic talent led him down different literary avenues.[6]
By that time, in fact, the project had served its purpose: Lorenzo
had appointed Poliziano as tutor to his oldest son, Piero, and his
future, at the age of twenty-one, seemed secure.

In the years following his acceptance into the Medici household, Poliziano continued his classical studies, focusing in particular on the poetry of Catullus, Martial, and Statius. His own poetic
production during those years was increasingly directed toward

independently inspired compositions, not translation. Many of the Latin poems later collected in the *Book of Epigrams* date from the early seventies, although there is no evidence that at the time of their composition Poliziano contemplated ever publishing them. The same may be said of the poems in the *Book of Greek Epigrams* that date from this period. But two major poems of 1473 gave some indication of the direction his literary interests were heading. In the *Elegy to Fonzio*, Poliziano in 127 discursively formulated couplets addresses his slightly older contemporary, Bartolomeo Fonzio, on his literary and philological pursuits. The poem ranges over the literary scene of the day before turning to Poliziano's own vicissitudes. His interest in translating Homer had not necessarily waned, but his taste for variety was taking him into different realms of poetic activity, since, as he put it (136–37), "the dishes of a varied table are pleasing, and grasses gleam more sweetly when mixed with flowers."

With the *Elegy for Albiera*, Poliziano sought out a larger stage. The poem commemorates Albiera degli Albizzi, the fifteen-year-old fiancée of Sigismondo della Stufa, a close associate of Lorenzo de' Medici, who died on the eve of her wedding on July 14, 1473. Poliziano's elegy formed part of a larger enterprise, an anthology of works in prose and poetry assembled in honor of the deceased. Participants in the volume included some of the most prominent names in the Medici orbit—Naldo Naldi, Ugolino Verino, Bartolomeo Fonzio, Marsilio Ficino, Alessandro Braccesi, Andronicus Callistus, Bartolomeo Scala, and others.[7] In what we should recognize as a characteristic move, Poliziano's contribution is by far the longest, a demonstration that the now nineteen-year-old young man not only belonged in this august company, he dominated it. The result is a tour de force combining influences from a startling variety of classical sources. Not only the poets who attracted him at the moment, especially Statius in his *Silvae*, but scientific and medical texts, upon which he drew for his portrayal of the personified Fever that kills the girl.[8]

In 1475 with his position in the Medici household now secured, Poliziano's career took a new turn, away from poetic composition in Greek and Latin. His affiliation with the Medici deepened, as he assumed the positions of tutor to Lorenzo's eldest son, Piero, born February 15, 1472, and private secretary to Lorenzo himself. At the same time, and surely not entirely by coincidence, his poetic efforts inclined increasingly to compositions in the vernacular. With his Homeric project now definitely abandoned, Poliziano took as his inspiration contemporary Florence, which forms the setting for the masterpiece of his younger years, the *Stanze*, composed in octaves commemorating the victory of Lorenzo's younger brother Giuliano in a joust that took place on January 28, 1475. Giuliano is the protagonist, together with the celebrated beauty Simonetta Cattaneo, the wife of Marco Vespucci and the object of adoration by both the Medici brothers.[9] The death of the young and beautiful Simonetta later in the spring of 1476 ignited a spark in Poliziano, who drew upon the same resources of imagination that had manifested themselves in his *Elegy for Albiera* two years earlier. Combining classical allusion with traditional elements of courtly poetry in the vernacular, Poliziano conjures up a supernatural atmosphere of heroic virtues colored by tragedy. It was against this background that in the same year, 1476, Poliziano penned for Lorenzo the influential introductory epistle to the *Raccolta aragonese*, an anthology of Italian poetry dedicated to Federico of Aragon. During these years Poliziano continued to compose occasional verse in Latin—elegies, epigrams, and odes—as one would expect of a man of letters in this period, but his interest in Greek epigrams had waned. And Poliziano may well have been on a path to becoming a figure of even greater transformational importance in Italian literature, had not events of a different sort intervened.

By the spring of 1478 Poliziano was firmly established as a leading figure in the Medicean entourage. As Lorenzo's personal secretary and tutor to his son, and with more sons on the way, Poliziano's position was secure, as was his financial situation with the concession to him of income from the priorate of San Paolo, thanks to Medici influence. But opposition to the Medici regime, which had never been absent, exploded on April 26 of that year, when supporters of the opposition party, led by members of the rival Pazzi family, attempted the assassination of Lorenzo and his brother Giuliano in the cathedral of Florence, Santa Maria del Fiore. The conspiracy failed in its objectives when Lorenzo managed to escape the would-be assassins with only a wound to the neck. He and a few of his entourage managed to barricade themselves in the sacristy with a few adherents, among them Poliziano. But Giuliano was killed before the altar, and chaos erupted in Florence.[10]

In the ensuing struggle between Lorenzo and his enemies, who were backed by Pope Sixtus IV, Poliziano contributed as only a scholar could. He penned a Medici propaganda piece, the *Coniurationis commentarium*, on the Pazzi conspiracy, modeled on the Roman historian Sallust's *De Catilinae coniuratione*. Open warfare broke out in the summer of that year when Ferrante of Aragon launched an assault on Florence. Poliziano was evacuated from the city, together with his two charges, Piero and his younger brother, Giovanni—the future Pope Leo X—and their mother, Clarice Orsini. For the remainder of 1478 they shuttled among Medici estates, but the already existing tensions between Poliziano and Lorenzo's wife were only exacerbated by this situation. She was unhappy with Poliziano as tutor to her children, and in May 1479 she engineered his ouster from the Medici household at Cafaggiolo. Later in the year, on December 6, when Lorenzo left Florence for Naples on a dangerous mission to conclude a treaty with Ferrante of Aragon, Poliziano did not accompany him. Instead, he left Florence and embarked upon a series of visits to some of the centers of learning of northern Italy—Venice, Padua, Mantua, and Verona.

But if Poliziano was contemplating a transfer to another locale—and we do not know for certain that he was—he soon repented of the idea. Although he had been well received during his peregrination and had made good use of the opportunity to make the acquaintance of some of the most celebrated humanists of northern Italy, the attractions of Florence soon beckoned again. Lorenzo returned to the city in triumph in March 1480, and in a famous letter, known as his *Apology*, Poliziano implored his former patron to receive him back.[11] In August Poliziano returned to Florence, and although he was not reinstalled in the Medici household, he did return to a significant position. With Lorenzo's backing he was appointed as Professor of Rhetoric and Poetry in the Florentine Studio, where he soon began to offer courses of study. And soon thereafter he was restored to the position of tutor to Lorenzo's sons. It was probably in the months leading up to his return that Poliziano composed the bizarre *Silva on Scabies*, another virtuoso performance in Latin elegiacs. Drawing on a wide variety of disparate sources, including Ovid, Statius, Vergil, and Seneca, Poliziano describes a horrific wasting disease that has afflicted him. The disease is probably a macabre metaphor for the folly that led to his break with Clarice Orsini and subsequently Lorenzo himself. The cure was his new position as a scholar primarily, and not a poet, except in the service of his scholarship, and this change in his situation at the still young age of twenty-six marks the end of a brilliant period of creative activity.

From the year of his first appointment to the Studio until his death in 1494, Poliziano's poetic output was intimately connected with his researches as a scholar. His four *Silvae*—the title was an homage to Statius, one of his favorite classical authors—are verse introductions in Latin hexameters to his lectures at the Studio.

Lecture courses on Vergil's *Eclogues* (1482–83), Vergil's *Georgics* and the Hesiodic *Works and Days* (1483), and Homer's *Iliad* (1485), were each accompanied by the publication of three of the *Silvae*. The last poem in the collection, the *Nutricia*, is devoted not to any one course of study, but to the art of poetry itself. It was composed in 1486 with a different title than the published version and dedicated to Matthias Corvinus, king of Hungary, himself a cultivated man of letters and patron of scholars.[12]

During this last phase of his life and career, Poliziano continued to compose some occasional verse, which was later collected in the *Book of Epigrams*. For example, in 1488 he composed a verse prologue for a performance of Plautus' *Menaechmi* staged in the church of San Lorenzo on May 12. The composition had been requested by his friend, Paolo di Giovanni Comparini da Prato, canon at the church, and was performed before an audience that included Lorenzo de' Medici. In his prologue Poliziano criticizes earlier Renaissance attempts at comedy and takes the critics of ancient comedy to task. This is among the latest manifestations of Poliziano's interest in the poetry of Greece and Rome, as his attention was increasingly drawn to Aristotle and philosophy. The publication of the first "century" of the *Miscellanea*, a collection of short philological studies of problems of exegesis in ancient texts, secured his reputation as a scholar. A second "century" of the *Miscellanea* was never completed, interrupted either by Poliziano's death or by his ever-diverging interests.[13] Philosophy was the reigning passion of the last five years of his life, and there is some reason to believe that during those years Poliziano himself gave thought to the idea of setting a final seal upon his career as a poet.

Poliziano published little of his poetry himself. Uniquely, the *Silvae* were printed after their public performances at the Studio, with the exception of the *Nutricia*, the final poem in the series. The original composition was probably never delivered to its intended dedicatee, Matthias Corvinus, who died in 1490. Five years after its composition, the poem was published in 1491, like its predecessors, at the press of Antonio Miscomini in Florence. It bore a new title, *Nutricia*, and was offered to a new dedicatee, Cardinal Antoniotto Gentili. But none of the creative works of his youth had yet appeared in print, when something spurred Poliziano to tend to his posterity in 1494, the last year of his life as it transpired. Perhaps it was the death of his patron, Lorenzo de' Medici, in the spring of 1492, an event commemorated by Poliziano in a famous letter to the humanist Jacopo Antiquari (*Epist.* 4.2), that triggered such thoughts.[14] Poliziano was at Lorenzo's deathbed together with his close friend, the philosopher Pico della Mirandola, and Savonarola, the Dominican friar whose role in the Florentine republic was becoming increasingly prominent and problematic.[15] Whatever the impetus, by 1494 Poliziano had formed the intention to collect and publish the great bulk of his poetical writings in Latin and Greek.

Poliziano was surely aware of the impending publication of the *Anthologia Planudea* by his rival Janus Lascaris, which appeared on August 15, 1494. In the last months of his life, Poliziano studied this edition, but he had already resumed the composition of epigrams in Greek, presumably in anticipation of this event. And to demonstrate his mastery of the genre, he had collected and arranged his earlier Greek poetry for publication, as he relates in a letter of June 1494 addressed to Antonio Urceo (*Epist.* 5.7):

> I have composed what is for all intents and purposes a little book of Greek epigrams, which my friends often urge me to publish. And they say that it will be not only to the glory of the Latins (for so they flatter me), but to the glory of the age altogether, if I, a man of Latin, awaken the Greek Muses that have been sleeping now for so long. For not one poem written by a Greek within these past six hundred years is to be found that can be read with patience. However, it is said

that today there are one or two persons who are making some attempt, although nothing is yet on view. For the purpose, therefore, of calling out or provoking these very persons, the thought occurred to me of publishing this book of mine, such as it is, as long as you don't disagree. You see, in this matter I want to have your unvarnished opinion in full. And so, either this little book will meet with the approval of those same persons who are thought to be working on their own compositions, and for that very reason I will be the recipient of altogether great fame; or it will be criticized and they will themselves then perhaps write something better, and so I will be well received on precisely that account.

Poliziano did not live to see this book through to publication. The same fate befell his other projects. The completion of the planned edition of his correspondence was announced in a letter of May 23, 1494, to his former pupil, Piero de' Medici.[16] But like the rest of his works, the letters did not appear in print until the publication of Poliziano's collected works in Greek and Latin, printed at the Venetian press of Aldo Manuzio in 1498.[17] A second collection of *Miscellanea* was left unfinished at his death, a further indication perhaps that Poliziano was now wholly devoted to his scholarly interests in philosophy. He was also planning an edition of his Latin epigrams during that year,[18] a more complicated task than the Greek collection because of the greater scope and variety of his compositions in Latin; but it too was never completed and published during the author's lifetime.

Poliziano died in Florence on the night of September 28, 1494, in circumstances that remain mysterious. In the aftermath, his enemies, who were not few, disseminated various unflattering diagnoses of the cause.[19] Militating against some of the more scandalous stories is the fact that, with Savonarola's approval, Poliziano was interred in the Church of San Marco wearing a Dominican habit. His close friend Pico della Mirandola died only a few weeks later, on November 17, and was buried nearby. That date marked the end of an era in Florentine humanism, when the French king Charles the VIII entered the city and put an end to the Medici regime.[20] Angelo Poliziano was perhaps its most characteristic representative, encompassing in his genius not only the qualities of a preeminent scholar but also the creative energies of a classically inspired poet. In the tumultuous years that followed, his papers were dispersed and his legacy imperiled, to be rescued only by the intervention of his executors, Pietro Crinito and Alessandro Sarti, who delivered his Greek and Latin works to Aldo Manuzio for publication. The texts in this volume are largely the fruit of their devotion.

I am very grateful to Nigel Wilson for his suggestions on the text, which are acknowledged in the notes, as well as for many other corrections and helpful comments. Francesco Bausi kindly made a number of bibliographical suggestions. In addition, the series editor, James Hankins, has improved this volume in every respect, in addition to rescuing it from numerous errors, for which I wish to offer thanks without implicating him in any that remain.

NOTES

1. For the details of Poliziano's early life, see Emilo Bigi's entry in *DBI* 2 (1960); for a somewhat more diverting, anecdotal account, Del Lungo, *Florentia*, is still worth consulting. There is a very useful biographical sketch in Bausi's introduction to his edition of Poliziano's *Poesie* (2006), 53–60. (Full references to editions and studies referred to in the notes to this volume may be found in the Bibliography; see also the abbreviations at the start of the Notes to the Translation.)

2. On the careers of Argyropoulos and Andronicus, in addition to the entries by Bigi in *DBI* 4 (1962) and 3 (1962), see Wilson, *From Byzantium to Italy*, 99–103, 131–34.

3. On Poliziano's education in Greek and continuing interests in translation and exegesis, Wilson, *From Byzantium to Italy*, 115–28.

4. The larger collection in the Palatine Anthology (Heidelberg, Universitätsbibliothek MS Pal. Gr. 23, and Paris, Bibliothèque Nationale de France, MS Suppl. Gr. 384) was not discovered until the end of the sixteenth century, and its contents were unknown to Poliziano and his contemporaries; see Cameron, *The Greek Anthology*, 178–201.

5. Poliziano's copy survives as Vatican City, Biblioteca Apostolica Vaticana, MS Vat. gr. 1373. On its source in Florence, Biblioteca Medicea Laurenziana, Plut. 31.28, see Mioni, "L'Anthologia Planudea."

6. On Poliziano's translation of the *Iliad*, see Maïer, *Ange Politien*, 83–98, and Rubinstein, "Imitation and Style."

7. On this anthology, see Patetta, "Una raccolta manoscritta," and Perosa, *Studi*, 2:189–94.

8. On Poliziano's literary sources in the personification, see Perosa, "Febris," and Orvieto, *Poliziano e l'ambiente mediceo*, 194–204.

9. It is possible that that an idealized version of her features was used by Botticelli in his female images of the 1470s, including *The Birth of Venus;* see David Alan Brown, et al., *Virtue and Beauty: Leonardo's Ginevra de'Benci and Renaissance Portraits of Women* (Princeton: Princeton University Press and National Gallery of Art, Washington DC, 2001), 180–85.

10. On the Pazzi conspiracy and the events of that turbulent time, see Martines, *April Blood*.

11. Edited by Maïer in Poliziano, *Opera omnia* (1970–71), 3:551–61.

12. See the edition by Charles Fantazzi in this I Tatti Renaissance Library (Cambridge, MA: Harvard University Press, 2004).

13. See the edition of Branca and Stocchi (1972). An edition of both centuries is in progress from this I Tatti Renaissance Library.

14. Edited by Shane Butler in Poliziano's *Letters* (Cambridge, MA: Harvard University Press, 2006), 1:226–50.

15. On Savonarola and subsequent events, see Polizzotto, *The Elect Nation*.

16. See the edition in Del Lungo, 85.

17. Aldus' preface to the edition may be found in Manutius, *Humanism and the Latin Classics*, edited by John N. Grant (Cambridge, MA: Harvard University Press, 2017), 182–87.

18. Writing to Antonio Zeno, probably in the summer of 1494, Poliziano says, "I am not sending you my [Latin] epigrams because I am planning to publish them soon together with the Greek."

19. The testimonia are collected by Del Lungo, *Florentia*, 255–79. In 2007 the bodies of Poliziano and Pico della Mirandola were exhumed, and press reports in 2008 that toxic levels of arsenic were discovered in the bones of both men lend some credibility to the suspicion that Poliziano's one-time student Piero de' Medici had had them poisoned.

20. On cultural developments in Florence in the years immediately before and after the death of Lorenzo de' Medici, see Godman, *From Poliziano to Machiavelli*.

GREEK AND LATIN POETRY

ANGELI POLITIANI ELEGIA, SIVE EPICEDION IN ALBIERAE ALBICIAE IMMATURUM EXITUM AD SISMVNDUM STUPHAM EIVS SPONSUM

Et merito (quis enim tantum perferre dolorem,
    Aut quis iam miseris temperet a lacrimis?),
Sed tamen, heu, frustra crudelia sidera damnas,
    Sismunde, et frustra numina surda vocas!
5   Pro dolor! A, quantos rapta pro coniuge fletus
    Ingeminas! Quanto perluis imbre genas!
Sollicitasque pios fratres miserumque parentem,
    Inque tuo tota est vulnere nigra domus.
Nigra domus tota est, flent maesti ad limina cives,
10   Flent socii lacrimis et tua damna piis.
Ipse ego qui dudum reges magno ore canebam,
    Dardanaque Argolica Pergama rapta manu,
Heu, nil dulce sonans taceo iam bella tubasque,
    Et refero ad nigros carmina maesta rogos!
15   Ac tecum, infaustus vates, consortia luctus
    En repeto, et querulam pectine pango lyram!
Nec, Sismunde, tuos gemitus aegrumque dolorem
    Arceo: sunt lacrimis funera digna piis.
Maius habes vulnus secreto in pectore, quam quo
20   Te deceat madidas non habuisse genas.
Nam poteras dudum nulli invidisse deorum,
    Dum subiit velis aura secunda tuis.
Nunc, ubi dira suum vertit Fortuna tenorem,
    Uxor abest, animae portio magna tuae.

AN ELEGY, OR RATHER
A FUNERAL LAMENT,
BY ANGELO POLIZIANO UPON THE
PREMATURE DEATH OF ALBIERA
DEGLI ALBIZZI[1] FOR SIGISMONDO
DELLA STUFA,[2] HER BETROTHED

Yes, it is right (for who could endure a grief so great,[3] or refrain
from bitter tears?), but, alas, Sigismondo, it is futile all the same
to blame the cruelty of the stars and futile, too, to call upon the
inexorable gods! Oh, the pain! Ah, how great the lamentations 5
you repeat for the wife taken from you! How great the rain of
tears that washes over your cheeks! Your devoted brothers and
your unhappy father are worried about you, and your entire
household is in mourning over your loss.[4] Your entire household is
in mourning, your countrymen weep in sorrow at your threshold,
and your friends shed pious tears at your loss. I myself, who but a 10
short time ago was singing of kings in the high style and the capture of Dardan Pergamum by the band from Argos,[5] alas, now
have nothing to say of wars and calls to battle. But it is not because I sing a sweet song; instead I recite sad poems at a burned-
out pyre. And look, unhappy bard, as I revisit our shared grief 15
with you, and with the plectrum I pluck the plaintive lyre! Sigismondo, I do not mean to keep you from the pains of mourning
and grief: this death calls for pious tears. The wound that you
harbor in the depths of your heart is so great that it would not be 20
right for you to have dry cheeks. Not long ago you could not have
envied any of the gods, while a favoring breeze filled your sails.
But now that Fortune has cruelly altered her course, your wife, the
greater portion of your soul,[6] is no more. Your wife is no more, 25

3

25 Uxor abest, heu heu, sed qualem nulla tulerunt
    Saecula, sed qualem tempora nulla ferent!
Uni quicquid habet dederat Natura decoris,
    Uni etiam dederat Gratia quicquid habet.
Candor erat dulci suffusus sanguine, qualem
30   Alba ferunt rubris lilia mixta rosis.
Ut nitidum laeti radiabant sidus ocelli:
    Saepe Amor accensas rettulit inde faces.
Solverat effusos quotiens sine lege capillos,
    Infesta est trepidis visa Diana feris.
35 Sive iterum adductos fulvum collegit in aurum,
    Compta Cytheriaco est pectine visa Venus.
Usque illam parvi furtim componere Amores
    Sunt soliti, et facili Gratia blanda manu,
Atque Honor et teneri iam cana Modestia vultus,
40   Et Decor, et Probitas, purpureusque Pudor,
Casta Fides, Risusque hilaris, Moresque pudici,
    Incessusque decens, nudaque Simplicitas.
Quae cuncta in cineres fati gravis intulit hora;
    Mors cuncta inmiti carpsit acerba manu.
45 Occidis, Albiere, prima fraudata iuuenta,
    Exigeres vitae cum tria lustra tuae;
Occidis amborum correpta ante ora parentum,
    Occidis ante tui lumina maesta viri.
A dolor! I nunc, et rebus confide secundis,
50   Quas Fortuna levi fertque refertque manu!
Tolle animum, et victo molire ex hoste triumphos:
    Laurigerum Morti subiciere caput.
Erige Taenareis radiantia tecta columnis:
    Parca tamen rapida te trahet inde manu.
55 Ingenio, formae, validae confide iuventae:
    Albiera ecce gravi morte soluta iacet.

alas, and alas again! But a wife the like of which no generation has borne before, the like of which no age shall bring again! To her alone Nature had given all the beauty in her possession; to her alone Grace too had given her all. Her fair complexion was suffused with a sweet blush, as when white lilies have been mixed with red roses. Her eyes gleamed with joy like a shining star: many times did Love light from them the torches that he carried. Whenever she unbound her hair and let it flow freely, she looked like Diana, the scourge of frightened beasts. If she pulled it back again and gathered it in a golden pin, she looked like Venus arrayed with a comb from Cythera.[7] Little Cupids always used to prepare her in secret, as did alluring Grace with her ready hand; and Honor and Self-Restraint, gray-haired now, but of youthful countenance; and Elegance, Probity, and blushing Modesty, chaste Fidelity, cheerful Laughter, and unassuming Character; and dignified Bearing and naked Sincerity. The heavy hour of fate has brought all this to ashes; bitter Death has torn all this away with his inexorable hand. You die, cheated out of your early youth, Albiera,[8] completing only thrice five years of your life; you die, carried off within the sight of both your parents; you die before the sorrowful eyes of your husband. Ah, the pain! Go now and trust in the prosperity that Fortune's fickle hand both gives and takes away! Lift up your heart, and make ready the triumphs that you've won over your vanquished foe: you'll be Death's minion, though you bear laurels upon your head. Raise up a house resplendent with columns from Taenarus:[9] the swift hand of Fate shall still drag you from it. Place your trust in intellect, beauty, the strength of youth, but consider that Albiera now lies undone by a painful

5

Tu mihi nunc tanti fuerit quae causa doloris,
    Attonito vati, maesta Thalia, refer.
Annua pelliti referentem sacra Iohannis
60   Extulerat roseo Cynthius ore diem,
Cum celebres linquens Sirenum nomine muros,
    Herculeumque petens regia nata torum,
Candida Sullanae vestigia protinus urbi
    Intulerat, longae fessa labore viae.
65 Pro se quisque igitur pueri iuuenesque senesque
    Matresque et tenerae, splendida turba, nurus
Illius adventum celebrant; atque unicus urbis
    Est vultus, festo murmure cuncta fremunt.
Est via (Panthagiam Sullani nomine dicunt):
70   Omnibus hic superis templa dicata micant.
Hic domus aethereas perrumpens Lentia nubes
    Prouehit ad rutilos culmina celsa polos;
Quam prope ridentes submittunt prata colores,
    Pictaque florifero germine vernat humus.
75 Hic, dum cornipedes primi sub carceris oras
    Tyrrhenae expectant signa canora tubae,
Regia nata leves gaudet celebrare choreas,
    Iamque nurus certa bracchia lege movent.
Emicat ante alias vultu pulcherrima nymphas
80   Albiera, et tremulum spargit ab ore iubar.
Aura quatit fusos in candida terga capillos,
    Irradiant dulci lumina nigra face;
Tamque suas vincit comites, quam Lucifer ore
    Purpureo rutilans astra minora premit.
85 Attoniti Albieram spectant iuvenesque senesque;
    Ferreus est quem non forma pudorve mouet.
Mentibus Albieram laetis plausuque secundo,
    Albieram nutu, lumine, voce probant.

death. O sad Thalia,[10] tell me now, your bewildered poet, the reason for a grief so great.

The rosy-faced Cynthian[11] had just brought forth the day that brings back the annual feast of John the Baptist,[12] when the king's daughter, leaving behind the famous walls that take their name from the Sirens on her journey to the bridal bed of Hercules, turned her bright steps straight for Sulla's city, tired from the effort of the long journey.[13] And so, everyone—boys as well as men young and old, mothers and their sons' young wives, a splendid throng—celebrates her arrival, each according to his own; the city wears a single expression, and the clamor of celebratory shouting is everywhere. There is a street that the locals call Borgo Ognissanti:[14] here gleams a church dedicated to all the saints. Here the Palazzo Lenzi breaks through the clouds in the sky above and raises its lofty crests to the glittering pole. Nearby there is a meadow that produces cheerful colors and the ground blooms as if painted with flowering buds.[15] Here, while the stallions wait for the echoing signal from the Tuscan trumpet at the edge of the starting gate, the king's daughter happily joins in light-footed dances, and the young brides now move their arms in tempo. Albiera stands out among the other girls as the most beautiful in appearance and diffuses a tremulous radiance from her face. The breeze stirs the hair spread upon her fair shoulders, her dark eyes gleam with a sweet fire; and she surpasses her companions just as the Evening Star obscures the lesser stars, sparkling with his gleaming visage. Men young and old gaze in astonishment at Albiera; the man who is not moved by her beauty or modesty must be made of iron. With joyful hearts and approving applause, with a nod, a look, a word, they voice their approval of Albiera. The

Vertit in hanc torvos Rhamnusia luminis orbes,
90   Exiguoque movet murmura parva sono.
Tum miserae letale favens, oculisque nitorem
   Adicit, et solito celsius ora levat;
Tantaque perturbans extemplo gaudia, tristem
   Qua pereat virgo, quaerit acerba, viam.
95 Hic Febrim aethereas carpentem prospicit auras,
   Exserere Icarius dum parat ora Canis.
Illam Erebo Noctuque satam comitantur euntem
   Luctusque et tenebris Mors adoperta caput,
Et Gemitus gravis, et Gemitu commixta Querela,
100   Singultusque frequens, Anxietasque ferox,
Et Tremor, et Macies, pavidoque Insania vultu,
   Semper et ardenti pectore anhela Sitis,
Horridus atque Rigor, trepidaeque Insomnia mentis,
   Inconstansque Rubor, terrificusque Pavor.
105 Marmaricique trahunt dominae iuga curva leones,
   Ignea quis rabido murmure corda fremunt.
Vertice diva feras ardenti attollit echidnas,
   Quae saniem Stygio semper ab ore vomunt.
Sanguinei flagrant oculi, cava tempora frigent,
110   Colla madens sudor, pectora pallor obit;
Atque animi interpres liventi lingua veneno
   Manat, et atra quatit feruidus ora vapor,
Spiritus unde grauis taetrum deuoluit odorem.
   Letifera strident guttura plena face,
115 Sputa cadunt rictu croceo contacta colore,
   Perpetuo naris laxa fluore madet.
Nulla quies nullique premunt membra arida somni,
   Faucibus in salsis tussis acerba sonat.
Risus abest, rari squalent rubigine dentes,
120   Sordida lunato prominet ungue manus.

goddess of Rhamnus[16] turns to her with a grim look in her eyes, and in a low voice lets out a short murmur. Then a gleam comes 90 to her eyes as she bestows her lethal favor to the poor girl, and she lifts her head higher than usual. And as she plots to confound such great happiness without delay, the bitter goddess searches out some unhappy way for the girl to die. At this moment she spots 95 Fever passing through the upper airs, just as Icarius' Dog was preparing to show its snout.[17] Accompanying the daughter of Erebus and Night[18] are Mourning and Death, her head covered in shadows; and heavy Moaning, and Lamentation mingled with Moaning; repeated Sobbing and savage Anxiety; Trembling, and Wast- 100 ing, and Madness with her fearful look; and Thirst, always gasping with her breast on fire; shuddering Cold, and Insomnia, her mind unsettled; inconstant Flush and terrifying Dread. Lions from Mar- 105 marica[19] pull their mistress' curved yoke, their fiery hearts roaring in a furious growl. Upon the goddess' blazing head fierce vipers rise up, continually spewing gore from their infernal mouths. Her eyes are ablaze with blood, her hollow temples stiff and cold; a 110 damp sweat settles upon her neck, a pallor upon her breast. Her tongue, the soul's interpreter, drips with livid poison, and a fiery vapor rattles her black mouth, from which her heavy breath pours out a noisome stench. Her throat hisses, filled with death-dealing flame; spittle, stained with a yellow color, drips from her maw, her 115 open nostrils are wet from never-ending flux. No rest, no sleep ever comes over her arid limbs, in her briny jaws a harsh cough sounds. She has no smile; her few teeth are stained and filthy, her 120 foul hand extends in a hooked claw. Her gleaming right hand

Dextera fumiferam praefulgens lampada quassat,
    Sithonasque gerit frigida laeva niues.
Olli templa olim posuit Romana propago,
    Abstinuit saevas nec tamen inde manus.
125 Sacra illam Actiaco tenuere Palatia Phoebo,
    Quique olim vicus nomine Longus erat;
Area quin etiam dirae templa ardua Febris
    Ostendit, Marii quae monumenta tenet.
Hoc ubi crudelis vidit Rhamnusia monstrum,
130   Exacuit saevo lurida corda sono:
'Aspicis hanc,' inquit, 'virgo sata Nocte, puellam,
    Cuius et hinc radiis ora serena micant,
Quae gaudet, fati sortisque ignara futurae,
    Quam digito atque oculis densa caterua notat?
135 Hanc nive tu gelida, rapidis hanc infice flammis:
    Sic opus est vires sentiat illa tuas.'
Dixerat, et pariter gressumque avertit et ora:
    Non oculos poterat iam tolerare truces.
Continuo ardentes stimulis citat illa leones,
140   Saepius et ducto versat in orbe facem.
Interea umentem noctis variantia pallam
    Hesperus in rutilo sparserat astra polo.
Albiera in patrios iam candida membra penates
    Intulerat, molli constiteratque toro.
145 Iam tenero placidum spirabat pectore somnum,
    Venit ad obstrusos cum dea saeva lares.
Quo dea, quo tendis? Non te lacrimabilis aetas,
    Non te forma movet, non pudor aut probitas?
Nonne movent lacrimaeque viri lacrimaeque parentum?
150   Mortalem potes (a!) perdere, saeua, deam?
Limina contigerat: tremuerunt limina, pallor
    Infecit postes, et patuere fores.

10

shakes a smoky lamp, and her cold left hand bears the snows of
Sithonia.[20] In ancient times the Roman race built temples to her,
and even so she did not keep her cruel hands off them. The Pala-   125
tine, sacred to Actian Apollo, was her home, as was what was formerly known as Long Street; and what's more, the district where
the monument of Marius is located boasted of a lofty temple to
pitiless Fever.[21] As soon as the cruel goddess of Rhamnus caught
sight of this monster, she whipped up her lurid heart with these   130
savage words, saying, "Virgin daughter of Night, do you see this
girl, whose serene countenance shines brightly even from this distance, who rejoices, ignorant of her fate and her advancing destiny,
whom the packed crowd points to with gesture and with glance?
Infect her with icy cold, infect her with consuming flames: let her   135
feel your power in this way." So she spoke, simultaneously averting
her gaze and her gait, for she could no longer tolerate those savage
eyes. Immediately she spurs on her impatient lions with the whip,
repeatedly whirling her torch around in a circle.   140

Meanwhile Hesperus[22] had sprinkled stars in the glittering sky,
embroidering the moist mantle of the night, and Albiera had entered her father's house and settled her fair limbs in her soft bed.
Within her delicate breast she was already breathing peacefully in   145
sleep, when the savage goddess came to her shuttered home.
Where, goddess, where are you going? Doesn't her heartbreaking
youth move you to pity, her beauty, her modesty and her good-
ness? Don't the tears of her husband move you, and the tears of
her parents? Ah, can you bring yourself, fell being, to destroy a   150
mortal goddess? She had barely set foot on the threshold when it
began to tremble, a pallor stained the doorposts, and the door

Virgineum petit illa torum, pavidaeque puellae
    Pectore ab obsceno talia dicta refert:
155 'Quae placidam carpis secura mente quietem,
    Et fati et sortis nescia virgo tuae,
Nondum saeva meae sensisti vulnera dextrae,
    Quae tibi ego et mecum quae tibi fata parant.
Stat vacua tua Parca colo. Moritura puella,
160   Ne geme: cum dulce est vivere, dulce mori est.'
Sic ait, aestiferamque excussit lampada, et acres
    Virginis iniecit dura sub ossa faces.
Tum letale gelu invergens guttasque veneni,
    Inserta, heu, venis, effugit inde, nece.
165 Excitat illa graui geminos clamore parentes;
    Advocat absentem nuntia Fama virum.
Vicinae extemplo matres trepidaeque puellae
    Conveniunt, teneras imbre rigante genas.
Iam fera virgineas populatur flamma medullas,
170   Iam gelida torpent horrida membra nive.
Liquitur infelix: non ars operosa medentum,
    Non facta a misero coniuge vota iuvant.
Liquitur, et quamquam dirae vestigia mortis
    Cernit, et extremum sentit adesse diem,
175 Corde tamen gemitum premit et spem fronte serenat,
    Tristitiamque acie dissimulante tegit,
Scilicet augeret trepidi ne dura mariti
    Lamenta et curas anxietate graves.
Iam decima infaustam referebat lampade lucem
180   Cynthius, et picea texerat ora face,
Cum miserae extremus iam presserat error ocellos,
    Fugerat, heu, vultus, fugerat ore color.
Aspicit illa tamen dulcem moritura maritum,
    Illum acie solum deficiente notat,

opened. She tracks down the maiden's bed, and from the depths
of her foul heart she speaks the following words to the trembling
girl: "You who are now enjoying a peaceful rest, your mind free   155
from care, a maiden ignorant of fate and your destiny, you have
not yet felt the savage wounds dealt by my right hand, which I and
the Fates together with me are preparing for you. Your Fate's
thread has run out.[23] Though you are destined to die, girl, do not   160
mourn: it is a delight to die when life is sweet." So she spoke, and
then she shook her blazing lamp and cast piercing torches into the
girl's hard bones. Then Fever pours a lethal chill and drops of
venom into her, and flees from that place, with death, alas, infused
into the girl's veins.

The girl rouses both her parents with a terrible cry, and Fame[24]   165
is the messenger who summons her absent husband. Mothers and
their anxious daughters converge at once from the neighborhood,
tears drenching their delicate cheeks. A fierce flame is already rav-
aging the maiden to the marrow, her shivering limbs are already   170
growing numb from the icy cold. The poor girl is fading away:
neither the painstaking expertise of the physicians, nor the prayers
offered by her distraught husband have any effect. She is fading
away, and although she notices the signs of bitter death and she
understands that her final day is at hand, still she suppresses the   175
groan in her heart, setting hope unclouded upon her brow, and
hides her sadness with a dissembling look, clearly because she
wants to avoid adding to her anxious husband's bitter laments and
heavy cares.

Now upon the tenth day the Cynthian[25] was again bringing
an ill-omened light, his face concealed by a pitch-black torch,   180
when the final moment of confusion had just closed the poor girl's
eyes and any expressiveness had fled from her face, alas, and any
color too. And yet, on the verge of death, she looks upon her
sweet husband, she fixes upon him alone with her failing vision,

185 Illius aspectu morientia lumina pascit,
      Mens illum e media morte reversa videt.
    Quis tibi tunc, Sismunde, dolor, cum virginis artus
      Aspiceres, anima iam fugiente, mori?
    Non tamen illa tui, non illa oblita parentum,
190   Te vocat, et tales fundit ab ore sonos:
    'Pars animae, Sismunde, meae, si coniugis in te
      Quicquam iuris habent ultima vota tuae,
    Parce, precor, lacrimis: vixi cursumque peregi.
      Iam procul a vobis me mea fata vocant.
195 Immatura quidem morior, sed pura sub umbras
      Discedam, et nullis sordida de maculis.
    Discedam virgo, facibus nec vitta maritis
      Cessit: coniugii nil nisi nomen habes.
    Est mihi dulce mori vitamque rependere famae:
200   Edita mortali condicione fui.
    At nisi nunc morerer, fueram moritura subinde:
      Est mihi dulce etiam, te superante, mori.
    Nil mihi iam poterant anni conferre seniles:
      Vita brevis longi temporis instar habet.
205 Mi dederat teneri leges Natura pudoris,
      Mi dederat mores cum probitate pios.
    Nil mutari in me cuperes, nisi tristia fata:
      Humanae vici condicionis opus.
    Vidi ego te summi defunctum munere honoris,
210   Vidi omnem festa pace nitere domum,
    Et nisi me gemini possunt nil flere parentes.
      Parce igitur Manes sollicitare pios!
    Parce, precor, lacrimis, coniunx! Sic laetus in auras
      Evadet tenues spiritus inde meus.
215 Maesta sed amborum, nimis a nimis, ora parentum
      Solare! Heu, nostro torpet in ore sonus!

she feeds her dying eyes with the sight of him, and her mind turns   185
away from the midst of death to see him. What despair was there
for you then, Sigismondo, when you saw that the girl's body was
failing, her soul already in flight? And yet she did not forget you,
nor did she forget her parents. She calls out to you, pouring out   190
these words from her lips:

   "Sigismondo, my soul mate, if your wife's final wishes have any
claim upon you, spare your tears, I beseech you. I have lived a full
life, completed my voyage. Now my destiny calls me far away from
you. I am indeed dying before my time, but I shall depart for the   195
afterlife in purity and marked by no stain. I shall depart a virgin,
and the wedding torches have not taken the place of my headband:
of marriage you have nothing but the name. For me it is sweet to
die and to give my life in exchange for fame; mortality was a con-   200
dition of my birth. And if I were not dying at this moment, I
would still have had to die soon after: for me death is also sweet
since you survive me. There is no benefit that years of old age
could bring me: my short life is the equivalent of a long existence.
Nature had given me rules of conduct based on tender modesty, a   205
character both pious and upright. There is nothing about me that
you would wish to be different, other than my sad fate: I have
overcome the barrier of the human condition. I have seen you at-
tain the office of the highest distinction,[26] I have seen my home   210
gleaming in peaceful celebration, and my two parents can weep
over nothing other than me. So stop wearying the pious souls of
the departed, spare your tears, I beseech you, husband: thus shall
my joyful spirit thereafter ascend to the thin air. Ah, but do con-   215
sole the too, too melancholy countenances of my parents . . . Alas,
my voice sticks in my throat! Alas, I am being carried off! You

Heu, rapior! Tu vive mihi, tibi mortua vivam!
    Caligant oculi iam mihi morte graues.
Iamque vale, o coniunx, carique valete parentes!
220   Heu, procul hinc nigra condita nocte feror!'
Sic ait, et dulcem moriens complexa maritum
    Labitur, inque illo corpus inane iacet,
Corpus inane iacet cara cervice recumbens
    Coniugis. Heu, fati tristia iura gravis!
225 Hoc licuit vobis, o ferrea pectora, Parcae?
    Credo ego iam divum numina posse mori.
Quis nunc, quis gemitus miserorum et verba parentum
    Nesciat in tantis, heu, repetita malis?
Ora rigat lacrimis frater, rumpitque capillos
230   Maesta soror, teneras et secat ungue genas.
Non secus Hectoreo Troianae in funere matres
    Fleverunt scissis publica fata comis.
Implentur clamore lares, clamore resultant
    Atria, luctisonis fletibus aula fremit.
235 Heu, quid agas, coniunx? Quae vocem in verba relaxes?
    Quo fletu incuses tristia fata, miser?
Non lacrimas miserandus habes, non verba dolentum;
    Attonitus pigro torpet in ore sonus.
Extinctae ingeminas tantum misera oscula, et arte
240   Impedis[1] amplexu frigida membra tuo;
Dilectosque premis vultus, premis ora, nec ullum
    Invenit inclusus pectore luctus iter.
Quoque magis mersum premis alto in corde dolorem,
    Hoc magis ille furit, aestuat atque magis.
245 Sic magis inclusus furit intra obstacula torrens,
    Quae si dimoveas, lenior inde fluet.
Quin etiam invisae rupisses vincula vitae,
    Coniugis ut Manes prosequerere pios,

must live for me, as I shall live for you in death! My eyes are clouding over now, heavy with death. Farewell now, husband, and farewell, dear parents! Alas, I am carried far from here, enveloped 220 in the darkness of night."

So she spoke; and, embracing her sweet husband as she dies, she slips away. Her lifeless body lies upon him, lies resting upon her dear husband's shoulder — alas for the stern laws of inexorable fate! Were you allowed to do this, you hard-hearted Fates? Now I 225 believe that even gods can die. Who now, who could ignore the laments of her parents and the words they repeated, alas, in the midst of such great evils? Her brother waters his face with tears, her sister tears her hair in sorrow and scratches her delicate cheeks 230 with her fingernails.[27] At Hector's funeral the mothers of Troy lamented their country's fate in just this same way, by tearing their hair. The house is filled with cries, the halls reecho with cries, the courtyard resounds with mournful weeping. Alas, husband, what 235 are you to do? What words might your voice release? With what laments can you impeach the grim fates, poor man? In your pitiable condition tears fail you and the words that those in mourning typically say; grief-struck, the words stick in your paralyzed throat. All you can do is shower the dead girl with your desperate kisses and cling tightly to her cold limbs in your embrace. You press her 240 beloved face, and her lips, to yours, but the sorrow that is locked within your breast finds no outlet. And the more you repress the grief buried deep within your heart, the more it rages, the more it burns. In the same way a torrential stream rages more violently 245 when obstacles stand in its way, but once you remove them, it flows more gently from then on. You would even have burst the bonds of this hateful life to accompany the pious shade of your

Sed prohibent fratres et blandi cura parentis,
250   Sed prohibent socii, pectora fida, tui.
Iam virgo effertur nigro composta feretro,
    Desectas humili fronde revincta comas.
Heu, ubi nunc blandi risus, ubi dulcia verba,
    Quae poterant ferri frangere duritiem?
255 Lumina sidereas ubi nunc torquentia flammas,
    Heu, ubi puniceis aemula labra rosis?
Pro superi, quid non homini breuis eripit hora?
    A, miseri somnus et leuis umbra sumus!
Non tamen aut niveos pallor mutaverat artus,
260   Aut gelido macies sederat ore gravis,
Sed formosa levem mors est imitata soporem:
    Is nitidos vultus oraque langor habet.
Virginea sic lecta manu candentia languent
    Liliaque, et niveis texta corona rosis.
265 Hic, ceu nulla prius fuerint lamenta, novatur
    Luctus, et indignis imbribus ora madent.
Praecedit iam pompa frequens, iam maesta sacerdos
    Verba canit, sacris turribus aera sonant.
Funerea cives pullati veste sequuntur,
270   Et spargunt maestas rore madente genas;
Densaque plebs vidui deplorat fata mariti,
    Atque illum digito luminibusque notat.
O quantum impexi crines oculique genaeque
    Noctis habent! Quantus nubilat ora dolor!
275 Quid nunc exequias celebres opulentaque dicam
    Munera? Quid donis templa referta piis?
Omnis ceratis radiat funalibus ara,
    Omnis odoratis ignibus ara calet.
Aeternamque canunt requiem lucemque verendi
280   Sacricolae, et lymphis corpus inane rigant.

wife, but thoughts of your brothers stop you and concern for your
gentle father,[28] as well as thoughts of your truehearted friends.   250

Now the girl is being carried out, composed upon a dark bier,
her hair cut and bound back by a humble garland. Alas, where
now is that charming smile, where now those sweet words that
could burst the hardest iron? Where now those eyes spinning   255
starry flames? Alas, where now those lips that rival red roses? Oh
gods above, what is there that cannot be taken from a human in a
brief instant? Ah, we wretched beings are but a dream and a flick-
ering shadow! And yet pallor had not changed her snow-white
limbs, nor had emaciation settled heavily into her cold face.   260
Rather, her death was beautiful, mimicking a light sleep, such was
the stillness upon her splendid face and lips. White lilies gathered
by a maiden's hand fade like this, or a garland woven with snow-
white roses.

At this moment, the mourning starts anew, as if there had been   265
no lamentations before, and faces grow wet with indignant tears.
Now the packed procession moves forward, now the priest intones
the melancholy words, and from the sacred steeples the bells
sound. The people of the city follow, all dressed in black in their
funeral attire, and they bathe their sad cheeks with moist tears.   270
The packed commoners bemoan the fate of the widowed husband
and point him out with gestures and with glances. Oh, how black
the night that covers their disheveled hair, their eyes and their
cheeks! How great the sadness that clouds their faces! No need to   275
tell now of the crowded funeral mass and the rich offerings. No
need to tell of the church filled with pious gifts. Every altar gleams
with waxed tapers, every altar glows with the scent of burning incense. The reverend priests pray for her eternal rest and light, and   280
sprinkle her lifeless body with water. Finally a tomb of carved

Et tandem gelidos operosi marmoris artus
   Includit tumulus, et breue carmen habet:
'Hoc iacet Albierae pulchrum sub marmore corpus;
   Nulla quidem tantum marmora laudis habent.
285 Exornat tumulum corpus, sed spiritus astra:
   O quanta accessit gloria lausque polo!'

marble encloses her cold limbs, and it carries this short epitaph:[29] "Beneath this marble slab lies the beautiful body of Albiera; no other marble has so great a tribute. Her body adorns the tomb, 285 but her spirit adorns the stars: oh, what great glory and praise are added to heaven!"

LIBER EPIGRAMMATVM

: I :

Ad Laurentium Medicem

Cum referam attonito, Medices, tibi carmina plectro
    Ingeniumque tibi serviat omne meum,
Quod tegor attrita, ridet plebecula, veste,
    Tegmina quod pedibus sunt recutita meis,
5 Quod digitos caligae, disrupto carcere, nudos
    Permittunt caelo liberiore frui,
Intima bombycum vacua est quod stamine vestis,
    Sectaque de caesa vincula fallit ove.
Ridet et ignavum sic me putat esse poetam,
10   Nec placuisse animo carmina nostra tuo.
Tu contra effusas toto sic pectore laudes
    Ingeris, ut libris sit data palma meis.
Hoc tibi si credi cupis et cohibere popellum,
    Laurenti, vestes iam mihi mitte tuas!

: II :

Ad eundem gratiarum actio

Dum cupio ingentes numeris tibi solvere grates
    Laurenti, aetatis[1] gloria prima tuae,
Excita iam dudum longo mihi murmure tandem
    Astitit arguta Calliopea lyra.
5 Astitit, inque meo pretiosas corpore vestes
    Ut vidit, pavidum rettulit inde pedem,

THE BOOK OF EPIGRAMS

To Lorenzo de' Medici[1]

While I bring you songs upon my inspired lyre, Medici, and my talent is entirely at your service, the rabble make fun of me because I wear a shabby cloak; because my feet rattle in my shoes; because   5 my boots allow my bare toes to enjoy the open sky with their broken soles; because my undergarment has no silken thread, and conceals fastenings cut from a slaughtered sheep. They make fun of me, and likewise they think that I am a lazy poet, and that my   10 songs have not been to your liking. You, on the other hand, wholeheartedly heap such extravagant praise on me that the palm has been awarded to my books. If you want the credit for this and you wish to put a stop to the riffraff, Lorenzo, send me some clothes now — yours!

: II :

An expression of gratitude to the same person

While I was longing to show my vast gratitude to you in meter, Lorenzo, the first glory of your age, Calliope[2] finally came to my side with her melodious lyre after she had been summoned by me for a long time in a protracted murmur. She came to my side, but   5 when she saw the costly garments on my body, she drew back from

Nec potuit culti faciem dea nosse poetae,
    Corporaque in Tyrio conspicienda sinu.
Si minus ergo tibi meritas ago carmine grates,
10   Frustrata est calamum diva vocata meum.
Mox tibi sublato modulabor pectine versus,
    Cultibus assuerit² cum mea Musa novis.

: III :

In aridam populum, quae repente
ante domum Laurentii reviruit

Quod recidiva novas diffundit vertice frondes
    Quae Medicam surgit populus ante domum,
Cui quondam, Ogygio fierent cum sacra Lyaeo,
    Admovit rapidas ebria turba faces,
5 Quid mirum? Herculeis nam cum Laurentius armis
    Aemulus, Ausonios temperet arte lares,
Ipse suas iuveni Tirynthius explicat umbras,
    Implicet ut meritum lecta corona caput.
Sic quoniam dextro modulatur Apolline carmen,
10   Ante suas lauri circumiere comas.
Nunc igitur, duplici crines lambente corona,
    Se bello ostendet seque valere toga.

me in fear, and, goddess though she was, she could not recognize the face of this well-groomed poet, nor his body so resplendent in Tyrian garb.[3] So if I do not show you the thanks that you deserve in song, it's the goddess whom I invoked that has cheated my pen. 10 Soon I shall raise the lyre and compose verses for you, when my Muse has gotten used to my new wardrobe.

: III :

*On a dried out poplar, which suddenly bloomed again
in front of Lorenzo's house*

A poplar tree is coming back to life and spreading fresh leaves from its top, the one that rises in front of the Medici house, to which the drunken crowd once set burning torches, when the rites of Ogygian Lyaeus[4] were taking place—where's the surprise in 5 that? For since Lorenzo competes with the military exploits of Hercules while skillfully administering the households of Italy, the man from Tiryns himself is unfolding the shade of his tree for the young man, so that a garland can be gathered to wreathe his worthy head.[5] And since he composes poetry with Apollo's favor, leaves of laurel have likewise enveloped his locks.[6] Now then, with 10 two crowns encircling his hair, he'll show himself equally talented in war and peace.

: IV :

De cane hebro ad Laurentium Medicem

Quod canis Hesperio, Medices, tibi missus ab Hebro
    Terribiles vasto strangulat ore feras,
Ast hominem pavido metuit contingere rictu,
    Nil mirum: domino convenit ille suo.
5 Sic tua nam sontes, Laurenti, poena coercet,
    Sic referunt abs te praemia digna pii.

: V :

Ad Fontium, MCCCCLXIX, XIII aetatis suae anno

Dulce mihi quondam studium fuit, invida sed me
    Paupertas laceros terruit uncta sinus.
Nunc igitur, quoniam vates fit fabula vulgi,
    Esse reor satius cedere temporibus.

: VI :

Marsupino

Carle, quid abstrusas[3] sapientum quaerere mentes,
    Quid properas tetricos consuluisse senes?
Te decet exactos mordaci claudere versus
    Pumice, delitias et celebrare tuas,

: IV :

For Lorenzo de' Medici, on his Spanish hound

The dog that was sent to you, Medici, from the river Ebro in the West[7] throttles terrifying beasts in its vast mouth, but is afraid to touch humans with its timid maw—that's not surprising. He's a perfect match for his master: for in the same way, Lorenzo, the penalties that you impose serve as a check on criminals, and the pious receive from you the rewards that they deserve.[8]

5

: V :

To Bartolomeo Fonzio, written in 1469 at the age of 13[9]

Once scholarship was sweet for me, but envious Poverty, her torn cloak smeared with grease, terrified me. So now, since a poet can become the talk of the town, I think it better to give in to the pressure of the times.

: VI :

To Carlo Marsuppini[10]

Carlo, why are you in a rush to inquire into the abstruse wisdom of philosophers, to consult gloomy old men? It suits you to compose verses polished with sharp pumice[11] and to celebrate your

5   Ut cantata novo se carmine iactet amica,
      Subiciatque leves nuda Thalia iocos.
   Par est nequitia iuvenes gaudere proterva:
      Hanc Venus aetatem vindicat ipsa sibi.
   Si sapis ergo, graves procul o procul exige chartas:
10   Non facit aetati Musa severa tuae.
   Vince Philetaeos molli cum carmine *Lusus*:
      Invideat teneris Graecia docta modis.
   Sic tibi purpurea geminus cum matre Cupido
      Imponet meritae myrtea serta comae;
15 Aeternamque feres super aurea sidera famam,
      Quae tibi post cineres sola superstes erit.

∶ VII ∶

Ad Ponticum, MCCCCLXXII

   Pontice vis nostro cumulum superaddere amori,
      Inque dies fieri semper amabilior?
   Vis mihi vel tenera iucundior esse puella?
      Vis mihi vel geminis carior esse oculis?
5   Mitte leves numeros, calamo nec parce iocoso;
      Mitte tuae testes carmina nequitiae.
   Si facies, caro fies mihi carior auro,
      Et nitido Phoebi sidere fulgidior.
   At si non facies, vili mihi vilior alga
10   Atque asini fies stercore sordidior.

sweetheart. That way your girlfriend can brag that she is the sub-   5
ject of a new song and the naked Muse of Comedy can add in
some lighthearted jests. It's right for young men to take pleasure in
ribald levity: Venus claims this time of life for herself. So, if you're
smart, you'll toss those pages of highbrow writing far, far away: a   10
serious Muse does not suit a young man like you. Go one better
than Philetas' *Playthings* with your own love poetry, and let your
delicate measures be the envy of highbrow Greeks.[12] If you do,
twin Cupids and their luminous[13] mother will set garlands of
myrtle upon your worthy hair, and your fame, which alone shall   15
survive your death, you shall carry forever beyond the golden stars.

: VII :

To Ponticus (1472)[14]

Ponticus, do you want to do something extra to crown my affection for you, and become more lovable to me every day? Do you
want me to find you more pleasing than a young girl? Do you
want to be dearer to me than my own two eyes? Then send me   5
some light verse, and don't be stingy with your clever pen: send me
poems that will testify to your playful spirit. If you do this, you
will be dearer to me than gleaming gold and brighter than the
shining star of Phoebus. But if you don't, you'll be more worthless
to me than third-rate seaweed[15] and more contemptible than don-   10
key dung.

: VIII :

In Paulum, MCCCCLXXII

Quae tu condideras damnavi carmina nuper,
    Nec tua damnavi carmina, Paule, tamen.
Auctor eras, fateor; sed cum sunt edita, Paule,
    Auctoris non sunt carmina, sed populi.

: IX :

Antonio Benivenio medico Elegia, MCCCCLXXII

Ut sonipes geminas attollit Martius aures,
    Cum raucae belli signa dedere tubae,
Sic mihi languenti surgunt in pectore vires,
    Ingenii laudas cum monumenta mei.
5 Et merito; neque enim, tanto sub iudice tutus,
    Pertimeo vulgi scommata vana rudis.
Nam quoniam Stygiam facile est tibi pellere mortem,
    Quam facile Invidiae frangere colla potes!
Felix cui liceat Fati pervertere legem,
10   Quem propter cumba stet leviore Charon,
Stamina qui valeas invita nectere Parca
    Atque animas vacua restituisse colo.
Felix grata domus Lycio Benivenia Phoebo,
    Cui sua concessit munera cuncta deus!
15 Namque Coronidem tibi cedere iussit Apollo,
    Iussit et Haemonium cedere Phillyriden.

: VIII :

Regarding Paul (1472)[16]

I recently criticized the poems that you had composed, and yet it wasn't actually *your* poetry that I criticized, Paul. You were the author, I admit, but once they've been published, Paul, poems belong not to the author, but to the public.

: IX :

An elegy for the physician Antonio di Paolo Benivieni (1472)[17]

Just as a warhorse pricks both its ears when the trumpets have sounded the signal for battle, so the strength in my weary breast swells when you praise the monuments of my intellect. And rightly 5 so, because I have no fear of the vulgar mob's empty insults[18] while under the protection of so great a critic. For, considering that it is a simple thing for you to repel the darkness of death, how easy it is for you to be able to break the neck of Envy! Fortunate you are that you can overthrow the laws of Fate, that because of you 10 Charon's boat is lighter, that you have the ability to bind Destiny's threads against her will and restore the breath of life when her distaff is empty![19] Fortunate is the house of the Benivieni and pleasing to Lycian Phoebus, who has granted it all his gifts! For 15 Apollo commanded the son of Coronis to take second place to you, and he has given the same command to the Thracian son of

Ast alius simili frater virtute recenset
    Quae medicam surgens herba ministret opem.
Tertius Aoniis satur ille Hieronymus undis
20   Ad querulam docto barbiton ore canit.
Bis senos alius modo cum transcenderit annos,
    Pectore iam canos vincit et ore senes.
Cederet huic Thamyras docti certamine cantus,
    Cederet aurata Calliopea lyra.
25 Argumenta etiam logicis miranda figuris
    Implicat, et magnum versat Aristotelem.
Di tibi dent Pyliam longe superare senectam,
    Antoni, Euboicos et superare dies!
Di tibi dent geminos longum superasse parentes!
30   Di servent fratres, pignora cara, tuos!
Tu modo praecipiti quae nuper carmina penna
    Scripsimus, ingenii munera parva mei,
Excipe, meque tuum memori sub mente reconde,
    Mutuaque alternus pectora servet amor.

: X :

Ad Xystum Cardinalem

Quod dubia incerto variantur nubila Phoebo,
    Dum petis Etruscos, maxime Xyste, lares,
Quid mirare? Suae[4] sol ipse umbracula fronti
    Obiicit, et radios temperat ipse suos.
5 Sic te, Xyste, videt, sic te non laedit, et uno
    Tempore sic geminum perficit officium.
Iure igitur parent homines cui sidera parent:
    Spes hominum prima es primaque cura deum.

Phyllyra.[20] And the second brother, who is endowed with a similar talent, evaluates which herbs grow to supply a healing balm. The third brother, the famous Girolamo, filled with the inspirational waters of Aonia, sings to the accompaniment of the querulous lyre 20 with a well-trained voice. Another brother has only just passed the age of twelve, and already he surpasses the white-haired old men in sense and eloquence: Thamyras would lose to him in a contest of learned song, and even Calliope of the golden lyre would lose to him.[21] He also makes marvelously intricate arguments with figures 25 of logic and is always reading great Aristotle. May the gods grant that you far surpass Nestor in old age, Antonio, and surpass the age of the Sibyl too![22] May the gods grant that you long survive both your parents! May the gods preserve your dear brothers! 30 Only please receive the poems that I recently wrote with a precipitous pen, the tiny gifts of my inspiration. Receive them and remember to stash me away as a possession in your mind; and let our shared affection keep our hearts mutually disposed.

: X :

To Cardinal Sixtus[23]

Why are you surprised that the clouds are colored by uncertain sunlight, while you head for your home in Tuscany, O most excellent Sixtus? Of its own accord the sun is covering its face with a parasol and softening its rays. That way it sees you, Sixtus, but 5 doesn't harm you, and that way it performs these two functions at the same time. Therefore it's right for men to obey the man whom the stars obey: you are the first hope of humankind and the first care of the gods.

: XI :

Ad eundem

Tenderet Etruscam nuper cum Xystus in urbem,
    Aurea quae magni signa leonis habet,
Viderat assiduis pallentes solibus herbas,
    Et cava limoso flumina sicca sinu.
5 Viderat et querulis poscentem vocibus imbres
    Effusas populum congeminare preces.
Ergo salutiferos suspendit in aethere nimbos,
    Dum pergit Lydas Xystus adire domos.
Inde ubi iam laetum mediae sese intulit urbi,
10   Obtulit et Tuscis ora serena piis,
Ardua laxato discussit nubila caelo,
    Et liquido arentem nectare pavit humum.
An quisquam neget esse deum te, Xyste, tenentem
    Imperium terris imperiumque polo?

: XII :

Ad eundem

Verba dedi Xysto: decet haec dare dona poetam.
    Aera decet Xystum reddere: verba refert.
Verum habet ille alios qui dent sibi verba, fatemur;
    Aera tamen qui nunc det mihi nullus adest.

: XI :

To the same man

Recently, while Sixtus was traveling to the city in Tuscany that has a golden lion as its symbol,[24] he saw grasses parched by constant sunlight and deep-channeled streams dried out in their muddy course. He saw too the people redouble the prayers that they 5 poured out, calling for rain with plaintive voices. And so Sixtus kept the salubrious clouds hanging in the sky as he pressed on to reach his Lydian home.[25] Then when he had joyfully entered the city center and presented his serene visage to the pious Tuscans, 10 he released the heavens, broke open the clouds above and fed the parched soil with liquid nectar.[26] Is there anyone who could deny that you are a god, Sixtus, holding sway over the earth and dominion in the sky?

: XII :

To the same man

I gave a gift of words to Sixtus, the right kind for a poet to give. Sixtus ought to repay me in cash, but in return he cheated me.[27] Yes, he has others who could give him words, this I admit; but there is no one else around now who could give me cash.

: XIII :

Ad eundem propter aliquos poetas detractores

Credebam demens Xystum mihi verba dedisse.
    Fallebar, vates nam mihi verba dabant.
Nil queror: insanis mos est dare verba poetis.
    Di faciant ne sis, Xyste, poeta mihi!

: XIV :

Ad eundem

Dicenti te, Xiste, deum si dona dedisses
    Quae petiit, iam te diceret esse Iovem.

: XV :

In picturam puellae quae in deliciis Laurentio Medici est

Ne dubita, picta est quam cernis virgo, sed acres
    Hisce oculis flammas eiaculatur Amor.
Hisce oculis vocem dedit ars, linguaeque negavit.
    Heu fuge! Sed nulla est iam fuga: vulnus habes.

: XIII :

To the same man, concerning certain derogatory poets

In my folly I used to believe that Sixtus had cheated me, but I was wrong: it was some poets who deceived me. I'm not complaining: cheating is normal practice for crazy poets. But Heaven forefend, Sixtus, that you should play the poet with me!

: XIV :

To the same man

Sixtus, if you had given the gifts he asked for to the one who said you were a god,[28] he would now be saying that you are Jove.

: XV :

On a painting of a girl, whom Lorenzo de' Medici fancies

Make no mistake, the girl you see is a painting, but Love does launch piercing flames from these eyes. To these eyes art has given voice, while denying it to her tongue. Alas, you should flee! But flight is not possible anymore, now that you're wounded.

: XVI :

Ad Franciscum Salviatum

Quam peto, si dederis, dulcis Salviate, salutem,
    O quam convenient nomina tanta tibi!
Parva peto, dare magna soles: da parva petenti.
    Parva tamen nescis si dare, magna dato.
5 Parva tibi, sed magna mihi sunt ista. Rogamus
    De nobis Xisto haec dicere verba velis:
'Est iuvenis: te, Xiste, colit, veneratur amatque.
    Spes sibi tu prima es, primaque cura sibi.[5]
Nec malus est vates, nec pessima carmina condit,
10   Sed nullo hic vates est tamen aere gravis.'
Hoc satis est; divo mandamus cetera Xisto.
    Sat bene perspiciet quid tua verba petant.

: XVII :

De Domitio et Marsilio

Audit Marsilius missam, missam facis illam
    Tu, Domiti: magis est religiosus uter?
Quis dubitet? tanto es tu religiosior illo,
    Quanto audire minus est bona quam facere.

: XVI :

To Francesco Salviati[29]

If you grant me the salvation that I seek, my dear Salviati, oh, how your great name will suit you! I ask for but a little, you usually give a lot: so grant this modest petition. But if you don't know how to give only a little, go ahead and give me a lot. It's a small 5 thing to you, but for me it's a lot. I'm asking you, please, to say these words about me to Sixtus: "There is a young man, Sixtus— he cherishes you, he worships you, he loves you. You are his principal hope, his principal care. He's not a bad poet and the poems he writes are not the worst, but still this poet is not loaded with 10 cash." That will do it. We leave the rest to saintly Sixtus: he will understand well enough what your words mean.

: XVII :

On Domizio Calderini[30] and Marsilio Ficino[31]

Marsilio is attending mass, but you are giving it a miss, Domizio. Which of you is the more devout? Can there be any doubt? You are more devout than he, to the extent that good attendance counts less than good deeds.[32]

∶ XVIII ∶

In Pamphilum

Mittis vina mihi: mihi, Pamphile, vina supersunt.
  Vis mage quod placeat mittere? Mitte sitim.

∶ XIX ∶

In Corydonem

'Sum puer,' exclamas, Corydon, subigisque fateri.
  In te reclamat sed tua barba: vir es.

∶ XX ∶

In Mabilium

Innumerae tibi sunt, Mabili, in carmine mendae,
  Atque ubi sint quaeris? Per mare quaeris aquam.

∶ XXI ∶

De Antonio Tusco ex temperanti poeta, Ad Fabianum

Tuscus ab Othrysio, Fabiane, Antonius Orpheo
  Hoc differt: homines hic trahit, ille feras.

: XVIII :

On Panfilo[33]

You send me wine, but I've wine to spare and then some, Panfilo.
Would you like to send me something more pleasing? Send thirst.

: XIX :

On Corydon[34]

"I am a boy," you exclaim, Corydon, and you compel me to agree.
But your beard tells against you: you are a man.

: XX :

On Mabilio[35]

There are countless flaws in your poetry, Mabilio, and yet you ask
where they are? You might as well be looking for water in the
ocean.

: XXI :

On Antonio of Tuscany, an extempore poet, to Fabiano[36]

Fabiano, the difference between Antonio the Tuscan[37] and Orpheus the Thracian[38] is this: the one attracts human beings, the
other beasts.

: XXII :

In Laurentium Medicem

Ante erat informis, Laurens, tua patria truncus;
    Nunc habet ecce suum, te tribuente, caput.
Namque tuis nimia est frenata licentia nuper
    Legibus: hoc patriae quis neget esse caput?
5 Caeca fuit quondam tua dicta Fluentia, sed nunc
    Cuncta, oculos illi te tribuente, videt;
Otia namque piis statuisti dulcia Musis,
    Quas patriae veros dixeris esse oculos.
Consilium dic esse aures, quo consulis illi.
10   Quod fugit insidias te duce, nare valet.
Cum dederit largas illi tua dextera fruges,
    Os habet: hoc totum patria corpus alit.
Impensis ductuque tuo Volaterra repulsas
    Accepit leges: haec sua dextra fuit.
15 Paene puer laevamque manum clipeumque dedisti,
    Cum tuta a misera seditione fuit.
Praemia certa manent iustos, rata poena nocentes:
    Hisce urbem pedibus comprobat ire Solon.
Praeterea auratos posito squalore capillos
20   Compsit, et aurata candida veste nitet.
Hoc decus educti templorum ad sidera sumptus,
    Hoc Medicae praestant ardua tecta domus.
Sic patriam gignis, Laurens, educis et ornas,
    Patria sic vero te vocat ore patrem.

: XXII :

On Lorenzo de' Medici

Lorenzo, your country was a misshapen trunk before, but look, thanks to you it now has its proper head. For its excessive immorality was recently reined in by your legislation, and who would deny that this constitutes a country's head? Your city, Fluentia,[39] as it used to be called, was once blind,[40] but now she sees all, since you have given her eyes. For you have established a sweet repose for the pious Muses, and it is they whom one might call the true eyes of a country.[41] Let's say that the wisdom, with which you advise her, is the equivalent of her ears. The fact that she escapes treachery under your leadership amounts to a nose. Since your right hand gave her abundant crops,[42] she has a mouth, by means of which the country feeds the entire body. Because of your expenditures and your leadership Volterra accepted the terms it had formerly rejected:[43] this has been her right hand. While still but a boy you gave her a left hand and a shield, when she was saved from the misery of sedition.[44] Certainty of reward awaits the just, sure punishment the guilty: Solon[45] approves of a city proceeding on this path. Furthermore, she has cast aside her former shabbiness, adorned her hair with gold, and gleams resplendently in golden raiment. This honor is bestowed by sumptuous churches raised to the stars, and by the lofty peaks of the Medici house.[46] This is how you give birth to your country, Lorenzo, this is how you raise her and adorn her; this is why your country truly calls you father.

: XXIII :

In eundem

Cui tua gesta licet brevibus comprendere, Laurens,
    Ille brevi caelum claudet et astra manu.

: XXIV :

In Philippum fratrem pictorem

Conditus hic ego sum, picturae fama, Philippus.
    Nulli ignota meae est gratia mira manus.
Artifices potui digitis animare colores,
    Sperataque animos fallere voce diu.
5 Ipsa meis stupuit Natura expressa figuris,
    Meque suis fassa est artibus esse parem.
Marmoreo tumulo Medices Laurentius hic me
    Condidit; ante humili pulvere tectus eram.

: XXV :

Ad Laurentium extemporaneum epigramma

O ego quam cupio reducis contingere dextram,
    Laurenti, et laeto dicere laetus ave!
Maxima sed densum capiunt vix atria vulgus,
    Tota salutantum vocibus aula fremit.

: XXIII :

On the same man

The man who can encompass your achievements in a few lines,
Lorenzo, will enclose heaven and its stars in his little hand.

: XXIV :

On Fra Filippo the painter[47]

I, Filippo, famous for my painting, am buried here. The wondrous
grace of my hand is known to all. With my fingers I could bring to
life the artist's colors, and trick minds into waiting a long time to
hear a sound. Nature herself was amazed when portrayed in my   5
compositions, and she admitted that I was her equal in the arts.
Lorenzo de' Medici laid me here in a marble tomb, where before I
had been covered by humble dust.

: XXV :

An extemporaneous epigram addressed to Lorenzo de' Medici[48]

Oh, how I long to touch your right hand now that you've returned, Lorenzo, and say, as one happy man to another, "Greetings!" But your great halls can scarcely contain the teeming
mob, and the whole palace resounds with the voices of well-

5 Undique purpurei Medicem pia turba senatus
    Stat circum; cunctis celsior ipse patet.
  Quid faciam? Accedam? Nequeo: vetat invida turba.
    Alloquar? At pavido torpet in ore sonus.
  Aspiciam? Licet hoc, toto nam vertice supra est:
10   Non omne officium turba molesta negas!
  Aspice, sublimi quem vertice fundit honorem!
    Sidereo quantum spargit ab ore iubar!
  Quae reducis facies, laetis quam laetus amicis
    Respondet nutu, lumine, voce, manu!
15 Nil agimus; cupio solitam de more salutem
    Dicere, et officium persoluisse meum.
  Ite mei versus, Medicique haec dicite nostro:
    Angelus hoc mittit Politianus ave.

: XXVI :

Ad eundem

Invideo Pisis, Laurenti, nec tamen odi,
  Ne mihi displiceat quae tibi terra placet.

: XXVII :

In eundem cum ruri querna corona fronte redimitum
viderem ex tempore

Quam bene glandifera cingis tua tempora quercu,
  Qui civem servas non modo, sed populum!

wishers. All around Medici stands a devoted throng of senators[49] 5
dressed in purple, while he himself towers conspicuously above all
of them. What am I to do? Approach? I can't: the envious mob
prevents it. Address him? But my voice sticks in my trembling
throat. Gaze at him? This I can do, for he towers over them by a
full head: you do not deny me every service, you annoying mob! 10
Look at how he radiates dignity from his head on high! What
splendor he radiates from his heavenly face! Look at the returnee's
expression, how happily he responds to his happy friends with a
nod, a look, a word, a touch! It's pointless, yet I want to offer my 15
customary good wishes in the usual way and fulfill my obligation.
Go then, my verses, and say this to our friend Medici: "Angelo
Poliziano sends you this greeting."

: XXVI :

To the same man

I am envious of Pisa,[50] Lorenzo, but I don't hate it, lest the land
that pleases you displease me.

: XXVII :

On the same man, extemporized when I saw him at his country estate wearing an oak garland on his brow[51]

How well it is that you garland your brow with acorn-bearing oak,
you who are the savior not just of a citizen, but a people!

: XXVIII :

In eundem votum

Det tibi Nestoreos, Laurenti, Iuppiter annos,
    Nestoreum quoniam pectus et ora dedit.

: XXIX :

In Laurentium Medicem

Cum commissa sibi tellus malefida negasset
    Semina et agricolae falleret herba fidem,
Protinus optatas patriae tua dextera fruges
    Obtulit, et celerem iussit abire famem.
5 Nec mora, Piseis commutas sedibus urbem
    Servatam, et nimio tempore lentus abes.
Heu, quid agis? Patriae, Laurens, te redde gementi.
    Non facta est donis laetior illa tuis.
Maesta dolet, malletque famem perferre priorem
10   Quam desiderium patria ferre tui.

: XXX :

In Laurentium Iuliumque Petri filios,
fratres piissimos

Nec tanta Oebalios tenuit concordia fratres,
    Nec tanto Atridas foedere iunxit amor,
Implicuit quanto Medicum duo pectora nexu
    Mitis amor, concors gratia, pura fides.

: XXVIII :

A prayer to the same man

May Jupiter grant you Nestor's[52] years, Lorenzo, since he granted you Nestor's wisdom and eloquence.

: XXIX :

On Lorenzo de' Medici

When the fickle earth had rejected the seeds consigned to it and the crops were failing the farmer's trust,[53] it was your right hand that straightway brought your country the grain it longed for, and commanded the famine to speed off. But immediately thereafter 5 you traded the city you had saved for a place in Pisa, and you tarry there for far too long. Alas, what are you up to? Lorenzo, come back to your grieving country: she has not been made any the happier by your gifts. Your nation mourns in sorrow and would rather suffer the earlier famine than endure this longing for you. 10

: XXX :

On Lorenzo and Giuliano, the sons of Piero, the most devoted of brothers[54]

The harmony that held those famous Spartan brothers[55] together was not so great, nor did love join the sons of Atreus[56] by so strong a bond as the tie that has bound the hearts of the two Medici in gentle Love, harmonious Grace, and sincere Faith.

5 Unum velle animis, unum est quoque nolle duobus,
     Corque sibi alterna dant capiuntque manu.
    Esse quid hoc dicam, Iuli, et tu, maxime Laurens?
     Anne duos una mente calere putem?

: XXXI :

In Laurentium Medicem

    Num tibi litorea collectum Anthedone gramen
     Divinum extemplo pectus et ora dedit?
    Nil mortale sapis, Laurens, sed pectore caelum,
     Sed caelum lingua mente animoque refers.
5 Cum referas caelum, caelum tibi praemia fiet:
     Tu cito parta tamen praemia sero pete.

: XXXII :

In eundem

    Quicquid habent Natura tibi et Fortuna dederunt,
     Sed tamen haec superas munera consilio.
    Nam sunt illa quidem paucis communia tecum;
     Maxima consilii gloria tota tua est.
5 Consilio quid agis cupiunt imitarier omnes,
     Laurenti, rerum maxime; nemo potest.

Their two spirits have the same likes and dislikes, and they alter- 5
nately hand their hearts to each other and reclaim them. I ask you,
Giuliano, and you, Lorenzo the Magnificent, what shall I say is
the cause? Am I to think that two men are inspired by one mind?

: XXXI :

On Lorenzo de' Medici

Was it herbs gathered on Anthedon's[57] shore that instantly gave
you divine wisdom and eloquence? There is no hint of mortality
in you, Lorenzo, and in your heart it's heaven that you recall, and
heaven, too, in your speech, your thoughts, your soul. And since 5
it's heaven you recall, heaven shall be your reward: but please be
slow to collect this reward, so swiftly won.

: XXXII :

On the same man

Nature and Fortune have given to you all that they have, but still
you surpass these gifts with your judgment. For, while those are
things that you possess in common with a few others, the great
glory of judgment is all yours. What you achieve by your judg- 5
ment, Lorenzo, greatest in all the world, all want to imitate. But
none can.

: XXXIII :

In Marsilium

Mores, ingenium, Musas, sophiamque supremam
    Vis uno dicam nomine? Marsilius!

: XXXIV :

In Laurentium Medicem

Nescio quos media caeli de sede petitos
    Luminibus radios suspicor esse tuis.
Nam quotiens oculos in me convertis amicos,
    Complector cunctas pectore laetitias.
5 Tunc faciles subeunt Musae, tunc ipse videtur
    Purus Apollinei sideris esse nitor.
At quotiens oculos a me deflectis amicos,
    Complector nullas pectore laetitias,
Non faciles subeunt Musae, non ipse videtur
10   Purus Apollinei sideris esse nitor.
Cur ergo avertis, Laurenti, lumina? Redde,
    Redde meis, quaeso, lumina luminibus!
Laetitias mihi redde meas! Redde, invide, Musas
    Quas tua mi rapiunt lumina! Sed propera.

: XXXIII :

On Marsilio[58]

Character, intellect, poetry and wisdom supreme: shall I say them all in a single name? Marsilio!

: XXXIV :

On Lorenzo de' Medici

I suspect that some kind of rays from the very center of heaven were found for those eyes of yours. For whenever you cast a friendly look toward me, my heart is filled with every sort of happiness. Then the Muses come easily to me, then the very gleam of   5
Apollo's star[59] seems pure to me. But whenever you turn that look of friendship away from me, my heart is filled with no happiness at all, the Muses do not come easily to me, the very gleam of   10
Apollo's star seems impure to me. So why do you avert your gaze, Lorenzo? Give back, I pray you, give back the light of your eyes to mine! Give me back my happiness! Give me back the Muses, my jealous friend, whom your eyes steal from me! And hurry up about it!

: XXXV :

Ad eundem

O ego si possem laqueo subducere collum,
 Et pedicis vinctos explicuisse pedes!
Haud equidem dubitem volucres superare canendo
 Quas aluit campis unda Caystra suis.
5 At nunc, Phoebeos inter velut anser olores,
 Agrestem rauco gutture fundo sonum.
Sed facile expediar, Medices, fiamque canorus,
 Si modo tu dicas 'Politiane, veni.'

: XXXVI :

Ad eundem

Celsa triumphatis, Medices, Florentia Pisis
 Invidet: ut dominam se putet ipsa, redi.

: XXXVII :

In Gaddium

Delicias tibi Roma suas, Florentia, Gaddi,
 Datque suas: o quam deliciosus homo es!

: XXXV :

To the same man[60]

Oh, if only I could take the noose from my neck, and free my feet that are bound in shackles! Indeed I would speedily outdo in song those birds that the waters of the Cayster[61] nurture in their fields. But as things stand now, I pour out a bumpkin sound from my 5 raspy throat, like a goose among the swans of Phoebus. But it would be easy to set me free, Medici, and I'd become a songster, if only you would say: "Poliziano, come."

: XXXVI :

To the same man

Medici, proud Florence envies Pisa, whom she triumphed over. For her to think herself its mistress, you must return.[62]

: XXXVII :

On Francesco Gaddi[63]

Rome bestows her delights upon you, Gaddi, as does Florence. Oh, what a delight-full man you are!

: XXXVIII :

In libellum elegiarum Naldi poetae

Dum celebrat Medicem Naldus, dum laudat amicam,
  Et pariter gemino raptus amore canit,
Tam lepidum unanimes illi ornavere libellum
  Phoebus, Amor, Pallas, Gratia, Musa, Fides.

: XXXIX :

In aedes publicas octo virorum Florentiae

Si qua fides, scelerum procul o procul ite ministri!
  Hic vos iustitiae poena severa manet.

: XL :

In easdem

Hos etiam caelo praefert Astraea penates:
  Non illi in toto est gratior orbe domus.

: XXXVIII :

On the book of elegies by the poet Naldi[64]

While Naldo celebrates Medici, praising his girlfriend, singing his songs, captured in equal measure by two loves, his quite charming little book has been adorned wholeheartedly by Phoebus, Love, Pallas, Grace, Muse, and Faith.

: XXXIX :

On the public building of the Eight Men of Florence[65]

Trust me, go far, far away from this place, you agents of crime: the harsh punishment of justice awaits you here.

: XL :

On the same building

Astraea[66] prefers this house even to heaven: no home is more welcome to her in all the world.

: XLI :

In Albieram Sismundi Stufae sponsam
fato immaturo ereptam

Vivebam (fato sum rapta) Albiera; coniunx
  Sismundus vitam reddidit en iterum!
Nam faciem et claram caelato marmore formam,
  Ingenium et mores carmine restituit.

: XLII :

In eandem

Viva tibi fueram, coniunx, Albiera semper
  Cara quidem; nunc sum mortua cara magis.

: XLIII :

In eandem

Debebam vivens tibi, sed mage rapta: voluptas
  Illa fuit, verum haec proxima religio est.

: XLI :

On the fiancée of Sigismondo della Stufa, Albiera,
who was taken by a premature death[67]

In life I was Albiera, but I was taken by fate. But look, my husband Sigismondo has given me a second life! For he has restored my face and fair form in sculpted marble, my nature and character in verse.

: XLII :

On the same woman

In life, my husband, I was always your dear Albiera; I am even more so now that I am dead.

: XLIII :

On the same woman

I was in your debt while I lived, but I am even more so now that I've been taken. That former debt was a pleasure, but this latter one is more in way of a religious obligation.

: XLIV :

In eandem

Morte una geminam sum nacta Albiera vitam;
    Fama etenim terras, spiritus astra colit.
Fama olim, numquam sed spiritus occidet. Haec mi
    Vita quidem semper vivet, at illa diu.

: XLV :

In eandem

Mortalis fueram dum vixi Albiera, coniunx,
    Sismunde; at nunc sum, mortua, facta dea.

: XLVI :

In eandem

Quod tibi, vir, tenera sum rapta Albiera iuventa,
    Ne geme: cum dulce est vivere, dulce mori est.

: XLIV :

On the same woman

By a single death I, Albiera, have found life twice; for while my fame dwells on earth, my spirit inhabits the stars. My fame will perish one day, but my spirit never. This latter form of life indeed will last forever, while the former will endure, but only for a time.

: XLV :

On the same woman

I was mortal while I lived as Albiera your wife, Sigismondo. But now that I am dead, I've become a goddess.

: XLVI :

On the same woman

Do not mourn, my husband, because I, your Albiera, was taken from you in the tenderness of youth; when life is sweet, so is death.[68]

: XLVII :

In eandem

Quid quereris, genitor? vivit tua filia caelo
  Albiera. Anne deam progenuisse doles?

: XLVIII :

In Demetrium Cretensem et Dionysium Paravisinum,
Graecorum voluminum impressores

Qui colis Aonidas, Graios quoque volve libellos;
  Namque illas genuit Graecia, non Latium.
En Paravisinus quanta hos Dionysius arte
  Imprimit, en quanto cernitis ingenio!
5 Te quoque, Demetri, ponto circumsona Crete
  Tanti operis nobis edidit artificem.
Turce, quid insultas? Tu Graeca volumina perdis;
  Hi pariunt. Hydrae, nunc age, colla seca.

: XLIX :

In puellam morientem

Quaerenti venerem diu negasti.
Sed dum mi totiens pudet negare,
Tandem occasio iusta pernegandi
Inventa est: moreris. Vafra es sagaxque!

: XLVII :

On the same woman

Why do you complain, father? Your daughter, Albiera, lives in heaven. You don't regret having fathered a goddess, do you?

: XLVIII :

On Demetrius of Crete and Dionigi Parravicino,
printers of Greek books[69]

You must turn the pages of Greek books too, you who cultivate the Muses,[70] for it was Greece, not Latium, that gave birth to them. Observe how artfully Dionigi Parravicino prints these books! Observe the great skill he employs! Crete, encircled by the sounding sea, gave birth to you too, Demetrius, who have crafted   5 such a wonderful work for us. Why do you scoff, Turk? You destroy Greek books; these men produce them. You might as well try to cut off the Hydra's heads.

: XLIX :

On a dying girl

For a long time you said no when I wanted sex. But while it's embarrassing that you say no to me so many times, a fitting occasion for your persistent refusal has finally been found: you're dying. You *are* sly and crafty!

: L :

[Eidem] Bernardo Bembo Veneto oratori,
viro undecumque elegantissimo[6]

Ut miseros quondam nautas Acheloia Siren
    In poenam traxit carmine blandisono;
Sic, Bernarde, tuo quemvis succendis amore,
    Seu quid mente agitas seu geris aut loqueris.
5 Si causam Veneti tutaris, Bembe, Senatus,
    Mox Pitho in labris stat veneranda tuis.
Seria si tractas, credam tractare Minervam;
    Si ioca, dat puros Gratia nuda sales.
Carmina seu cantas, tibi Musae in pectore cantant;
10   Sive taces, tacito ridet in ore Lepos.
Si graderis, placido non dura Modestia vultu
    Est comes et dulcis cum Gravitate modus;
Blandus honos vestem furtim componit, ovansque
    Te circum plena ludit Amor pharetra.
15 Fronte Decor, sedet ore Fides, in pectore Candor,
    Inque tuis omnes sunt oculis Veneres.
Sic nos devincis nec vinctos, Bembe, relaxas;
    Sic te quisquis adit mox tua philtra bibit.
Frustra ad te florem Cylleni ferret Ulysses,
20   Sed pro te optasset linquere vel patriam.

: L :

To Bernardo Bembo,[71] the Venetian ambassador,
a most elegant man in every respect

Just as the Siren, Achelous' daughter,[72] once drew poor sailors to
their doom with her seductive song, so do you, Bernardo, fire all
with love for you, whatever you do by thought or deed or word. If   5
you are protecting the interests of the Venetian Senate, then es-
teemed Persuasion[73] stands poised upon your lips. If it is serious
matters you are dealing with, I'd believe it was Minerva in action;
but if its lighthearted affairs, naked Grace supplies your plain witticisms. If it's songs you sing, the Muses are singing in your heart;
but if you are silent, Charm is smiling upon your silent lips. If you   10
are stepping out, an unassuming Modesty in your tranquil expression is your companion, and sweet Moderation combined with
dignity. Gentle Honor secretly arranges your dress, while in celebration Love frolics about you with a full quiver. Grace rests upon   15
your brow, good Faith in your visage, Candor in your heart, and in
your eyes are all the charms of Venus. This is how you bind us to
you, Bembo, and once bound, you do not let us go; this is how
anyone who meets you imbibes your potion. It would be futile for
Ulysses to bring you the flower of Cyllene's god,[74] but for your   20
sake he would even have chosen to abandon his homeland.

: LI :

In Panaetium

Tantus amor tuus est in me, tamque omne, Panaeti,
    Exemplum veteris vincis amicitiae,
Ut tibi collatus iuvenis Phocaeus Orestem
    Oderit, et spernat Thesea Pirithous,
5   Sicanium Pyladen credatur fallere Damon,
    Vixque bonum frenis Castora frater amet.
Non tu unam pro me mortem, sed mille subires,
    Pro me Sisyphium non fugeres lapidem.
Nunc solum hoc tanto refero mercedis amori,
10   Quod me abs te solo victum in amore puto.

: LII :

In Iovianum Crassum Monopoliten⟨sem⟩

Non rara Atthaeae quod amem te gloria linguae
    Causa est, non Latiae copia, non Solymae,
Non acre ingenium, non lingua diserta, nec oris
    Gratia, nec versus vena benigna tui;
5   Sed quod inest rarus tibi, Crasse, in pectore candor,
    Quem nisi amem, rabida tigride natus ero.
Nec te ut amem causa est haec: me abs te cogit amari.
    Crede mihi, pretium est solus amoris amor.

: LI :

On Panezio[75]

So great is your love for me, Panezio, and so far do you surpass
every example of friendship from antiquity, that when compared
to you, the young man from Phocis[76] hates Orestes and Pirithous
despises Theseus; and one might believe that Damon cheats the 5
Sicilian version of Pylades,[77] and Castor the cavalryman is scarcely
beloved by his brother.[78] You would undergo not one, but a thousand deaths for me; for my sake you wouldn't recoil from Sisyphus' rock.[79] I now repay such great love, but with only this reward, the thought that I am surpassed in my affection by you 10
alone.

: LII :

On Gioviano Crasso da Monopoli[80]

The reason why I love you is not your rare command of the language of Attica,[81] nor that of Latium or Jerusalem, not your keen
intellect, eloquent tongue, nor the grace of your countenance, nor
the pleasing nature of your verse; but because there is a rare kind 5
of candor in your heart, Crasso. I'd have to have been born of a
rabid tigress, if I did not cherish that. And yet that's not the reason *I* love *you;* this is what leads *you* to love *me.* Trust me, love
alone is love's reward.

: LIII :

In Simonettam

Dum pulchra effertur nigro Simonetta feretro,
    Blandus et exanimi spirat in ore lepos,
Nactus Amor tempus quo non sibi turba caveret,
    Iecit ab occlusis mille faces oculis.
5 Mille animos cepit viventis imagine risus,
    Ac morti insultans, 'est mea,' dixit, 'adhuc!'
'Est mea,' dixit, 'adhuc! Nondum totam eripis illam!
    Illa vel exanimis militat ecce mihi!'
Dixit, et ingemuit; neque enim satis apta triumphis
10   Illa puer vidit tempora, sed lacrimis.

: LIV :

In eandem

Cum Simonetta decens media iam in morte labaret:
    'Mors,' illi quidam, 'iam prope,' dixit, 'adest.'
Sustulit illa graves oculos, nec territa dixit:
    'Hanc animam, nobis qui dedit, accipiat.'
5 Hactenus, et tacuit. Repete hic aevum omne, Vetustas;
    Nil par huic animo quod referatur habes.

: LIII :

On Simonetta[82]

While the beautiful Simonetta was being carried out on a black bier, and an alluring charm still breathed upon her dead lips, Love seized the moment when the crowd was not on its guard against him and cast a thousand torches from her closed eyes. He cap- 5 tured a thousand hearts with the vision of her living smile, and, taunting death, he said, "She's mine still! She's mine," he said, "still! You are not yet taking her entirely! Look, even in death she makes war on my behalf!" He spoke, and then he groaned; for the boy 10 saw that this was not the moment for gloating, but for tears.

: LIV :

On the same woman

While the lovely Simonetta was slipping away, now firmly in death's grip, someone said to her, "Death is at hand." She raised her heavy eyes, and, unafraid, said, "Let he who gave me this life, receive it again." That was all, and then she was still. If Antiquity 5 were to review the whole of time in this world, it could tell of nothing equal to this soul.

: LV :

In eandem

Hic Simonetta iacet, iacet hic simul omnis amorum
    Turba, iacent omnes deliciae et veneres.

: LVI :

In Simonettam. Iulii est sententia a me versibus inclusa

Aspice ut exiguo capiatur marmore quicquid
    Mortali possit a superis tribui!
Hic Simonetta iacet, cuius mortalia cuncta
    Concipere immensum non poterant animum;
5 Quam neque mors potuit visa exterrere, Deumque
    Mox petiit cui se nympha dedit moriens.

: LVII :

In Archeanassam, Plato. Epigramma e graeco versum

Archeanassa mihi meretrix Colophonia nunc est,
    Cuius et in rugis insidet acer Amor.
A miseri, a prima tetigit quos illa iuventa
    Igne suo! Medii vos rapuere rogi.

: LV :

On the same woman

Here lies Simonetta; here too lies the entire troop of Loves; here lie all the delights and charms of passion.

: LVI :

On Simonetta. The sentiment is Giuliano's, set to verse by me

See how all that can be bestowed upon a mortal by the gods can be contained in just a bit of marble! Here lies Simonetta, whose boundless soul could not be contained by all the mortal world. Not even the sight of death could terrify her, and then she went in 5 search of God, to whom, as she died, she gave herself as bride.

: LVII :

Plato on Archeanassa, an epigram translated from Greek[83]

Archeanassa of Colophon is now my mistress, on whose very wrinkles sits passionate Love. Ah, the poor souls whom she touched from her early youth with her flame! You were carried off in the midst of a blazing pyre.

: LVIII :

Sapphus Epithaphion in Timada[7] e graeco versum

Timados[8] hic pulvis, quae dulces ante hymenaeos
   Excepta est nigro Persephones thalamo.
Illius, heu, fato cunctae de vertice amatam
   Aequales ferro subsecuere comam.

: LIX :

Antipatri in Homerum e graeco versum

Troiam canens, Homere, flammis erutam,
Urbes gravi livore stantes concutis.

: LX :

Ad Galeotum principem Faventinum

Cur promissa tibi tuus poeta
Nondum praestiterit, rogas? Poeta est.

: LVIII :

Sappho's epitaph on Timas,[84] *translated from the Greek*

This is the dust of Timas, who was received in the black chamber of Persephone before the sweet wedding songs could be played. Upon her death, alas, all her companions clipped their lovely locks from their heads.

: LIX :

On Homer, by Antipater, translated from the Greek[85]

Homer, as you sing of Troy's destruction in flames, you rattle cities still standing with profound jealousy.

: LX :

To Galeotto, Prince of Faenza[86]

Why has your friend, the poet, not yet fulfilled his promises, you ask? He's a poet.

: LXI :

In Ptolomaei Geographiam e graeco

Si caelum e terra spectes, caelum omne videbis;
Si terram e caelo, penitus tibi terra patebit.
Nunc terram penitus cernis, caelum isse[9] putato.

: LXII :

In Herculem et Antaeum e Graeco

Incaluere animis dura certare palaestra
    Neptuni quondam filius atque Iovis.
Nec certamen erant operoso ex aere lebetes,
    Sed quod vel vitam vel ferat interitum.
5 Occidit Antaeus: Iove natum vincere fas est,
    Estque magistra pales Graecia non Libya.

: LXIII :

In Niobem lapidem

Hoc est sepulcrum intus cadaver non habens,
Hoc est cadaver et sepulcrum non habens,
Sed est idem cadaver et sepulchrum sibi.

: LXI :

On Ptolemy's Geography,[87] *from the Greek*

If you look at the sky from the earth, you'll see the entire sky; if you look at the earth from the sky, the earth will be wide open to you. Now that you see the earth completely, you must imagine that you have mounted the sky.

: LXII :

On Hercules and Antaeus from the Greek[88]

Once upon a time the son of Neptune and the son of Jove[89] burned with a passion to compete on the hard ground of the wrestling-floor. And the contest was not for caldrons made of crafted bronze, but that one might win life or death. Antaeus it   5 was who fell: it is right that the son of Jove should triumph, for it is Greece that is the mistress of wrestling, not Libya.

: LXIII :

On Niobe turned to stone[90]

This is a tomb that does not have a corpse within it, and this is a corpse that also does not have a tomb, but is at once both a corpse and its own tomb.

: LXIV :

In Mabilium Novatum Insubrem

Quod vestes oleo geris perunctas,
Mucco et pulvere sordidas, Mabili;
Quod lardum madido fluit capillo,
Pleno furfuribusque vermibusque
5 Et cadaveribus pedunculorum;
Quod fuligine squalet atra barba,
Quam rodunt tineae pulexque saltans;
Quod mucosa tibi seges pilorum
Extat naribus usque polyposis,
10 Qua septem lepores queant latere;
Quod gingivaque buxeique dentes
Sordent ploxonio, ac putente in ala
Educas olidae marem capellae;
Quodque unguis sanie rubet cruenta,
15 Saepe ut lucifugam putem esse blattam,
Cenae reliquiasque pridianae
Incrementa manus habent voracis;
His te ex omnibus esse quis poetam,
Vatem, fatidicum neget, Mabili?
20 Tales Caecilios fuisse credo,
Plautos Pacuviosque Naeviosque
Aut si quis Curium boves sequentem
Traxit versibus ulmeum in theatrum.
Caeli numina quod negas deumque,
25 Lucreti fuit hoc et Euripidis.
Paedicas: fuit hoc Maronianum,
Paedicavit Anacreon Bathyllum.
Insanis: Colophonius poeta es.

: LXIV :

On Mabilio from Insubrian Novate[91]

Because you wear clothes that are drenched in olive oil, Mabilio,
filthy with mucus and dust; because grease flows from your damp
hair, which is full of dandruff scales and worms and dead bodies   5
of lice; because there's soot in your filthy, black beard, which is
gnawed by moths and a prancing flea; because a snotty crop of
hairs protrudes from your polyp-ridden nose, where seven rabbits   10
could hide out; because you have filthy gums and teeth the color
of boxwood in your slack jaw,[92] and in your stinking armpit you
are raising a smelly she-goat's mate; because your fingernail is red
with bloody matter, to the point that I often think it's a light-   15
shunning cockroach; and because those appurtenances to your voracious hand contain the remnants of yesterday's dinner; for all of
these reasons, who would deny that you are a poet, a seer, a
prophet, Mabilio? I believe that the likes of Caecilius looked like   20
this, and Plautus and Pacuvius and Naevius, and anyone who used
verses to attract Curius the cowherd into a wooden theater.[93] As to
the fact that you deny the divine power of heaven and the gods,
you have this in common with Lucretius and Euripides.[94] You   25
practice anal sex; this was Vergil's thing,[95] and Anacreon buggered
Bathyllus.[96] You are out of your mind; that makes you a poet from

77

Iam iam phthiriasi scaturiente
30　Semesus cadis et foraminatis
Membris: hoc Pherecidae habes tragoedi.
De cunctis maledicis: hoc poeta es.
Es mendax, levis, insolens, ineptus,
Insulsus, petulans: et his poeta es.
35　Quid multis moror? Es poeta totus.
Possum hoc indiciis probare centum.
Quo vulgus negat esse te poetam,
Id quiddam est minimum neque adnotandum,
Quod vexas miseras subinde chartas
40　Plenis versibus inficetiarum.

: LXV :

In eundem Mabilium obicientem Angelo Politiano
quod neque curtum carmen neque longum sciat componere,
in quo responso Mabilium ludit
quod curtum et longum improprie usurparit,
simulque obicit quod ⟨expedivit⟩
ante penultima producta posuerit Mabilius

Quod me scire negas vel curtum scribere carmen
　　Vel longum, fateor: solus utrumque facis.
Nil breve, nil medium est, longum est curtumve, Mabili,
　　Quicquid habes, quicquid aut geris aut loqueris.
5　Proximus a primo tibi pes est tempore curtus,
　　Quando *expedivit* inseris hexametro.
Altera curta tibi solea est, curtumque, Mabili,
　　Subligar: erumpunt hinc digiti, hinc veretrum.

78

Colophon.[97] And now, half consumed by raging phthiriasis, your   30
limbs bored through, you collapse: this you have in common with
Pherecydes the tragedian.[98] You badmouth everyone; in this respect you are a poet. You're dishonest, petty, arrogant, tasteless,
insipid, and impudent: in these respects, too, you are a poet. Why   35
waste time on all the details? You are the complete poet. I can
show this by a hundred proofs. The point on which the public
denies that you are a poet is something quite minor and hardly to
be noted, namely that you continually torment your wretched
pages with verses full of infelicities.   40

: LXV :

On the same Mabilio, who criticized Angelo Poliziano
for not knowing how to compose either a short poem
or a long one, in response to which he makes fun of Mabilio
because he used the Latin for "short" and "long" improperly,
and at the same time he objects that Mabilio scanned
"expedivit" with a lengthened antepenultimate syllable

You say that I do not know how to write either a short poem or a
long one. Point conceded: only you do both. There's nothing "little," nothing "moderate," Mabilio; with you it's "long" or "short,"
whatever you're about, whatever you do or say. The foot following   5
the first is "short" by a measure, when you insert "expediuit" into a
hexameter. One of your sandals is "short," and so are your under-
pants, Mabilio; your toes protrude from the one, your dick from

Siquis forte tuas studeat componere laudes,
10   Uno longus erit[10] hic quoque versiculo.
At siquis scribat quot habent tua carmina mendas,
       Conficiet curtas hic vel hic Iliades.
Quae semper fellat dicit periuria semper:
       Longa tibi lingua est; hac cito curtus eris.
15   Quod vacat, est longum caput atque enorme, Mabili,
       Iudice vel cerebro: si quod inest, rogita.
Verum alia est aliis sententia, namque Phrenesis
       Conqueritur capitis de brevitate tui.
Qui cerebro tenus id lacerant, curtum esse fatentur:
20   Tu quoque mox curto curtus eris capite.
Quamquam id carnifices nondum statuere, sed ingens
       De te certamen est gladio et crucibus.
Hoc est quod vultur, quod corvus gestit, et escam
       Te fore uterque sibi praevidet augurio.
25   Hoc spurci mores, impura hoc vita meretur,
       Obscenoque animus corpore sordidior.
Quid moror his? Nam si prolixum singula narrans
       In te ego nunc librum scripsero, curtus erit.

: LXVI :

In Mabilium, minitantem
novum se fulgur verosque tonitrus missurum

Quod fulgur mihi te novum, Mabili,
Missurum et tonitrus minere veros,
Nil est: novimus hos neque esse fictos,
Nam veros tuus esse odor probavit.

the other. If by chance anyone should take a fancy to write in your praise, with just one little verse he too will be "long." And if anyone should write up all the faults your poetry contains, the *Iliads* that he completes will seem "short." The tongue that always fellates always lies: you've got a "long" tongue, but soon you'll be "short" of it. The head that's lacking judgment and a brain, Mabilio, is "long" and irregular; just keep asking whatever's in there. But different people feel differently, for Madness complains about the smallness of your head. Those who tear into it right up to the brain agree that it is "short"; you too will soon be "short" your short head. Although as a matter of fact the executioners haven't made that decision yet, but there is a huge contest over you between the sword and the cross. This is what the vulture and the crow are itching for, and each one predicts that you will be their tasty morsel. This is what your filthy character deserves, your impure life, and your heart which is more squalid than your filthy body. Why do I linger on these points? For if I now go on to write an extensive book on you, relating each and every detail, it will be "short."

: LXVI :

On Mabilio, who keeps threatening that he will let loose a fresh flash of lightning and real thunder

There's no reason for you to threaten to send a fresh flash of lightning and real thunderbolts my way, Mabilio. I know about them and I know they're not fake; for your stench has proved them real.

: LXVII :

In eundem Mabilium

Si iam carmina nostra te, Mabili,
Urgent ad laqueum, miser, crucemque,
Ne, quaeso, propera mori, tuum ne
Fraudes carnificem suo lucello.
5 Namque est percupidus tui, ac libenter
Is tantum tibi dempserit laboris.
Quid? Nostin' hominem? Negas? At idem est
Aurem qui secuit tibi sinistram.

: LXVIII :

In Mabili inertem maledicentiam

Ore tibi pauci, sed nulli in carmine dentes
    Cum sint, atque illi sint putridi et veteres,
Allatras, ut cum nequeas mordere, Mabili,
    Latratu ostendas te tamen esse canem.

: LXIX :

In Mabilium, quod perturbatus respondeat

Iratus nimium nobis, sed iure, Mabili,
    Urgeris nostris iam, puto, carminibus.
Ipse iocor tecum ridens, sed iure, Mabili:
    Quis non rideret carmina, quaeso, tua?

: LXVII :

On the same Mabilio

Mabilio, if my poems are now driving you to the noose and cross,
do not, poor fellow, speed up your death, lest you cheat your executioner of his small profit. For he is quite partial to you and   5
would gladly unburden you of so much toil. What? You know the
fellow? No, you say? But he's the same one who cut off your left
ear.

: LXVIII :

On Mabilio's clumsy verbal abuse

Since you have only a few teeth in your mouth and none at all in
your poetry (and those are old and rotten at that), you bark at
people, so that by barking, Mabilio, you can show that though you
cannot bite, you are nonetheless a dog.

: LXIX :

On Mabilio, for making an angry response

Your anger at me is excessive, Mabilio, and yet justified, since you
are now, I think, feeling the pressure of my poetry. I myself am
laughing when I jest with you, Mabilio, and yet justifiably: who
wouldn't laugh at your poetry, I ask?

: LXX :

In Mabilium responsum

Quod nasum mihi, quod reflexa colla
Demens obicis, esse utrumque nostrum
Assertor veniam vel ipse; nam me
Nil nasutius est sagaciusque,
5   In te dum liceat vibrare nasum.
Nam quis te, rogo, sic inelegantem,
Insulsum, illepidum videns, ineptum,
Versus scribere prorsus infacetos,
Non centum cupiat sibi esse nasos?
10 Centum rhinocerotas atque barros,
Ronchos, auriculas, ciconiasque
Cum splene et petulantibus cachinnis?
Condas te in putidum licet lupanar,
Mergas te in mediis licet cloacis,
15 Non cedas olida licet latrina.
Quoquo diffugias pavens, Mabili,
Nostrum non poteris latere nasum.
Prendam te, miser, utque trux molossus
Frangam dentibus imbecille tergum.
20 Sed nasus superest tibi, Mabili,
Curtus, dimidiatus, osseusque,
In quo polypus exurit,[11] vel ipse
Quo cimex posuit sibi cubile,
Quo tutas pulices habent latebras,
25 Qui iam pervius est adusque frontem,
In quo nidificare vespa possit,
Qui neutro patet indecens hiatu,
Clausus sentibus hic quibus, sed ille

: LXX :

On Mabilio, a response

Since you are crazy enough to fault me for having a nose and a hunched neck, I shall come, in person no less, to make a legal assertion that I have both. For nothing is more long-nosed and keen-scented than I,[99] so long as I can wrinkle my nose in your 5 direction. For who, I ask, would not wish to have a hundred noses, when he sees someone as uncultured, unattractive, unrefined, unskillful as you writing utterly unsophisticated verses? One hundred 10 rhino snouts and elephant trunks, snorting, ear wagging, and flipping the bird, accompanied by wild and angry laughter? You can hide yourself in a putrid whorehouse, submerge yourself in the middle of the sewers, but you won't be able to get out of the stink- 15 ing latrine. Wherever you flee in terror, Mabilio, you won't be able to hide from my nose. I'll catch you, you wretch, and like a vicious hound[100] I'll break your feeble back with my teeth. But you've got 20 more than enough of a nose yourself, Mabilio, broken, halved, and bony, with a burning polyp in it, where even a bug has made a bed for itself, where fleas have a safe hiding place, which is now perfo- 25 rated right up to your forehead, in which a wasp could make a nest, which is unsightly because it's open in neither nostril, one of which is closed off with brambles, while the other is filled with

Plenus cassibus est araneorum.
30 Sed quid te cruciat, reflexa colla
Si interdum gero? Num parum videtur,
Si pronos statuis tuos cinaedos,
Si pronum statuent, miser Mabili,
Mox te carnificis manus, velut nunc
35 Pronum te statuunt mutoniati?
Atqui tu resupina colla demens
Posthac desine iam mihi exprobrare.
Nam qui pronus obambulas popinas,
Spurcatum caput erigas libenter,
40 Si pondus sinat herniae, Mabili.

: LXXI :

Iambicum trimetron de domo
nuper a Mabilio empta in desertissimo urbis loco
qui 'Ad Caballum' dicitur

Heres relictus a parente sordido,
Ille impudicus, temulentus, aleo,
Spurcus, lutosus, pedicosus, hispidus,
Pannosus, unctus, caprimulgus, horridus,[12]
5 Edax, ineptus, insolens Mabilius,
Uno expatravit patrimonium die
Gula helluante, cunnilingis osculis,
Vorace culo et exfututa mentula.
Mox cum super vix quindecim nummi forent,
10 Rebus cavendi iam suis tempus ratus,
Emit lacertis et colubris hospitam
Domum, rigentem senticetis et rubis,
Familiarem vulturi et bubonibus;

spiders' webs. But why does it torture you, if now and then I bend   30
my neck back? It doesn't strike you as sufficient that you bend
your catamites forward; that soon the executioner's hands will
bend you forward, poor Mabilio, just as those well-hung fellows   35
are bending you forward now? But from here on out now, stop
criticizing me for having a hunched neck, since you, who shuffle
round the taverns with your face to the ground, would happily lift
up your disgusting head, if only the pressure of your hernia would   40
let you, Mabilio.

: LXXI :

Iambic trimeters on the house that was recently
purchased by Mabilio in the most deserted part of the city,
which is called "Ad Caballum"[101]

When he was left as heir by his filthy father, that immoral,
drunken, gambling, foul, dirty, lice-ridden, hairy, ragged, greasy,
shaggy, bumpkin, gluttonous, cloddish, arrogant Mabilio squan-   5
dered his inheritance in a single day with his guzzling appetite, his
taste for cunnilingus, his voracious anus, and his fucked-out dick.
Then when there were scarcely fifteen florins left, thinking that   10
now was the time to watch out for his affairs, he bought a house
that's a haven for lizards and snakes, bristling with shrubs and
bushes, a home to vultures and owls; in which a throng of beggars

87

In qua solebat turba mendicantium,[13]
15 Longis coactos esuritionibus,
Mandare terrae turgidi ventris cibos;
Qua contumaces Aeolus ventos solet
Punire clausos; qua recuset Tantalus
Siticulosam Ditis horridi Styga
20 Mutare, et Aetnae centiceps gigas onus.
Nec vendere illam nec locare, si velit,
Donare nec Mabilius cuiquam potest:
Mutare dominum domus[14] haec nescit suum.
Quantum libet Mabilius sit prodigus,
25 Profundat ore, pene, podice et manu,
Quam nunc sit esse non potest pauper magis:
Fecit lucrum ingens, hanc emens, Mabilius.

: LXXII :

In violas a Venere mea dono acceptas

Molles o violae, Veneris munuscula nostrae,
    Dulce quibus tanti pignus amoris inest,
Quae vos, quae genuit tellus? Quo nectare odoras
    Sparserunt Zephyri mollis et aura comas?
5 Vosne in Acidaliis aluit Venus aurea campis?
    Vosne sub Idalio pavit Amor nemore?
His ego crediderim citharas ornare corollis
    Permessi in roseo margine Pieridas.
Hoc flore ambrosios incingitur Hora capillos;
10   Hoc tegit indociles Gratia blanda sinus.
Haec Aurora suae nectit redimicula fronti,
    Cum roseum verno pandit ab axe diem.

regularly deposits on the ground the food from their swollen bel- 15
lies that has been congealed from going too long without eating;
where Aeolus[102] regularly locks up his disobedient winds as punishment; for which Tantalus would refuse to trade the Grim Reap-
er's thirsty river Styx,[103] and the hundred-headed giant would not 20
trade the weight of Etna.[104] Mabilio couldn't sell that house or
rent it or give it to anyone, even if he wanted to: this house can't
change ownership. No matter how wasteful Mabilio is, how much
he squanders with his mouth, his penis, his arse or his hand, he 25
can't be more of a pauper than he is now: Mabilio made a huge
profit when he bought this house.

: LXXII :

On the violets I received as a gift from my Venus

O gentle violets, tiny presents from my Venus, in which there is a
sweet token of such great love, what soil produced you? With
what nectar did the gentle breezes of Zephyr sprinkle your fragrant leaves? Did golden Venus raise you in the fields of Acidalia? 5
Did Love feed you in some Idalian grove?[105] I could believe that
with garlands such as these the Muses adorn their lyres on the
rose-covered banks of the Permessus;[106] with a flower such as this
Hora[107] binds her ambrosial hair; with a flower such as this Grace 10
seductively covers her untrained bosom. Flowers like these make
up the chaplet that Aurora binds to her brow, when she spreads
the rosy daylight in the springtime sky. From buds such as these

Talibus Hesperidum rutilant violaria gemmis,
    Floribus his pictum possidet aura nemus.
15 His distincta pii ludunt per gramina manes,
    Hos fetus verna Chloridos herba parit.
Felices nimium violae, quas carpserit illa
    Dextera quae miserum me mihi subripuit!
Quas roseis digitis formoso admoverit ori,
20   Illi unde in me spicula torquet amor!
Forsitan et vobis haec illinc gratia venit,
    Tantus honor dominae spirat ab ore meae!
Aspice lacteolo blanditur ut illa colore,
    Aspice purpureis ut rubet haec foliis!
25 Hic color est dominae, roseo cum dulce pudore
    Pingit lacteolas purpura grata genas.
Quam dulcem labris, quam late spirat odorem!
    En, violae, in vobis ille remansit odor.
O fortunatae violae, mea vita, meumque
30   Delicium, o animi portus et aura mei!
A vobis saltem, violae, grata oscula carpam,
    Vos avida tangam terque quaterque manu,
Vos lacrimis satiabo meis quae maesta per ora
    Perque sinum vivi fluminis instar eunt.
35 Combibite has lacrimas, quae lentae pabula flammae
    Saevus Amor nostris exprimit ex oculis.
Vivite perpetuum, violae, nec solibus aestus
    Nec vos mordaci frigore carpat hiems.
Vivite perpetuum, miseri solamen amoris,
40   O violae, o nostri grata quies animi.
Vos eritis mecum semper, vos semper amabo,
    Torquebor pulchra dum miser a domina,
Dumque Cupidineae carpent mea pectora flammae,
    Dum mecum stabunt et lacrimae et gemitus.

the violet beds of the Hesperides take on a reddish glow, and their grove is painted with flowers like these as the breeze fills it. The 15 pious souls of the departed frolic through meadows adorned with flowers like these; these are like the fruits produced by Chloris'[108] crops in springtime. Far too fortunate you violets that were plucked by the hand that has stolen my wretched self from me! Those violets that her rosy fingers brought to that shapely mouth from which Love aims his arrows at me! Perhaps this grace came 20 to you too from that same source, so great is the dignity that breathes from the mouth of my mistress! Look at how alluring she is with her milky complexion! Look at how the flower blushes with its purple foliage! This is my mistress' coloring when a pleas- 25 ing purple paints her milk-white cheeks with sweet rosy modesty. How sweet the fragrance from her lips, how far and wide it breathes! Look, you violets, that fragrance remained within you. O blessed violets, my life and my delight, O safe harbor and life- 30 breath of my soul! From you at least, my violets, I shall gather pleasing kisses. I shall touch you three times, four times with my eager hands. I shall sate you with my tears, which flow like a run- ning river over my sad visage and the folds of my cloak. Drink in 35 these tears, which savage Love expresses from my eyes as fuel for a lingering flame. May you live for all time, violets; may the summer not consume you with the heat of its suns, nor winter with biting cold. May you live for all time, a consolation for my wretched love, O violets, a grateful relief for my soul. You will be with me always, 40 I shall love you forever, so long as my beautiful mistress continues to torture this poor wretch, so long as flames of desire consume my heart, so long as tears and lamentation are with me.

: LXXIII :

Ode dicolos ad Alexandrum Curtesium adolescentem bene
litteratum, qui ut Politianum videret, Florentiam petierat, cum
ille se commodum in Cafasolanum contulisset

Nil me iam patula iuvat
    Saevo letiferum lumine Sirium
Devitare sub ilice,
    Exceptum torulo gramineo caput
5 Bullantem prope rivulum.
    Iam sordet tremulo murmure palpitans
Illabens aqua calculis,
    Longis Dauliados garrula questibus.
Iam sordent aviaria;
10   Nil blandum est oculis, nil placet auribus.
Odi rura nemusque
    Et vallem et Zephyros et gelidos specus.
O qui moenibus inferat
    Iam me? O qui medio sistat in atrio
15 Urbani cupidum laris,
    Curtesi, o placido qui locet in sinu?
Cur mi non teneros datur
    Totis versiculos imbibere auribus
Coram dulciter asperos?
20   Cur dextrae cupidam iungere dexteram?
Tu me, dulcis amicule,
    Tu visum propera. O saeva necessitas!
O cur frangere compedes,
    Detrectare mihi cur iuga non licet?
25 Sed quid fundere iam iuvat
    Nequicquam ad superos tot querimonias?

: LXXIII :

An Ode in two cola[109] addressed to Alessandro Cortesi,[110] a
very learned young man, who had come to Florence to see
Poliziano when he had just moved to Cafaggiolo

I take no pleasure now in avoiding the savage light of the death-
dealing Dog Star under the spreading oak tree, resting my head on
a small cushion of grass by the bubbling brook. Now there is no   5
charm for me in the tremulous, babbling murmur of the water rip-
pling over the pebbles, chattering with the long complaints of the
bird from Daulis.[111] The wild birds hold no charm for me now;
nothing is charming in my sight, or pleasing to my ears. I hate the   10
countryside and the forest groves, the valley and the west winds
and the cool grottoes. Oh, who would take me inside their walls?
Oh, who would settle me in the midst of their court, desirous as I   15
am of a home in the city? O Cortesi, who would take me to his
peaceful bosom? Why am I not allowed to be in your presence and
imbibe with all my sense of hearing your delicate, bittersweet
verses? Why can I not join my eager right hand to yours? Do   20
hasten, my dear sweet friend, to come to visit me. Oh, destiny is
cruel! Oh, why can I not burst my bonds, why can I not shirk this
yoke? But what good is it now to pour out in vain so many com-   25
plaints to the gods above? Each man has his own lot, weighing

Sors cuique est sua, caelitus
   Dependens homini: quin etiam Iovem
Urget dura necessitas.
30   Quod Parcae annuerint, haud revocabile est.

: LXXIV :

In poste cubiculi sui

Blanda quies habitet: duri procul este labores.

: LXXV :

In cubiculo pro Iuliano Salviato

Pectoris interpres, genii domus, hospita curis,
   Cellula sum domini conscia deliciis.
Hic faciet te Iuno patrem, Cytherea maritum,
   Libertas regem, semideumque Sopor.

: LXXVI :

*E Graeco Theocriti
versum per Angelum Politianum*

Pulchra quidem nobis haud primis pulchra videntur.

down on him from heaven: indeed, even Jupiter is burdened by the harshness of destiny. That which the Fates have approved cannot   30 be recalled.

: LXXIV :

Upon the doorpost of his bedroom

May soothing rest reside here: away with you, harsh toils!

: LXXV :

Upon a bedroom, composed for Giuliano Salviati[112]

Interpreter of his heart, home of his character, host to his cares, I am the chamber of my master, privy to his delights. Here Juno will make you a father, Venus a husband, Liberty a king, and Sleep a demigod.

: LXXVI :

From the Greek of Theocritus, translated by Angelo Poliziano[113]

We are not at all the first to whom beautiful things seem beautiful.

∶ LXXVII ∶

Ex eodem versum

Et vanis in basiolis iucunda voluptas.

∶ LXXVIII ∶

Ex Hesiodo versum

Ipsa dies nunc est genitrix, nunc saeva noverca.

∶ LXXIX ∶

Ex eodem versum

Consilio perit ipse suo consultor iniquus.

∶ LXXX ∶

In leges extemporale

Inventum Actaei dicuntur iura Draconis.
    Vera est fama nimis: nil nisi virus habent.

⁚ LXXVII ⁚

Translated from the same poet[114]

Even in empty kisses there is sweet delight.

⁚ LXXVIII ⁚

Translated from Hesiod[115]

At one time the day is itself a mother, at another a cruel step-mother.

⁚ LXXIX ⁚

Translated from the same poet[116]

The unjust counselor is himself done in by his own counsel.

⁚ LXXX ⁚

An improvisation on the laws

They say that laws were invented by the Athenian Draco. The story is too true, for they contain only poison.[117]

: LXXXI :

In Theodorum Gazam

Heu sacrum caput occubuit Theodorus, et hora
    Una obiere omnes reliquiae generis!
Nec tamen hoc querimur (nimis est potuisse videri);
    Non erat hic nostro tempore dignus honos.
5 Hoc dolet, heu, quod neutra patri est nunc lingua superstes
    Quae mittat iustas manibus inferias.

: LXXXII :

In eundem

Cum terram hinc nosset Theodorus et äera et undas,
    'Iam restant,' inquit, 'sidera; terra, vale.'

: LXXXIII :

In somnos

O mihi quanta datis fallaces gaudia somni!
    Invideo, Endymion, Latmia[15] saxa tibi.
Iam si nil sopor est gelidae nisi mortis imago,
    Omnia mors superat gaudia: vita, vale!

: LXXXI :

On Theodore Gaza[118]

Alas, Theodore, our sacred guide, is dead! And in a single season all traces of his race have perished! But it is not this that we lament; our age was not worthy of this honor and it's more than we deserve that it could have seemed so. This is what pains me, alas,   5 that neither language[119] now survives its parent to deliver fitting rites to the dead.

: LXXXII :

On the same man

While Theodore yet knew the earth and air and waters on this side, he said, "Now the stars await; Earth, farewell."

: LXXXIII :

On dreams

Oh, what pleasures you give me, deceitful dreams! Endymion, I envy you your grotto on Latmos.[120] Now if sleep is nothing more than an image of death's chill, then death surpasses all other joys: so long, life!

: LXXXIV :

Basso

Basse, licet veterum monimenta revolvat avorum,
    Vix quem Fama tibi conferat inveniet.
Omnia nam tibi sunt, fuerant quae singula priscis,
    Fecisset triplex qualia vix Erulus.
5 Tu mittis Lydos aeterna in saecula fastos;
    Tu conferre audes cum Cicerone manum;
Tu brevibus claudis lasciva epigrammata chartis,
    Et tener exiguos ludis amans elegos.
Idem et Pindaricos gaudes recludere fontes,
10   Ut Venusina tibi barbitos astupeat.
Ecce Syracusias tentas inflare cicutas:
    Non iam hic in silvis Tityrus unus erit.
Iam Chaos antiquum primamque evolvere molem
    Incipis, et grandi protinus ore tonas.
15 Iam Maro te torva respectat fronte secundum,
    Iam pavet et sceptris gloria prisca suis.
Utque intret biferi si virgo rosaria Paesti,
    Quam primo carpat vix sciat illa rosam,
Sic tot Fama tuae cernens miracula laudis,
20   Palmam cui primum deferat in dubio est.

: LXXXIV :

To Bassus[121]

Bassus, were Fame to scroll through the memorials of our ancestors of old, she would scarcely find any to compare with you. For
to you have been granted each and every trait the ancients had, the
kind of things that Erulus,[122] the triple threat, could scarcely have
performed. You transmit the history of the Lydians[123] to the ages, 5
you have the chutzpah to match yourself with Cicero; you set
down short, playful epigrams on the page, and you play the part of
the tender lover, turning out trifling elegies. You also take pleasure
in revealing Pindaric springs, with the result that the lyre of Ve- 10
nosa[124] is astonished at you. Look, now you set your hand to play
upon Syracusan reeds![125] No longer will there be but one Tityrus
here in the forests. Now it's the tale of ancient Chaos and the
primeval ooze that you begin to unroll and it's like continuous
thunder from your great lips. Now Vergil with a furrowed brow 15
casts a glance at you following behind, and his ancient glory even
trembles for its scepter. And just as when a maiden enters the rose
gardens of twice-blooming Paestum[126] and scarcely knows which
rose to pick first, so too when Fame beholds the many wonders of
your renown, she is in doubt about which one to bestow the palm 20
to first.

: LXXXV :

Eidem

Carmina cum Basso deberem, carmina misi;
    Rettulit ille meis carmina carminibus,
Qualia sub densis volucris nec Daulias umbris
    Eridani in ripis, nec canit albus olor.
5 Sic sua cum Lycio donasset aenea Glauco,
    Aurea Tydides rettulit arma domum.

: LXXXVI :

In Argum

Quid tibi vis gelidos servans, vigil Arge, liquores?
    Quid nitidum ad fontem ferre gradum prohibes?
Obscenos hinc pelle sues, armenta, ferasque:
    Non peto membra istis fontibus abluere,
5 Non lymphas turbare paro. da tingere fauces,
    Exiguo liceat rore levare sitim.
Hostibus hoc Langia dedit, potumque vetantes
    Ruricolae in nigro gurgite nunc saliunt.
Quid, quod adest aestas? Quid, quod[16] sitis ipse volensque
10   Supplicio infelix Tantaleo frueris?
Ista quidem dives sed non est vena perennis:
    Iam custoditas prohibet aestus aquas.
Quod serves nil postmodo erit. Quid, inepte, moraris?
    Unda perit: bibe tu. vel sine, quaeso, bibam.

⁚ LXXXV ⁚

To the same person

When I owed Bassus some poems, I sent them to him. He repaid
my poems with poems, the likes of which neither the bird of
Daulis[127] sings under the dense shade, nor the white swan on the
banks of the Po. It's the same as when, after giving his own bronze   5
armor to Glaucus of Lycia, the son of Tydeus took home his armor of gold.[128]

⁚ LXXXVI ⁚

On Argus[129]

What do you mean by guarding these cool waters, watchful Argus? Why do you block me from approaching the glistening
spring? Keep away filthy swine, cattle and wild beasts, but I'm not
planning to wash my limbs in these springs, I'm not getting ready   5
to pollute the waters. Just let me wet my throat, let me relieve my
thirst with a bit of water. Langia[130] let her enemy do this, and the
mythical farmers who denied access to liquid refreshment now
leap about in the dark pool.[131] Consider the fact that summer is
here, that you yourself are thirsty, and that, unhappy though you   10
are, you're willingly enjoying the punishment of Tantalus.[132] That
stream is rich, to be sure, but it's not never-ending: the heat is already slowing the waters you're protecting. Before long there won't
be anything for you to guard. Why delay, you clod? The water's
going: go ahead and take a drink! But if not, please let me have
one.

: LXXXVII :

In Mabilium epitaphion

Flecte, viator, iter: fetet. nam putre Mabili
    Hac fovea corpus conditur atque animus.

: LXXXVIII :

In Lalagen

Laetior ut cervus, protracto naribus angui,
    Exuit annoso cornua cum senio;
Aurea Callaicis ut nuper dempta caminis
    Lamna repercusso dulcius igne tremit;
5 Pulchrior Eois ut Phosphorus emicat undis,
    Phosphorus Idaliae fax adamata deae;
Sic mea, frigidulo nuper languore soluta,
    Purpureo Lalage fulgurat ore magis.
Aspice sidereis ut blandum arridet ocellis,
10   Utque sub his geminam lampada quassat Amor,
Aureoli ut ludunt per lactea colla capilli,
    Quantus in explicita fronte superbit honos!
Quam non mortalem se fert! Quae haec ora manusque!
    O superi, anne Iovis dignior ulla toro?
15 Nunc lacrimae, nunc ipsa iuvant suspiria; sed tu
    Quam mage formosa es, tam mage mitis ades.
Omnibus ante aliis, nunc te quoque pulchrior ipsa es,
    Deque avida volucer Febre triumphat Amor.
Sed tu ne posthac per tanta pericula formam
20   Quaesieris, metam contigit illa suam.

: LXXXVII :

An epitaph on Mabilio

Traveler, take a detour. This way stinks, for in this pit are buried
Mabilio's putrid body and soul.

: LXXXVIII :

On Lalage[133]

Just as a deer more joyfully sheds its horns along with years of
decay after it has lured out a snake by breathing into its lair;[134] just
as a sheet of gold freshly plucked from a Galician forge trembles
more sweetly from the reflected flames; and just as the Morning   5
Star flickers more beautifully from the eastern waves, the Morning
Star beloved by the Idalian goddess;[135] so does my Lalage glisten
the more in her bright face, now that she has been released from
the slight chill that accompanied her languor. See how she smiles
at us seductively with her starry eyes, how in both of them Love   10
rattles his torch, how her golden hair plays across her milky-white
neck, and what great beauty is on display upon her open brow!
How unlike a mortal she carries herself! What a face is this, what
hands! O gods above, is any woman more worthy of Jove's bed?
Now her tears, now her very sighs are pleasing. But the more   15
lovely you are, the more fitting it is that you come gently. You were
more beautiful than all others before; now you are more beautiful
than yourself too, and winged Love triumphs over greedy Fever.
But in case you are thinking of acquiring beauty at such great
peril again, that beauty has reached its limit. You cannot be more   20

Pulchrior esse nequis; vel si potes, aequius est te
    Iam, Lalage, nostris parcere luminibus.
Vix te, vix talem ferimus; quod si auxeris illam,
    Fiam ego, qui nunc sum nil nisi flamma, cinis.

: LXXXIX :

Ad Laurentium pro sacerdotio accepto
in templo divi Pauli
cum adhuc sub iudice lis esset

Gratatur, Laurens, venienti nuper in urbem
    Quantum hominum tota vivit in urbe mihi.
Utque[17] omnis taceam, studium quos copulat aut tu,
    Quosque vetus nobis vinxit amicitia,
5 Caupo, auceps, lanius, pistor, cocus, institor urgent.
    Hinc me ungit tactu fartor, at inde cocus;
Hic me veste trahit, hinc basior, inde salutor.
    Occurro his vultu, lumine, voce, manu.
'Gratamur, Paulum quod habes,' vox omnibus haec est.
10   'Non habeo Paulum,' dico. 'Quid ergo?' 'Nihil.'

beautiful, but even if you could, it would be better now for you to spare our eyes, Lalage. We can barely, just barely, take you as you are now, but if you add more to your beauty, I, who now am naught but flame, shall be reduced to ashes.

: LXXXIX :

To Lorenzo de' Medici, in return for the gift
of the priesthood in the church of S. Paolo,
composed while the matter was still being decided[136]

Lorenzo, just recently, when I came into the city, every person living in the entire city came out to congratulate me. Leaving aside all those who are connected to me either by their interest in scholarship or by you as well as those bound to me by ancient ties of friendship, I was thronged by shopkeepers, fowlers, butchers, bak-   5
ers, cooks, and tailors. On one side a greasy poulterer touches me, on the other a cook. One man tugs on my cloak, another kisses me, and another slaps me on the back. I am confronted by their expressions, looks, voices, hands. "Congratulations on getting St. Paul's!"—this is what they all say. "I haven't got St. Paul's," say I.   10
"What've you got, then?" "St. Zilch!"[137]

: XC :

In Floram

Plectron habet citharae mea Flora et plectron amoris;
 Hoc mentem plectro percutit, hoc citharam.
A miserum sicui dura est, siquem aspicit illa!
 Alter is Anchises, alter Adonis erit.

: XCI :

In invidum

Carpit libellos invidus meos quidam,
Gibber, pusillus, crispulus, macer, blaesus.
Meos libellos meque (si libet) carpat,
Et calcet, et commingat. Haec feram cuncta,
5 Dum nec libellos invidus meos iste
Gibber, pusillus, crispulus, macer, blaesus,
Nec me ausit umquam basiare! Cur? Fellat.

: XCII :

In equum Laurentii Medicis

Et volucrem et Zephyros cursu praevertitur ipsos
 Quem tibi misit equum barbara, Laure, Nomas.
Cesserit huic pavidas submittens Pegasus alas,
 Iamque deo parens Cyllarus Oebalidae.

: XC :

On Flora[138]

My Flora has a plectrum for her lyre and a plectrum for her love; with the one she plays on my heart, with the other her lyre. Alas, the poor wretch to whom she is cold, as well as the one who catches her eye! The one will be her Anchises, the other her Adonis.[139]

: XCI :

On a jealous man

My books are being criticized by a certain jealous man, a hunch-backed, scrawny, curly-haired, skinny stammerer. Let him criticize my books, and me too, if he wants, and stomp on them and piss all over them. I can put up with all that, as long as he doesn't take   5 my books, that hunchbacked, scrawny, curly-haired, skinny stam-merer, and plant a kiss on them! Or me! Ever! Why? He's a cock-sucker.

: XCII :

On the horse of Lorenzo de' Medici

The horse that you received from barbarous Numidia, Lorenzo, outruns the birds and the west wind itself. Pegasus would lower his trembling wings and submit to him, as would Cyllarus who

5 Hunc aut carceribus aut meta cernere in ipsa,
   Laure, licet; medio non licet in stadio.

: XCIII :

Domitii epitaphion

Hunc Domiti siccis tumulum qui transit ocellis,
   Vel Phoebo ignarus vel male gratus homo est.
Intulit hic vatum caecis pia lumina chartis,
   Obstrusum ad Musas hic patefecit iter.
5 Hunc Verona tulit, docti patria illa Catulli,
   Huic letum atque urnam Roma dedit iuveni.

: XCIV :

Donati Azaroli

Donatus nomen, patria est Florentia, gens mi
   Azarola domus; clarus eram eloquio.
Francorum ad Regem patriae dum orator abirem,
   In Ducis Anguigeri moenibus occubui.
5 Sic vitam impendi patriae, quae me inde relatum
   Inter maiorum nunc cineres sepelit.

obeys the Oebalian god.[140] It's possible to get a good look at him 5
in the starting gate or at the turning post, Lorenzo, but not when
he's in the middle of the course.

: XCIII :

Domizio's[141] epitaph

The man who passes this, Domizio's tomb, with dry eyes, is either
ignorant of Phoebus or unwelcome to him. This man shone a
reverent light on the incomprehensible pages of the poets, he
opened up the hidden path to the Muses. Verona sired him, the 5
celebrated home of learned Catullus; Rome gave him his death
and a tomb, while he was still a young man.

: XCIV :

Donato Acciaiuoli's epitaph[142]

Donato is my name, Florence my homeland, my family the house
of the Acciaiuoli. I was famous for eloquence. While on my journey as my country's ambassador to the king of the Franks, I met
my end within the walls of the Duke who wears the serpent.[143]
Thus I gave my life for my country, which brought me back from 5
there to bury me now among the ashes of my ancestors.

: XCV :

Campani

Ille ego laurigeros cui cinxit et infula crines,
    Campanus, Romae delicium hic iaceo.
Mi ioca dictarunt Charites; nigro sale Momus,
    Mercurius niveo, tinxit utroque Venus.
5   Mi ioca, mi risus, placuit mihi uterque Cupido.
    Si me fles, procul hinc, quaeso, viator, abi.

: XCVI :

Angelus Politianus Laurentio Medici patrono
suo salutem

*Qua ode Gentilem nostrum nuper sum consolatus, eandem quoque ad te
mittendam statui. Visa est enim mihi res, quae non minus ad te quam ad
eum atque ad me ipsum pertineret. Omnia collegi quae communem hunc
nostrum dolorem, etsi minus tollere, levare procul dubio aliqua ex parte
possint. Tu cum tot videas tuae saluti tam diligenter invigilare, potes admo-
neri quam tibi necesse sit magni te ipsum facere, neque tuam, hoc est publi-
cam totius (ita me Deus amet) Italiae salutem, neglectam pati. Lege et
vale.*

Ad Gentilem episcopum ode dicolos

Gentiles, animi maxima pars mei,
Communi nimium sorte quid angeris?
Quid curis animum lugubribus teris,
    Et me discrucias simul?

: XCV :

Campano's epitaph[144]

I, that Campano, whose brow was bound with a laurel fillet, the
darling of Rome—here I lie. The Graces often told their jokes to
me. Momus imbued me with his coarse wit, Mercury with his refined wit, Venus with both.[145] A joke and a laugh gave me plea-   5
sure, as did both kinds of love. If you weep for me, pilgrim, please
go far from here.

: XCVI :

To Lorenzo de' Medici, his patron,
from Angelo Poliziano, greetings

I have decided to send to you also the same ode with which I recently con-
soled our friend Gentile.[146] For the subject seemed to me to be of a sort that
was as relevant to you as it was to him and to me myself. I have collected
all the thoughts which, I have no doubt, can at least to some degree lessen
this shared grief of ours, even if they cannot remove it. When you see how
many people are diligently watching over your welfare, you can be reminded
of how essential it is that you yourself place a high value on it and do not
allow your welfare—that is, so help me God, the common welfare of all
Italy—to be neglected. Read it and be well.

An Ode in two cola[147] to Bishop Gentile

Gentile, you who are the greatest part of my soul, why are you so
anguished over our common lot? Why do you wear out your soul
with doleful cares and put me on the rack as well? We have indeed   5

5   Passi digna quidem perpetuo sumus
      Luctu, qui mediis, heu miseri, sacris
      Illum, illum iuvenem vidimus, o nefas,
          Stratum sacrilega manu.

      At sunt attonito quae dare pectori
      Solamen valeant plurima: nam super
10   Est qui vel gremio creverit in tuo
          Laurens, Etruriae[18] caput.

      Laurens, quem patriae caelicolum pater
      Tutum terrifica Gorgone praestitit;
      Quem Tuscus, pariter quem Venetus leo
15   Servant et draco pervigil.

      Illi bellipotens excubat Hercules;
      Illi fatiferis militat arcubus;
      Illi mittit equos Francia Martios,
          Felix Francia regibus.

20   Circumstat populus murmure dissono,
      Circumstant iuvenem purpurei patres.
      Causa vincimus et robore militum:
          Hac stat Iuppiter, hac favet.

      Quare, o cum misera quid tibi nenia,
25   Si nil proficimus? quin potius gravis
      Abstersisse bono laetitiae die
          Audes nubila pectoris?

      Nam cum iam gelidos umbra reliquerit
30   Artus, non dolor hanc perpetuus retro
      Mordacesve trahunt sollicitudines
          Mentis curaque pervicax.

endured things worthy of endless lament, we who witnessed — oh the pity of it! — that young man — oh the crime! — that young man laid low by the hand of a blasphemer. But there are a great many things that can offer consolation to a broken heart, for there is one who survives who grew up in your very bosom, Lorenzo, the 10 leader of Tuscany. Lorenzo, whom the father of the gods in heaven has kept safe for his country by the power of the terrifying Gorgon,[148] whom the lions of Tuscany and of Venice guard and the 15 ever-vigilant serpent.[149] For him mighty Hercules keeps watch, for him he wages war with his death-dealing bow; for him France sends her warhorses — France, which is fortunate in her kings.[150] The people make a confused murmur as they rally round him, and 20 the senators, clad in purple, rally round the young man. We are triumphant in our cause and in the might of our soldiers. Here stands Jupiter, favoring our side. And so why, oh why do you waste time on a mournful dirge, since we accomplish nothing that 25 way? Why not steel yourself instead on this good day of happiness to sweep away the dark clouds of a heavy heart? For when once the spirit has left our cold limbs behind, pain does not perpetually 30 drag it back, nor do the mordant disquiets of the mind and stubborn care.

: XCVII :

In amicam

Allicis, expellis; sequeris, fugis; es pia, et es trux.
    Me vis, me non vis; me crucias, et amas.
Promittis, promissa negas; spem mi eripis, et das.
    Iam iam ego vel sortem, Tantale, malo tuam.
5 Durum ferre sitim circum salientibus undis,
    Durius in medio nectare ferre sitim.

: XCVIII :

In Domitium Scazon

Adsta, viator! Pulverem vides sacrum,
Quem verticosi turbat unda Benaci?
Hoc mutat ipsum saepe Musa Libethron
Fontemque Sisyphi ac vireta Permessi.
5 Quippe hoc Domitius vagiit solo primum,
Ille, ille doctus, ille quem probe nosti,
Dictata dantem Romulae iuventuti,
Mira eruentem sensa de penu vatum.
Abi, viator: sat tuis oculis debes.

: XCVII :

On a girlfriend[151]

You entice me, you reject me; you pursue me, you run away; you're kind and you're savage. You want me, you don't; you torture me and you love me. You make promises, you break them; you steal hope from me and you give it back. By this point I prefer even your fate, Tantalus.[152] It's hard to be thirsty with the waters lapping about you, but it's harder still to be thirsty when surrounded by nectar. 5

: XCVII :

On Domizio in limping iambics[153]

Stop, pilgrim! Do you see the sacred soil that the eddying waters of Lake Garda disturbs? The Muse often trades Libethron[154] itself for it, and the spring of Sisyphus[155] and the greensward of Permessus.[156] Indeed it was here on this soil that Domizio first cried as 5
an infant—that man, that famous learned man whom you know so well, dictating lessons to the youth of Rome, extracting marvelous meanings from the storehouse of the poets. Go now, pilgrim! You owe enough to your eyes.

: XCIX :

Ad Franciscum distichon

Scripsit in invidiam quidam, Francisce, poeta
    Tam bene, tam docte, nullus ut invideat.

: C :

In Amorem arantem ex Graeco Moschi

Peram humeris habilem posito nunc induit arcu,
    Et posita baculum lampade sumpsit Amor.
Subque iugum missos stimulo citat ecce iuvencos
    Improbus, et cultae semina mandat humo.
5   Suspiciensque polos, 'imple,' inquit, 'Iuppiter, arva,
    Ne cogam Europae te iuga ferre bovem.'

: CI :

Innocentio Pontifici Maximo

Si quod arcanis Helicon sub umbris
Carmen intactum fidibus priorum
Parturit, saxis iterum audiendum
    Arboribusque,

5   Quale nec triplex Achelois ausa est
Cautibus virgo residens marinis,
Nec puer Phoebi Ciconum remoto
    Dicere in antro;

: XCIX :

To Francesco, a couplet

Francesco, a certain poet wrote on the subject of jealousy so well, so learnedly, that no one was jealous.

: C :

On Eros as a plowman, from the Greek of Moschus[157]

Eros put aside his bow, donning a satchel that fit neatly on his shoulders and, setting aside his torch, picked up a staff. Look, the scamp is using a switch to drive the cattle that have been put under the yoke and he's sowing seeds in the tilled soil. And as he   5
looks up to the heavens, he says, "Jupiter, give me a full crop, or I'll make you carry the yoke as Europa's bull."

: CI :

To Pope Innocent[158]

If ever beneath its secret shades Helicon gives birth to a song untried by the lyres of old, something to be heard again by the rocks and trees, the kind of song that the three virgin daughters of   5
Achelous did not venture to sing as they sat upon their rocks by the sea, nor Phoebus' boy in his remote grotto among the

Illud attritas repetita chordas
10 Barbitos docto moduletur arcu,
    Dulcis interpres animi piaeque
            Conscia mentis.

    Namque te rerum caput, Innocenti,
    Turpe vulgato cecinisse plectro est,
15 Cuius aurata triplices refulgent
            Fronte coronae,
    Roma cui paret dominusque Thybris,
    Qui vicem summi geris hic Tonantis,
    Qui potes magnum reserare et idem
20   Claudere caelum,

    Blanda cui vultu Gravitas sereno
    Ridet, invisos abigitque fastus,
    Mitis et celsi radios potestas
            Temperat oris.

25 Sponte sublatos verecunda fasces
    Deprimit Virtus; apicata tristi
    Nube maiestas caret, et decoro est
            Splendida cultu.

    Ergo formosam redit in iuventam
30 Seque iam laetos parat ad triumphos
    Roma, septenos hilaratque colles
            Praeside tanto.

    Urbsque quae Phryxi speculatur undas
    Exuet saevas propere catenas,
35 Ac suas nobis opulenta palmas
            Mittet Idume.

Cicones,[159] let that be the one that I play as I take up my lute   10
again with its practiced bow, striking again the well-worn strings,
the sweet interpreter of my soul and confidant of my pious heart.
For it would be a disgrace to sing of you upon a vulgar instrument,
Innocent, leader of the world, you upon whose gilded brow gleams   15
a three-tiered crown, whom Rome obeys and the lordly Tiber, you
who here perform the role of the Thunderer on high, you who can
expose the greatness of the firmament and likewise close it up; on   20
whose serene face Dignity smiles seductively, banishing hateful arrogance, and the gentle power of your lofty visage tempers its rays.
Of her own accord modest Virtue lowers her raised fasces, and the   25
majesty of your tiara, free from any cloud of sadness, is resplendent with proper ornament. And so Rome returns to the time of
its lovely youth and now prepares for joyful triumphs, gladdening   30
each of the seven hills with so great a protector. And the city that
overlooks the waters of Phrixus shall soon shed her cruel chains,
and sumptuous Idumea shall send her palms to us.[160] Indeed, our   35

Quippe concordes animos manusque
Devovent reges tibi, seque ad arma
Concitat Turci sitiens cruoris
40   Vesper et Arctos.

Scilicet tales meditatus annos
Iuppiter fesso comes it parenti,
Quo tibi felix simul atque faustum
          Proroget aevum.

: CII :

In fontem Hungari regis

Usque Fluentina vectum est hoc marmor ab urbe,
     Mathiae ut regi largior unda fluat.

: CIII :

In eundem

Tusca manus, Tuscum marmor, rex Ungarus auctor:
     Aureus hoc Ister surgere fonte velit.

kings devote their hearts and hands to you in harmony; West and North rouse themselves to arms, thirsting for the blood of the 40 Turk. Clearly Jupiter contemplated years such as this when he accompanied your exhausted father,[161] that he might propagate for you an age at once happy and blessed.

: CII :

On the King of Hungary's fountain[162]

This marble was brought all the way from the city of Fluentia[163] so that water might flow more copiously for King Matthias.

: CIII :

On the same fountain

Tuscan the hand that fashioned it, Tuscan the marble it's made from, and the King of Hungary commissioned it: the golden Danube would be happy if this fountain were its source.

: CIV :

In Ciccham Senensem

Mnemosyne audito Senensis carmine Cicchae,
   'Quando,' inquit, 'decima est nata puella mihi?'

: CV :

In fontem Laurentii Medicis Ambram

Ut lasciva suo furtim daret oscula lauro,
   Ipsa sibi occultas repperit Ambra vias.

: CVI :

In eundem

Traxit amatrices haec usque ad limina nymphas,
   Dum iactat laurum saepius Ambra suum.

: CIV :

On Cecca of Siena[164]

Mnemosyne, upon hearing the poetry of Cecca da Siena, said, "When did I give birth to a tenth daughter?"

: CV :

On Ambra, a spring belonging to Lorenzo de' Medici[165]

That she might give playful kisses to her laurel[166] in private, Ambra contrived secret paths for herself.

: CVI :

On the same fountain

Ambra attracted the amorous nymphs all the way to this threshold by boasting about her laurel too often.

: CVII :

Ad Laurentium Medicem Iuniorem
epistola paene extemporanea

Quae petis omnifera, Laurenti dulcis, ab Ambra
    Carmina praeposita mitto salute tibi,
Ille domi vestrae tenero nutritus ab ungui,
    Sed tuus ante omnes, Politianus, amor.
5 Si quid agam quaeris, valeo, rurisque benigni
    Secessu gaudens otia lenta tero.
Et modo pascentes speculor de colle iuvencas,
    Nunc repeto ductus prosilientis aquae,
10 Iactaque magnificae miror fundamina villae.
    Saepe fruor studio versiculisque meis;
Aut ego florentem moneo ne cesset alumnum
    Ardua Pieridum per iuga ferre gradus;
Aut varios cantu procul alliciente volucres
15   Captamus, viridi tectus uterque casa.
Te tamen absentem mea mens oculique requirunt,
    Et desiderio torqueor usque tui.
Nam puerum iuvenis (potes hoc meminisse) colebam,
    Qui nunc te iuvenem vir quoque factus amo.
20 Indolis istius iam tum praesagia vidi,
    Scilicet et vatem vera monebat avis.
Viderat haec eadem, pueri cognomine gaudens,
    Publica res uno quo stabilita manet,
Cum sibi te comitem, lugubria patris habentem,
25   Seu pede ducebat sive iter esset equo;
Exemploque sui studium probitatis alebat,
    Ne labes annos tangeret ulla rudes.

: CVII :

To Lorenzo de' Medici the younger,[167] an almost extemporaneous epistle

The poems that you ask for, sweet Lorenzo, I send to you from
bountiful Ambra,[168] prefixing my greeting, I, that very Poliziano,
who was raised in your household from early childhood, but the
object of your affection above all. If you ask me how I am doing, I   5
am well, and rejoicing in the seclusion of this bounteous estate, I
slowly while away my time in leisure. Sometimes I watch the cattle
grazing from the hilltop, at other times I follow the track of the
babbling stream and admire the sturdy foundations of this mag-   10
nificent villa. Often I enjoy my studies and my poetic trifles, or I
warn my thriving pupil[169] not to slack off in making his way along
the arduous ridges of the Muses. Sometimes the two of us try to
catch some brightly colored birds, luring them from afar with bird
calls, each of us concealed in a brush-covered blind. And yet my   15
mind and my eyes search for you, absent though you are, and I am
continually tortured by my longing for you. For, as you might recall, when you were a boy and I a young man, I respected you, and
now that I am a grown man and you a young one, I cherish you.
Already back then I saw the evidence of your character, and it's   20
clear that the signs read by this seer were true. The one man upon
whom the stability of the republic depends had seen these same
qualities, when, pleased with the boy's name, he made you his
companion while you wore mourning for your father,[170] whether   25
the journey was on foot or by horseback. And by his example he
nurtured your passion for integrity, so that your no stain could

Ergo a se factis fruitur quoque moribus auctor,
    Iudicioque sibi iam placet ipse suo.
30 Quare aut Pontificem magnis de rebus adire
    Atque galeritos te iubet ille Patres,
Aut sua dat Gallo regi mandata referre,
    Imponitque umeris pondera tanta tuis.
Nam tibi nec gravitas, nec amica gratia frontis,
35   Nec deest proceri verticis altus honor,
Ingeniumque capax et par civilibus actis,
    Quaeque animi largas lingua ministret opes.
Iudice cum facias et Apolline carmina primus,
    Prima favore tamen nostra Thalia tuo est;
40 Utque ligustra novo superas candore nivemque,
    Praefers carminibus carmina nostra tuis.
Neve meae pereant cura est tua maxima nugae,
    Cogis et invito me patre ferre diem;
Neve nihil scribam, blande nova carmina poscis,
45   Officioque foves qualiacumque pio.
Et nunc, quae magnum longe testentur amorem,
    Scripta repentino fusa calore damus,
Non ut ab his nostrum censeri debeat orsis
    Ingenium, summa deficiente manu,
50 Sed tamen ut studium vatis tibi constet amici,
    Lapsa putes animo nec tua dicta meo.

    En tibi quam flagitabas elegiam, paene illam quidem
extemporaneam; siquidem mane, dum se rei divinae sacerdos parat,
inchoatam, absolvi dein post meridiem, dum rediens carrucae adequito.
    Quod etiam unum stilus quoque ipse satis superque probabit.
    Vale, dulce decus meum.

besmirch your tender years. So the man who molded your character enjoys the fruit of his labors, and he is himself quite pleased
with his own perspicuity. That is why he commissions you to go   30
to the Pope and the Cardinals on weighty matters,[171] or to remit
his demands to the French king,[172] so weighty a responsibility
does he place upon your shoulders. For you lack neither serious-
ness, nor a welcoming grace upon your brow, nor the high honor   35
of lofty status, and you have a capacious intelligence that is equal
to the affairs of state, and a tongue that serves up the ample riches
of your mind. Although you write poetry that is of the first rank
even in Apollo's judgment, nonetheless my Muse[173] comes out first
in your rating, and as you surpass the privet or snow in your fresh   40
brilliance, you prefer my poems to yours. It is your chief object of
care that my trifles not disappear, and though I am an unwilling
parent, you compel them to bear the light of day. And to prevent
me from not writing anything, you make flattering requests for
new poems, and out of your sense of duty and devotion, such as   45
they are, you promote them. And now, to bear witness to my great
devotion to you, I present you with these writings, poured out in
the sudden heat of inspiration, not so that my talent should be
judged by these works, lacking the final touch as they do, but so   50
that the devotion of your friend the poet may nonetheless be clear
to you, and you will not think that your words have slipped from
my mind.

There you have it, the elegy that you asked for, and practically
extemporized at that, since it was begun in the morning, when the priest
was getting ready for the sacrament, and I finished it off in the afternoon
while accompanying a coach on horseback on my return.
The style[174] itself will more than sufficiently certify that one fact.
Farewell, my dear, distinguished friend.

⁚ CVIII ⁚

Ode, MCCCCLXXXVII

Iam cornu gravidus praecipitem parat
Afflatus subitis frigoribus fugam
Autumnus pater, et deciduas sinu
    Frondes excipit arborum.

5 Cantant emeritis, Bacche, laboribus
Te nunc agricolae, sed male sobrios
Ventosae querulo murmure tibiae
    Saltatu subigunt frui.

Nos anni rediens orbita sub iugum
10 Musarum revocat, dulce ferentibus;
Porrectisque monent sidera noctibus
    Carpamus volucrem diem.

I mecum, docilis turba, biverticis
Parnassi rapidis per iuga passibus,
15 Expers quo senii nos vocat et rogi
    Consors gloria caelitum.

Nam me seu comitem seu, iuvenes, ducem
Malitis, venio; nec labor auferet
Quaerentem tetricae difficili gradu
20   Virtutis penetralia.

: CVIII :

An Ode (1487)[175]

His horn of plenty now filled, Father Autumn makes ready his
precipitous flight with sudden blasts of cold air and receives in his
bosom the leaves falling from the trees. Their labors now com-   5
plete, the farmers sing of you, Bacchus, but in their state of inso-
briety the plaintive murmur of the wild flutes inspires them to
enjoy the dance. The recurring circuit of the year recalls me to the   10
Muses' yoke, a pleasant burden to those who bear it, and as the
nights grow long, the stars warn us to enjoy the day as it speeds
by. Come with me, my troop of students, with rapid steps across
the ridges of the twin peaks of Parnassus,[176] where, free from old   15
age and the funeral pyre, the glory that is shared with the gods
calls us. For whether you prefer to think of me as your companion
or your leader, young men, I am coming anyway. Nor will the ex-
ertion keep me from seeking out the inner recesses of strict Virtue
by a difficult path.   20

: CIX :

In quendam

Hunc quem videtis ire fastoso gradu
    Servis tumentem publicis,
Vel hinniente per forum vehi capax
    Equo, quod omnes despuant,
5 Turbam superbo praeterit fastidio
    Qui civium stomachantium,
Gravique cunctos ora torquentes retro
    Despectat insolentia,
Intraque tutum moenibus pomerium
10   Agros patentes possidet,
Villamque diues publico peculio
    Insanus urbanam struit,
Ubi otietur inter obscenas lupas
    (Ne turpiora dixerim),
15 Ubi ampla pergraecetur inter pocula,
    Senex podagra rancidus—
Hunc vos putatis stirpe forsan inclita,
    Virtutis aut insignibus
Ad hoc volasse protinus fastigium?
20   Falsum putatis, hospites.
Molas hic inter natus est aquaticas,
    Gratus sodalis muribus.[19]
Fortuna ludens furfuris plenum tulit
    Ad usque supremos gradus,
25 Monstrare gaudens arroget quantum sibi
    Mortalis impudentia.
Ergo iste tantis arduus suffragiis
    Nunc immemor natalium,

: CIX :

On a certain person[177]

This man whom you see strutting about with his affected air, puffed up over his public slaves, or riding on a neighing horse through the open square that everybody spits on; who passes by 5 the crowd of bellyaching citizens with nauseating superciliousness, and looks down with unbearable arrogance upon everyone as they turn their faces away; who possesses wide-open fields within the 10 secure bounds of the city's walls, a madman, enriched from the public coffers, building a villa within the city,[178] where he will take his ease among filthy whores (not to mention more disgusting go-ings-on), where he will carry on like a Greek, cups filled to the 15 brim, an old man rank with gout—you perhaps think that this fellow comes from noble stock, or that it is because of his distinc-tive virtue that he has flown straight to this lofty perch? My 20 friends, you are mistaken. This man was born among the water mills, the mice's best friend. Fortune amused herself by raising this scab all the way to highest ranks, taking pleasure in showing just 25 how much human impudence can arrogate to itself. And so that fellow has now risen to a position of such great influence, oblivi-ous to the conditions of his birth. And whenever he sees someone

Ut quemque longo stemmate clarum videt
30   Aut dote rara nobilem,
Tristi veneno spargit et rodit statim
      Rubiginosis dentibus.
Non ipse se, fortuna non ipsum capit
      Aura favoris ebrium.
35   Sic culmen altum lubrico premens pede,
      Ventisque turbidis patens,
Casurus usque nutat et iam iam cadet,
      Sed non 'gradatim' scilicet.

: CX :

In invidum carmen

Quisquis es obscuro vatem qui dente lacessis
      Maiorem, tristi degener invidia,
Usque late lucemque pave, blattarius auctor,
      Lividior Graecis barbariorque tuis.
5 Quosque fames opicis ad nos emisit Athenis,
      Hos audi; gens est auribus apta Midae.

who comes from a long and illustrious line or is ennobled by a rare   30
talent, he spatters them with bitter venom and immediately sinks
his tartarous teeth into them. He can scarcely contain himself;
Fortune itself is too small for him now, intoxicated as he is with
the winds of popularity. So as he sets foot on the high and slip-   35
pery peak, exposed to the swirling winds, he totters continually on
the point of falling and soon, very soon he will fall, but certainly
not "by degrees."[179]

: CX :

A poem on a jealous person[180]

Whoever you are, you degenerate, nipping at a greater poet with
your black teeth out of your depressing jealousy, you should stay
in hiding and avoid the light of day, you cockroach of an author,
more invidious and more barbaric than your fellow Greeks. And   5
those people whom hunger has sent our way from the stupid city
of Athens, listen to them: that's a race fit for Midas' ears.[181]

: CXI :

De Angeli puella

Puella delicatior
    Lepusculo et cuniculo,
    Coaque tela mollior
    Anserculique plumula;

5 Puella qua lascivior
    Nec vernus est passerculus,
    Nec virginis blande sinu
    Sciurus usque lusitans;

Puella longe dulcior
10   Quam mel sit Hyblae aut saccarum.
    Ceu lac coactum candida
    Vel lilium vel prima nix;

Puella, cuius non comas
    Lyaeus aequaret puer,
15   Non pastor ille Amphrysius
    Amore mercenarius,
    Comas decenter pendulas
    Utroque frontis margine,
    Nodis decenter aureis
20   Nexas, decenter pinnulis
    Ludentium Cupidinum
    Subventilantibus vagas,
    Quas mille crispant annuli,
    Quas ros odorque myrrheus
25   Commendat atque recreat;

: CXI :

On Angelo's girlfriend[182]

A girl more skittish than a bunny or a rabbit, softer than Coan[183]
thread or a gosling's plume; a girl no less playful than a sparrowlet   5
in spring or a squirrel sweetly frolicking over a maiden's lap; a girl
far sweeter than honey from Hybla[184] or sugar; white as pressed   10
milk or lilies or the first snow; a girl whose hair the youthful Lyaeus[185] could not match, nor that famous shepherd on the Amph-   15
rysus,[186] love's hired hand—her hair that hangs becomingly on
both sides of her forehead, fetchingly bound in knots of gold,
flowing fetchingly, fanned by the little wings of playful Cupids;   20
covered by thousand ringlets, favored and refreshed by rosemary   25

Puella, cuius duplices
   Sub fronte amica fulgurant
   Amoris arcani faces,
   Quas contueri non queo
30   Nec stare contra vel procul,
   Quin occuper flamma gravi,
   Miser, miser, quae mollibus
   Furtim medullis adsilit:
   Non non ocellus, hospites,
35   Ille est et ille, sed faces,
   Faces Amoris igneae,
   Quas laeta suscitat Venus,
   Quas blanda pascit Gratia.

Quid narium dulcem modum
40   Vel quid genarum levium
   Dicam rosam cum lilio?[20]
   Labella quid coraliis
   Rubore praenitentia,
   Tam saepe tam longum mihi
45   Mordente pressa basio?

Quid margaritas dentium
   Praecandidorum proloquar,
   Linguamque perpleabilem,
   Utcumque iuncto anhelitu,
50   Amanti amantem copulans
   Festinat ad calcem Venus,
   Cum suave olentem spiritum
   Semiulca sugunt oscula,
   Lenocinante gaudio
55   Subinde murmurantia?
   Mentumve quid tornatile,
   Gulamque teretem et lacteam,

and essence of myrrh; a girl whose two eyes gleam beneath her
friendly brow, the torches of a secret love, eyes that I cannot look
upon or stand opposite, even at a distance, without being con-   30
sumed by powerful flame, eyes that furtively assail me — oh, the
misery! — in the soft of the marrow: neither the one nor the other
of them is actually an eye, my friends; they are torches, the blazing   35
torches of Love, which Venus happily waves and seductive Grace
feeds.

What shall I say of the sweet proportions of her nose or the   40
roses mixed with lilies of her smooth cheeks? Or her lips shining
brighter than red coral, so often and for so long pressed by me in   45
a clinging kiss? What am I to say of her pearly white teeth? Her
entwining tongue? Or how, when our gasping breaths conjoin,
coupling lover to lover, Venus hastens to the finish line, while her   50
sweet-smelling breath is imbibed by my half-ulcerated lips, mum-
bling afterwards upon the ministrations of happiness? Or her   55
well-turned chin, her smooth and milky throat, the shoulders that

Et quae lacertis milies
Ut arbor hedera incingitur,
60   Incincta cervix est meis?

Nam quae tibi mamillulae
Stant floridae et protuberant
Sororiantes primulum
Ceu mala punica arduae,
65   Quas ore toto presseram
Manuque contrectaveram,
Quem non amore allexerint?
Cui non asilum immiserint?
Quem non furore incenderint?

70 O qui lacerti, quae manus!
Quos Iuno, quas Aurora habet;
O quale pectus et latus!
O venter, o crus, o femur!
O qui Thetin decent pedes!
75   Pedes choreis nobiles,
Saltatibus mirabiles,
Statu, gradu spectabiles;

O verba iucundissima,
Tam nequiter ludentia,
80   Arguta, plena aculeis,
Decore, suavitudine,
Dicacitate, gratia!

O carminum dulces notae!
Quas ore pulchra melleo
85   Fundis lyraeque succinis,
Ut non Thalia blandius
Non ipse Apollo doctius

have a thousand times been entwined by my arms, as ivy is en- 60
twined upon a tree?

For those dear blossoming breasts of yours, firm and swelling
like a pair of sisters at first, standing out like pomegranates, which 65
I had pressed with my whole mouth and fondled in my hand,
what man could they not lure with passion? What man could they
not provoke? Whom could they not inflame with lust?

Oh, what arms, what hands! Arms like Juno's, hands like Au- 70
rora's! Oh, what a breast and hip! Oh, the stomach, the legs, the
thighs! Oh, those feet worthy of Thetis! Those feet so remarkable 75
in the choruses, marvelous at the dances, standing or walking—
well worth watching!

Oh, your words are so utterly pleasing, so playfully naughty,
lively and filled with edginess, elegance, sweetness, wit and grace! 80

Oh, the sweet notes of your songs flow so beautifully from your
honeyed lips as you sing to the accompaniment of the lyre that 85
Thalia could not play more seductively, nor Apollo himself more

Feras canendo mulceant,
Fluenta vertant in caput,
90   Et saxa cum silvis trahant.

O cuncta salsa et dulcia,
Festiva, laeta et mollia,
Referta amoenitatibus,
Amoribus lubentia,
95   Protervitate, lusibus
Risu, ioco, leporibus!

O quicquid est pulchrum et decet
Puella sola continens,
O praepotens cultu nimis,
100   Nimisque non culta placens,
Quis te deus mihi invidet?
Quae te mihi fors eripit?
Quo te repente proripis?
Quo, quo fugis, bellissima,
105   Risu serenans aethera?
Heu mea voluptas, mel meum,
Meum, puella, corculum,
Mihique longe carior
Lapillis auro purpura;
110   Ac nec lapillis carior
Auroque solum et purpura,
Sed spiritu mi carior,
Sed carior mi sanguine.

Memento tu tamen, precor,
115   Memento, formosissima,
Amoris atque compedum,
Quas a tenellis unguibus
Mecum tibi circumdedit,

skillfully to soothe the savage beasts with song, turn the rivers on
their heads, or attract the rocks and trees!   90

Oh, all is cleverness and charm with you, lively, happy and delicate, filled with delights, pleasing with love and lust, games and 95
laughter, jests and delight!

Oh, you are the girl who alone possesses all that is beautiful
and lovely! O you who are far surpassing in adornment, and far 100
too pleasing even unadorned, what god begrudges you to me?
What chance steals you from me? Where are you stealing yourself
to so suddenly? Where, oh where are you running away to, beautiful girl, making the heavens serene with your smile? Alas my dar- 105
ling, my honey-sweet, my sweetheart girl, dearer to me by far than
jewels, gold, or ermine! And not only dearer than jewels and gold 110
and ermine, but dearer to me than breath, dearer to me than life!

But remember, I pray you, my beautiful one, remember, our 115
love and the bonds that have been placed around you and me since

Heu, lacrimis amantium, heu,
120   Suspiriis ridens, Venus.

: CXII :

De se ipso semper amante

Sex ego cum plena perago trieteride lustra,
    Nec placet in speculo iam mea forma mihi,
Nec responsurum spes improba fingit amorem,
    Blanditiisque levem suspicor esse fidem.
5 Cum tamen haec ita sint, capior miser illice vultu,
    Et numquam a dura compede solvor amans.
Iam iam, militia nostrae contenta iuventae,
    Desinat, aut ceston commodet alma Venus.

: CXIII :

De Alcone et serpente

Vidit ut implicitum puero pater anxius anguem,
    Intendit dubia cornua flexa manu,
Inque ferae fauces calamum sic torsit, ut audax
    Terruerit natum non minus angue senex.
5 Sed numquam pius errat amor: puer hoste perempto
    Salvus erat. Stupuit morte direpta salus.
Victor ab hac pharetram quercu suspendit et arcum,
    Fortunae atque artis quae monumenta suae.

childhood by Venus, who laughs, alas, at the tears of lovers and   120
their sighs.

⁖ CXII ⁖

Concerning his own state of being constantly in love

I have now completed six lustrums plus a full three years,[187] and
what I see in the mirror no longer pleases me. My expectations are
not excessive in imagining that love will respond to me, and I suspect that no one puts much stock in my smooth talk. And yet,   5
even so I am captured by an alluring face, wretch that I am, and I
am always in love, never to be released from those hard fetters. Let
Gracious Venus at long last put a stop to it, and be content with
my service in my youth, or else let her lend me her magic bras-
siere.[188]

⁖ CXIII ⁖

On Alcon and the serpent[189]

When the anxious father saw the serpent entwined around his
son, with a trembling hand he bent his bow and stretched it tight;
and he shot an arrow into the jaws of the beast so violently, that
the daring old man terrified his son no less than the snake. But a   5
faithful love never misses: the boy was saved and the enemy destroyed. His deliverance, thus snatched from death, was stupefy-
ing.[190] The victor hung his quiver and bow from this oak tree, as
memorials to his good fortune and his skill.

: CXIV :

In puellam

Nix ipsa es virgo, et nive ludis. Lude, sed ante
   Quam pereat candor, fac rigor ut pereat.

: CXV :

Ad fures

Ite alio, fures, nulla hic occasio lucri:
   Nam fida est custos addita pauperies.

: CXVI :

Ad hirundinem nidificantem sub Medeae statua

Medeae statua est, misella hirundo,
Sub qua nidificas. Tuos ne credas
Huic natos, rogo, quae suos necavit.

: CXIV :

On a girl

You are like the snow itself, young lady, as you play in the snow. Play on, but before you lose your fair complexion, see that you lose your iciness.

: CXV :

To thieves[191]

Go elsewhere, thieves, there's no opportunity for lucre here, for a steadfast guardian has been set here — poverty.

: CXVI :

To a swallow building her nest under a statue of Medea[192]

This is a statue of Medea, my poor little swallow, under which you build your nest. Please, do not entrust your children to this woman, who murdered her own.

: CXVII :

De lectulo meretricio e lauru[21]

Unius effugi torum,
Ut omnium fierem torus.

: CXVIII :

De lauro securi caesa

Cum Mars Daphne se miscuit
Apollo tunc ubi fuit?

: CXIX :

Distichon

Spem simul et Nemesin posita dicat Eunus in ara,
  Scilicet ut speres omnia, nil habeas.

: CXVII :

On a prostitute's bed made out of laurel[193]

I escaped one man's bed, only to become every man's bed.

: CXVIII :

On a laurel tree cut down by an ax[194]

When Mars had sex with Daphne,[195] where was Apollo then?

: CXIX :

A couplet[196]

Eunus consecrates both Hope and Nemesis[197] at the altar he has erected, evidently so you might hope for anything, but have nothing.

: CXX :

In oleam vitibus implicatam

Quid me implicatis, palmites,
Plantam Minervae, non Bromi?
Procul racemos tollite,
Ne virgo dicar ebria.

: CXXI :

Epitaphium

Stirpe fui, forma natoque opibusque viroque
    Felix, ingenio, moribus atque animo.
Sed cum alter partus iam nuptae ageretur et annus,
    Heu, nondum nata cum subole interii!
5 Tristius ut caderem, tantum mihi Parca bonorum
    Ostendit potius perfida quam tribuit.

Ioannae Albitiae uxori incomparabili
Laurentius Tornabonus
posuit beatae memoriae.

: CXX :

On an olive tree entwined with grape vines[198]

O grapevines, why do you coil around me? I am Minerva's plant, not Bromius'![199] Take away your grape clusters, lest I, a maiden, be called a drunk.

: CXXI :

An epitaph[200]

I was fortunate in my lineage, my looks, my son, my wealth and my husband, my nature, my character, and my intellect. But during my second pregnancy (which was also the second year of my marriage), alas, I perished along with my unborn child. That my   5 death should be the more tragic, Fate in her treachery gave me only a glimpse of so many good things but did not bestow them.

For Giovanna degli Albizzi, Incomparable Wife,
Lorenzo Tornabuoni
erected this to her good memory.

⁝ CXXII ⁝

In fonte baptismatis Florentiae

Quicquid ab antiqua manauit origine morbi
    Purgabunt istae (si modo credis) aquae.

⁝ CXXIII ⁝

In Michaelem Verinum

Verinus Michael florentibus occidit annis,
    Moribus ambiguum maior, an ingenio.
Disticha composuit docto miranda parenti,
    Quae claudunt gyro grandia sensa brevi.
5   Sola Venus poterat lento succurrere morbo;
    Ne se pollueret, maluit ille mori.
Sic iacet, heu, patri dolor et decus! Unde iuventus
    Exemplum, vates materiam capiant.

⁝ CXXIV ⁝

In Daphnen

Complexus virides frondosae virginis artus,
    'Sic quoque mutata,' dixit Apollo, 'fruar.'
Utque novas gustu bacas temptavit, 'Eandem
    (Ei mihi!) servat,' ait, 'nunc quoque amaritiem.'

: CXXII :

On the baptismal font in Florence

Any vice that has arisen from an ancient origin, those waters will wash away, if only you have faith.

: CXXIII :

On Michele Verino[201]

Michele Vieri passed away in the very flower of life—it's hard to say whether he excelled in character more or intellect. For his learned father he composed marvelous distichs, which encapsulate great ideas in brief compass. Only Venus could have come to the   5 aid of his lingering malady; he preferred to die rather than pollute himself. So he lies here, alas, a source of grief and pride to his father. In him our youth may find an example, our poets inspiration.

: CXXIV :

On Daphne

While embracing the green limbs of the leafy maiden, Apollo said, "Changed though you be, I shall enjoy you even so." But when he tried to taste her new fruits, he said, "Oh my! Even now she retains the same bitterness."

: CXXV :

Praefatio in Menaechmos

Heus heus, tacete, sultis, vos, ego ut loquar.
Nam nostra conducta est huc lingua, vestri oculi;
Vos spectare decet, nos loqui et fabulam agere.
Alioqui, capite ipsi hunc ornatum scaenicum,
5   Atque exporgite lumbos: tum nos sessum ibimus,
Spectabimusque nos taciti, aut ridebimus.
Vel si frigebit actio dormitabimus.
    Comoediam *Menaechmos* acturi sumus,
Lepidam et iocosam et elegantem ut nihil supra,
10 Sed mendosam alicubi tamen culpa temporum.
Inerunt in ea nonnulla ne nobis quidem
Satis intellecta, sed haec erunt pauca admodum.
Quae si minus placebunt auribus, expuite,
Aut devorate ceu soletis catapotia.
15   Romanus est hic sermo, Romani sales;
Nihil invenustum aut ineptum et graeculum,
Quale solent nugari molitores ceteri,
Quorum nec ullis versibus comoediae
Nec argumento constant perplexabili,
20 Nec quicquam habent comoediae praeter titulos.
Non ipsae secum congruunt, nec adest fides
Rebus agundis ac nec personis indoles,
Tantumque si quid furtivum est in eis placet—
Quippe alienis insidiantur laboribus.
Velim equidem nostra ne placeat quibus haec placent.
25   Facient profecto maiora operae pretia nunc
Longe adulescentes isti, siquidem insueverint
Puro sermoni Romae urbis vernaculo,

: CXXV :

Preface to "The Brothers Menaechmus"[202]

Hey, hey, quiet please! I mean you! Let me speak! You see, it's *my* tongue that's been hired here, and *your* eyes; it's your job to spectate, mine to speak and act the play. Okay now, why don't you take in this set design and give your gams a stretch: then we'll go sit 5 down and spectate in silence, or we'll laugh out loud. Or if the show is dull, we'll take a bit of a nap.

The comedy that we're about to put on is *The Brothers Menaechmus*; it's delightful and full of jokes and elegant as all get out, but 10 it has its faults here and there due to its age. There will be a few things in it that even I don't understand very well, but they will really be quite few. So if they don't tickle your ears, just spit 'em out, or swallow fast the way you do a bitter pill.

The dialogue is pure Roman, the witticisms too; nothing inel- 15 egant or clumsy or "Greeky," the sort of nonsense those other fuckers[203] usually make up. Their comedies aren't composed in any kind of verse and they don't have a plot that's at all perplexing, and 20 are comedies in name only. They don't have any consistency or believability in the action and their characters lack character. And the only thing in them that's any good is plagiarized—you see they prey upon the work of others. I mean, I wouldn't want my play to appeal to any who like theirs.

In my opinion those young lads of yours will do something 25 more worthwhile if they have gotten used to the pure native speech of the city of Rome, [of which our good friend Plautus is

[Cuius habetur Plautus hic noster pater,][22]
Quam si magistris freti trivialibus
30 Linguas tenellas polluant stribiligine;
Siquidem ita traditum est a laudatis viris:
Latine vellent etiam si Musae loqui,
Nullis usuras nisi Plautinis vocibus.
      Quod si qui clamitent nos facere histrionicam,
35 Atque id reprehendant, minime diffitebimur,
Dum nos sciant disciplinam antiquam sequi.
Etenim formandos comoedo veteres dabant
Pueros ingenuos, actionem ut discerent.
Sed qui nos damnant, histriones sunt maxumi,
40 Nam Curios simulant, vivunt bacchanalia.
Hi sunt praecipue quidam clamosi, leves,
Cucullati, lignipedes, cincti funibus,
Superciliosum incurvicervicum pecus.
Qui quod ab aliis habitu et cultu dissentiunt,
45 Tristesque vultu vendunt sanctimonias,
Censuram sibi quandam et tyrannidem occupant,
Pavidamque plebem territant minaciis.
      Sed iam valete, spectatores, et gregi
Favete nostro; vobis quod vortat bene.

Recitata Florentiae.

considered the father], rather than relying upon masters of no value whatsoever and polluting their delicate little tongues with 30 gibberish, since indeed the following maxim has been passed on to us from praiseworthy men: If the Muses, too, wished to speak in Latin, they would employ only the language of Plautus.[204]

But if anyone should rail about my practicing the art of drama and find fault with that, I won't disavow it one little bit, so long as 35 they know that I am pursuing a venerable discipline. For the ancients used to entrust freeborn boys to a comic poet for their education, so that they would learn how to perform. But it's my critics who are the real performers, for they pretend to be paragons of 40 virtue[205] while leading a life of bacchanals. Certain of these people are especially noisy and petty, running around in hoods and clogs, using ropes as belts,[206] a supercilious, hunchbacked flock. And because they don't agree with others about dress and culture, and 45 they go about grim-faced, peddling their pieties, they usurp for themselves a sort of tyranny over the policing of morals and they continually terrify the timid public with their threats.

But that's it for now. Farewell spectators, but do show your appreciation for our company of players. And may that turn out well for you.

Recited in Florence.

: CXXVI :

In anum

Huc huc, iambi! Arripite mi iam mordicus
Anum hanc furenti percitam libidine,
Tentiginosam, catulientem, spurcidam,
Gravedinosam, vietam, olentem, rancidam,
5 Cadaverosam, fronte rugosa, coma
Cana atque rara, depilatis palpebris,
Glabro supercilio, labellis defluentibus,
Oculis rubentibus, genis lacrimantibus,
Edentulamque (ni duo nigri et sordidi
10 Dentes supersint), auriculis exsanguibus
Flaccisque, mucco naribus stillantibus,
Rictu saliva undante, taetro anhelitu,
Mammis senecta putridis, praegrandibus,
Araneosis, deciduis, inanibus,
15 Laxoque ventre dissipato et fixili,
Cunno ulceroso, verminante podice,
Natibusque macris, aridis, et osseis,
Utroque sicco crure utroque bracchio,
Talo genuque utroque procul extantibus,
20 Calcaneoque pernionibus gravi,
Ut nil sit aspernabilius, nil taetrius
Monstrosiusque aut nauseabundum magis.
Quam pistor olim, caupo, calo, baiulus,
Et institores, et lanius, et carnifex,
25 Et muliones permolebant et coci,
Ceu prostitutam et sellulariam meram,
Nunc nemo iam vult visere, nemo colloqui.
Fastidit unusquisque et habet ludibrio

⁝ CXXVI ⁝

On an old woman

Here! Come here, my iambs! Now grab me this old woman with your fangs, the one that's aroused with mad lust, completely turned on, hot to trot, down and dirty, rasping with mucous, withered, stinking, rancid, like a corpse, with a wrinkly brow,   5 white hair and not much of it, plucked eyelashes, bald eyebrows, drooping lips, bloodshot eyes, tear-soaked cheeks, and missing her teeth (except for two surviving ones, black and filthy), with ear-   10 lobes bloodless and flaccid, her nostrils dripping mucous, her mouth swimming in saliva, her breath foul, her enormous breasts putrid from old age, full of cobwebs, pendulous and pointless, her   15 flapping belly distended in folds, her cunt one big sore, her anus crawling with vermin, and her skinny ass shriveled and bony, both her legs and both her arms desiccated, with both her ankles and both her knees sticking out, and her heels loaded with chilblain: 20 nothing could be more despicable, more disgusting, more monstrous or more nauseating. Once a miller "ground" her up, and a bartender, and a serf, and a porter, and peddlers, and a butcher, an executioner, some mule drivers and cooks, as if she were a straight-   25 up, full-time prostitute. Now no one even wants to visit her, or talk to her, they loathe her one and all, and treat the old woman as

Anum subante perditam prurigine.
30 Sed audet impudens tamen, audet impudens,
Procax, proterva, nec iam anus sed mortua,
Utcumque prurit (prurit autem iugiter),
Se postulare ut comprimam, sibi ut arrigam,
Quasi ipse verres, quasi asinus sim vel canis.
35 Abi hinc, abi, anus, in maximam malam crucem!
Abi scelesta, obscena; sive vera anus
Seu terriculum es seu larva bustuaria!
Nam si optio mi detur, edepol magis
Scrofam futuam quam te vel asinam vel canem.

: CXXVII :

Hymnus

O virgo prudentissima,
Quam caelo missus Gabriel
Supremi regis nuntius
Plenam testatur gratia;

5 Cuius devota humilitas,
Gemmis ornata fulgidis
Fidentis conscientiae,
Amore Deum rapit;

Te sponsam Factor omnium,
10 Te matrem Dei Filius,
Te vocat habitaculum
Suum Beatus Spiritus.

an object of derision when that old itch gets the wretch in heat.
But still that shameless woman has the nerve, brazen as she is,   30
barefaced, impudent, not even an old lady but a dead one, whenever she gets the itch (and she has it constantly), she has the nerve
to demand that I drill her, that I get it up for her, as if I were some
kind of wild pig or a donkey or some sort of a dog. Get away from   35
me, old lady, get away and go to hell! Get away you wicked slut!
Are you really an old lady, or some nightmare or a specter from
beyond the grave? If I had to choose, by god I would rather fuck a
sow than you, or even a donkey or a bitch.

: CXXVII :

A hymn[207]

O Virgin most wise, whom Gabriel, sent from heaven as messenger of the supreme king, affirms as full of grace; Whose devout   5
humility, adorned with the gleaming jewels of devout conscience,
seizes God with love; The Creator of all calls you his bride,
the Son of God calls you mother, the Holy Spirit calls you his   10

Per te de taetro carcere
Antiqui patres exeunt,
15 Per te nobis astriferae²³
Panduntur aulae limina.

Tu stellis comam cingeris,
Tu lunam premis pedibus,
Te sole amictam candido
20 Chori stupent angelici.

Tu Stella Maris diceris,
Quae nobis inter scopulos,
Inter obscuros turbines
Portum salutis indicas.

25 Audi, virgo puerpera
Et sola mater integra,
Audi precantes, quaesimus,
Tuos, Maria, servulos.

Repelle mentis tenebras,
30 Dirumpe cordis glaciem;
Nos sub tuum praesidium
Confugientes protege.

Da nobis in proposito
Sancto perseverantiam,
35 Ne noster adversarius
In te sperantes superet.

Sed et cunctis fidelibus,
Tuum qui²⁴ templum visitant,
Benigna mater, dexteram
40 Da caelestis auxilii.
     Amen.

dwelling place. Through you the Church Fathers of old are freed from their foul prison; through you the threshold of the starry 15 palace is open to us. You bind your hair with stars, your feet tread upon the moon; cloaked in the gleaming sun, the choruses of an- 20 gels are in awe of you. You are called the Star of the Sea, who shows us the harbor of salvation among the rocks and dark tem- pests. Hear us, O child-bearing virgin, the only mother without 25 blemish, hear our prayer, we beseech you, Mary, your humble ser- vants. Drive the shadows from our minds, shatter the ice in our 30 hearts. Keep us safe, who seek refuge under your protection. Grant us perseverance in the holy sacrament, lest our adversary 35 overcome those who hope in you. But to all the faithful too, who visit your church, kind mother, grant the pledge of Heaven's help. 40

Amen.

: CXXVIII :

Alius hymnus eiusdem

Ecce ancilla Domini,
Quam Pater ipse Omnipotens
Elegit ante saecula
Quietum tabernaculum.

5   Ecce cui sacras nuptias
Fortis indixit Angelus,
Ecce quam Sanctus Spiritus
Alto replevit numine.

Ecce virgo concipiens
10   Intacta Dei genitrix,
Ecce Iessaea virgula
De qua flos pulcher emicat.

Huc, huc omnes accurrite
Emanuelem visere,
15   Quem iacentem praesepio
Bos adorant et asinus.

Cuius natali iubilant
Celsi regis exercitus,
Et magnum nocte gaudium
20   Adnuntiant pastoribus.

Videte stellam praeviam
Sanctis Eois regibus,
Qui vagienti Domino
Aurum, myrrham, tus offerunt.

: CXXVIII :

Another hymn to Mary

Behold the handmaid of the Lord[208] whom the Father Almighty
himself chose before the ages as his peaceful tabernacle. Behold 5
the one to whom the Archangel proclaimed the sacred nuptials;
behold she whom the Holy Spirit filled with his high godhead.
Behold the virgin who conceives untouched, the mother of God; 10
behold the branch of Jesse from which a beautiful flower springs.
Here, come here, come running all to see Emanuel, lying in a man- 15
ger while ox and ass adore him. At his birth the host of heaven's
king rejoices, and in the night announces great joy to the shep- 20
herds. See the star that guides the holy kings of the East, who to
our mewling Lord bring offerings of gold, myrrh, and incense.

25 Heu, iam tenellum sanguinem
    Fundit ex lege veteri,
    Dum Symeonis gremio
    Desideratus incubat.

    Videte matrem virginem,
30 Herodis metu pavidam,
    Latentem cum filiolo
    Aegypti regionibus.

    Cernite mox sollicitam,
    Dum puer templo disputat;
35 Cernite rursus hilarem,
    Dum sacras replet hydrias.

    Spectate miserabilem,
    De cruce nati pendulam,
    Commendatam discipulo,
40 Cor saevo fixam gladio.

    Videte tandem radiis
    Magna vincentem sidera,
    Undantem plena gratia,
    Splendentem clara gloria.

45 Regina Caeli maxima,
    Sanctissima, pulcherrima,
    Sustenta tuos servulos,
    Defende tuum populum.
       Amen.

Oh, now he spills tender young blood according to the ancient law, 25
while in the arms of Simeon rests the one he longed for.[209] See the
virgin mother, trembling with fear of Herod, hiding with her little 30
son in the lands of Egypt. Now watch as she is upset, while the
boy disputes in the temple; watch how she is happy again, while 35
he refills the sacred vessels. Gaze at her in her misery hanging
upon her son's cross, entrusted to a disciple, her heart pierced by a 40
cruel sword. See her at last in radiance outshining the great stars,
overflowing with abundant grace, resplendent in bright glory. Most 45
mighty queen of Heaven, most holy and most beautiful, comfort
your poor servants, defend your people.

Amen.

: CXXIX :

Herodianus latinitate a Politiano
donatus in laudem traductoris
sui canit hendecasyllabum

Qui me transposuit Politianus
Verbis omnia reddidit Latinis,
Pulchro sensa revestiens nitore.
Mirum, transtulit Atticos lepores
5 Contextu numeroque blandiori.
Romanus (iuvat hoc) recens amictus,
Concinna speciem ferens ab arte,
Nobis conciliat patentiori
Gentes quae Latium sonant in orbe,
10 Ut posthac mihi latius vagari,
In plures liceat manus venire.
Felix historiae fide[25] renatae,
Felix exoriente luce tanta
Olim publica res Latina surget.
15 Iam debes, studiosa turba, plausus;
Laudis munere gratiam referto.
Aeger desinat utiles malignis
Livor carpere dentibus labores.

: CXXIX :

Having been given the gift of fluency in Latin by Poliziano,
Herodian[210] composes a hendecasyllabic poem
in praise of his translator

My translator, Poliziano, rendered everything in Latin words, re-
clothing my thoughts in a beautiful sheen. It's amazing how he
transferred the delights of Attic Greek into a more charming style 5
and meter. My brand new Roman cloak (I like this!), which dis-
plays its beauty from its polished art, makes me known to the
peoples who speak Latin in the wider world, so that from here on 10
I can travel more broadly and come into the hands of more people.
Happy now with faith in the rebirth of history, happy now in the
great light stirring, one day the Republic of Latin shall rise! Now 15
you ought to applaud, you congregation of scholars; show your
gratitude with the gift of praise. Let Envy grow weak and cease to
pick at practical works with her malignant teeth.

⁚ CXXX ⁚

Epitaphion Iocti Pictoris

Ille ego sum per quem pictura extincta revixit,
  Cui quam recta manus, tam fuit et facilis.
Naturae deerat nostrae quod defuit arti;
  Plus licuit nulli pingere nec melius.
5 Miraris turrem egregiam sacro aere sonantem?
  Haec quoque de modulo crevit ad astra meo.
Denique, sum Ioctus. Quid opus fuit illa referre?
  Hoc nomen longi carminis instar erat.

> *Obiit Anno MCCCXXXVI. Cives Posuerunt*
> *Beatae Memoriae MCCCCLXXXX Florentiae*
> *in Templo Divae Reparatae.*

⁚ CXXXI ⁚

Intonata per Arrighum Isaac

Quis dabit capiti meo
  Aquam, quis oculis meis
  Fontem lacrimarum dabit,
  Ut nocte fleam?
5 Ut luce fleam?

Sic turtur viduus solet,
  Sic cycnus moriens solet,
  Sic luscinia conqueri.
  Heu miser, miser!
10 O dolor, dolor!

: CXXX :

An Epitaph for the painter Giotto[211]

I am the one through whom the extinct art of painting came back
to life, whose hand was as true as it was effortless. What was missing in my art was also missing in nature; there was none who
could paint more or better. Do you marvel at the beautiful tower 5
that resounds with the sacred bell?[212] This, too, climbed to the
stars from my design. After all, I am Giotto. Why was it necessary
to recount all that? This name was the equivalent of a long poem.

> *Died in the year 1336. His fellow citizens placed this
> to his good memory in the year 1490 at Florence
> in the Church of Santa Reparata.*

: CXXXI :

Set to music by Heinrich Isaac[213]

Who will give water for my head, who will give my eyes a fountain
of tears,[214] that I might weep by night, that I might weep by day? 5
So is the widowed turtledove wont to mourn, so too the swan as it
dies, so too the nightingale. Alas, wretch that I am! Oh the pain, 10

Laurus impetu fulminis
    Illa illa iacet subito,
    Laurus omnium celebris
    Musarum choris,
15   Nympharum choris.

Sub cuius patula coma
    Et Phoebi lyra blandius
    Et vox dulcius insonat;
    Nunc muta omnia,
20   Nunc surda omnia.[26]

: CXXXII :

Amor fugitivus e graeco Moschi[27]

Cum Venus intento natum clamore vocaret,
'Si quisquam in triviis errantem vidit Amorem,
Hic fugitivus,' ait, 'meus est. Pretium feret index
Basiolum Veneris. Quod si ad me duxeris illum,
5 Non tantum[28] dabo basiolum; plus, hospes, habebis.
Insignis puer est. En omnia percipe signa:[29]
Non est candidulus,[30] verum ignem imitatur; ocelli
Acres, flammeoli; mala mens, suavissima verba;
Quod loquitur, non sentit idem; vox mellea, sed cum
10 Ira inflammatur, tum mens est aspera;[31] fallax
Fraudator, mendax; ludit crudele puellus.
Crispulus est olli vertex faciesque proterva
Exiguaeque manus. Procul autem spicula torquet:
Torquet in umbriferumque Acheronta et regna silentum.
15 Membra quidem nudus, mentem velatus, avisque

the pain! From the stroke of a thunderbolt our laurel,[215] that one
so dear, is suddenly laid low, the laurel celebrated in the choruses
of all the Muses and the choruses of all the nymphs. Beneath its   15
spreading foliage even Phoebus' lyre sounds more beguilingly and
his voice more sweetly. Now all is mute, now all is silent.[216]   20

: CXXXII :

Love the Runaway, from the Greek of Moschus[217]

When Venus was crying out intently and calling for her son, she
said, "If anyone has seen Love hanging around the street corners,
this runaway is mine. Any informer shall have as prize a little kiss
from Venus. But if you bring him to me, I shall give you not just a   5
little kiss, my friend, but something besides. The boy is easy to
spot. Look, learn all the signs: his complexion is not fair, but looks
like fire; eyes keen and fervent; his mind is evil, but his speech is
very sweet; he does not mean what he says; his voice is like honey,
but when he burns with anger, his heart is violent; treacherous,   10
cheating, lying; the little brat plays cruel jokes. His hair is curly,
his expression impudent, and his hands are tiny, though he can
shoot arrows quite a distance — he even shoots them into ghost-
filled Acheron and the dominions of the dead. His body is naked,   15

173

More quatit pinnas, et nunc hos nunc petit illos,[32]
Saepe viri pressans praecordia, saepe puellae.
Arcum habet exiguum, sed et[33] arcu imposta sagitta est;
Parva sagitta quidem, sed caelum fertur adusque.
20 Parva pharetra olli dependit et aurea tergo;
Sunt et amari intus calami, quibus ille protervus
Me quoque saepe ferit matrem. Sunt omnia saeva,
Omnia, seque ipsum multo quoque saevius angit:
Parvula fax olli, Solem tamen urit et ipsum.[34]
25 Verbere si prendes, age, ne miserare puellum.
Si flentem aspicies, ne mox fallare caveto.
Sin arridebit, magis attrahe. Basia si fors
Ferre volet, fuge tu: sunt noxia basia, in ipsis
Multa venena labris.[35] Si fors ita dixerit: "Heus tu,
30 Accipe, nempe tibi cuncta haec mea largior arma,"
Ne continge, cave,[36] fallacia munera Amoris:
Omnia quippe[37] igni sunt infecta illius arma.'

: CXXXIII :

In laudem Cardinalis Mantuani

O meos longum modulata lusus
Quos amor primam docuit iuventam,
Flecte nunc mecum numeros, novumque
    Dic, lyra, carmen:

5 Non quod hirsutos agat huc leones,
Sed quod et frontem domini serenet,
Et levet curas, penitusque doctas
    Mulceat aures.

but his mind is veiled. He flaps his wings like a bird, and attacks one person after another, sometimes oppressing a man's heart, sometimes a girl's. He has a tiny bow, but upon the bow is set an arrow too, a little arrow, yes, but it carries all the way to heaven. A 20 quiver, small and golden, hangs upon his back, and in it are the bitter shafts with which that scoundrel often wounds me too, his mother though I am. Everything about him is savage, everything, and he also inflicts far more savage torment on himself. His torch is very small, but it burns even the Sun himself. If you catch him 25 with your whip, go on, show the brat no mercy. If you see him weeping, be careful that he doesn't trick you next. But if he's laughing, pull him along all the more forcefully. If by chance he wants to kiss you, get yourself out of there! His kisses are deadly, and on his very lips there is poison aplenty. And if by chance he says, 'Hey you, I'm giving you all these weapons of mine, really, 30 take them,' watch out! Don't even touch the deceitful gifts of Love, for all his weapons have been dipped in fire."

⁝ CXXXIII ⁝

In praise of the Cardinal of Mantua[218]

O lyre, you who have long accompanied my trifles, first taught to me by Love in my youth, change now your measures, together with me, and sing a new song. Not the kind that could lead shaggy 5 lions here, but the kind that could soothe even our lord's brow, lighten his cares, and comfort his ever so learned ears. The prince

Vindicat nostros sibi iure cantus
10   Qui colit vates citharamque princeps;
Ille cui sacro rutilus refulget
      Crine galerus;

Ille cui flagrans triplici corona
Cinget auratam diadema frontem.
15   Fallor, an vati bonus haec canenti
      Dictat Apollo?

Phoebe, quae dictas rata fac, precamur!
Dignus est nostrae dominus Thaliae,
Cui celer versa fluat Hermus uni
20   Aureus urna;

Cui tuas mittat, Cytherea, conchas
Conscius primi Phaethontis Indus;
Ipsa cui dives properet beatum
      Copia cornu.

25   Quippe non gazam pavidus repostam
Servat, Aeaeo similis draconi,
Sed vigil Famam secat, ac perenni
      Imminet aevo.

Ipsa Phoebeae vacat aula turbae
30   Dulcior blandis Heliconis umbris,
Et vocans doctos patet ampla toto
      Ianua poste.

Sic refert magnae titulis superbum
Stemma Gonzagae recidiva virtus,
35   Gaudet et fastos superare avitos
      Aemulus heres.

who honors poets and the cithara rightly claims my songs for him-   10
self, the one upon whose sacred locks a red cap gleams, the one
whose gilded brow will be encircled by a diadem blazing with a
triple crown.[219] Am I mistaken, or is it good Apollo who dictates   15
these words to the poet as he sings? Phoebus, see that what you
dictate is fulfilled, we beseech you! This lord is worthy of our
Muse,[220] for whom alone the golden river Hermus[221] flows swiftly,
its urn upturned; to whom, the river Indus, which witnesses the   20
sun's first dawning, sends your pearls, Lady of Cythera;[222] to
whom rich Plenty herself dispatches her horn of wealth. To be   25
sure he does not guard his hoarded wealth out of fear, like that
famed serpent of Aea;[223] instead, ever alert, he follows fame and is
intent upon eternity. His palace itself is open to Phoebus' flock, a   30
more pleasant place than the seductive shade of Helicon, and his
generous door is wide open inviting the learned in. Thus is virtue
restored, bringing back the line of the great Gonzagas, proud in its
titles, and their ambitious heir takes pleasure in surpassing his   35

Scilicet stirpem generosa suco
Poma commendant, timidumque numquam
Vulturem feto Iouis acer ales
40   Extudit ovo.

Curre iam toto violentus amne,
O sacris Minci celebrate Musis!
Ecce Maecenas tibi nunc Maroque
      Contigit uni!

45   Iamque vicinas tibi subdat undas
Vel Padus multo resonans olore,
Quamlibet flentes animosus alnos
      Astraque iactet.

Candidas ergo volucres notarat
50   Mantuam condens Tiberinus Ocnus,
Nempe quem Parcae docuit benignae
      Conscia mater.

ancestors' record of accomplishments. Clearly the superior fruit
proves the worth of the stock, and never has Jupiter's spirited bird
produced a timid vulture when its egg is hatched. Run wild now   40
in full stream, O Mincius,[224] celebrated by the sacred Muses!
Look, now Maecenas and Vergil fell to you alone! And now the   45
river Po, which echoes to the sounds of many a swan, submits its
neighboring waters to you, although he proudly boasts of his
weeping alders and a constellation.[225] Ocnus, therefore, Tiber's
son, had observed white birds while founding Mantua, Ocnus   50
whom his mother, conscious of his propitious destiny, had indeed
taught well.[226]

LIBER EPIGRAMMATON
GRAECORUM

Zenobius Acciaiolus studiosis omnibus felicitatem

Angeli Politiani Graeca epigrammata sicut in archetypo volumine
scripta erant publicanda curavi, non quod ea censerem iudicio
auctoris ad aeternitatem probata, sed ut bonis adulescentibus ad
certam spem profectus extarent, cum Politianum viderent in hoc
quoque genere scriptionis, in quo Latini paulum modo mussi-
tantes gloriari solemus, eo tamen studio ac diligentia processisse,
ut horum permulta paene puer conscripserit. Quaedam vero inam-
bulanti etiam, aut cenanti veluti repentino calore fusa ipsi sciamus,
in quis tamen ipsis, ut mihi quidem videtur, eiusmodi multa sunt,
quorum si facilitatem ac copiam reputaris, magni quidem ingenii
Politianum, sed et multae lectionis fuisse ostendant planeque indi-
cent quantum vir ille operae pretium facere potuerit, si perficere
quae cogitabat per importunum obitum licuisset; ut quod effecit,
laude dignissimus, quod non potuit venia ac commiseratione
censendus sit. Florentiae, Kalendis Decembribus 1495.

THE BOOK OF GREEK
EPIGRAMS

Zanobi Acciaiuoli[1] to all scholars, good wishes

I have seen to the publication of the Greek epigrams of Angelo
Poliziano, just as they had been written out in his original volume,
not because I judged that in the opinion of their author they had
been approved for posterity, but so that they might be available to
young men of good breeding to give them sure hope that they can
achieve success when they see that, in this genre of writing, in
which we Latins typically turn to boasting when we are only stam-
mering along, Poliziano made such progress by virtue of his scholarship and diligence that he wrote many of these while he was still
practically a boy. Some of them we know from personal experience
came to him as if in the sudden heat of inspiration while he was
strolling about or dining. Nonetheless, it seems to me that among
those very epigrams there are many of such quality that, if you
ponder their fluency and verbal command, they reveal that Poliziano was indeed man of great genius, but also extremely well-read.
And they plainly indicate how much valuable work that man could
have done, if an untimely death had not prevented him from ac-
complishing what he intended. Accordingly, he should be considered as most deserving of praise for what he did accomplish, and
we should make allowances in evaluating him as we regret what he
could not. Florence, December 1, 1495.[2]

: I :

1471, aetatis meae anno 17. In invidum quendam

Ὦ φίλε, χαῖρε᾽ λέγεις, ὅτε σὸν ποτὶ δῶμα καθήκω,
Αὐτὰρ ἔμ᾽ οὐκ ἔλαθεν ῥῆμα χαριζόμενον.
Οὐδ᾽ ἐθέλεις φθονερὸς χαίρειν ἐμέ, οὔτε φιλεῖς με·
Καὶ γὰρ σημαίνει τοῦτο τὸ ᾽χαῖρε᾽ δύο·
5   Ἔστιν σώζεσθαι χαίρειν, ἔστιν δ᾽ ἀπολέσθαι.
Τοὶ γὰρ ἔγωγε λέγω σοί· ᾽φίλε, χαῖρε μάλα.᾽

: II :

In Corydonem

'Sum puer,' exclamas, Corydon, subigisque fateri.
In te reclamat sed tua barba: vir es.

Graece

᾽Εἰμί,᾽ λέγεις, ᾽παῖς,᾽ ὦ Κορύδων· δεῖ τοῦτο λέγειν με.
Ἀνὴρ δ᾽εἶ, κατὰ σοῦ σὸν τὸ γένειον ἔφα.

: I :

1471, when I was 17 years old. Against a jealous man

"Greetings, my friend," is what you say when I come to your
house, but I am not fooled by your fawning words. Out of jealousy you don't want me to be happy,[3] and you aren't my friend;
and in fact the word "Greetings" has two meanings: on the one   5
hand it means "to be well," on the other "to go to hell." And so I
say to you, "Special greetings to you, my friend."

: II :

On Corydon[4]

"I am a boy," you exclaim, Corydon, and you compel me to agree.
But your beard tells against you: you are a man.

In Greek

"I am a boy," so you say, Corydon, and this is what I must call you.
But you're a man: your beard contradicts you.

: III :

1472, *anno aetatis* 18. Εἰς Χάρολον Βριξιέα

Σοῦ γ' ἔτι παιδαρίου κροτάφους περίδησεν Ἀπόλλων
Κωρυκίοις δάφνης πλέγμασι χρυσοκόμου·
Καὶ σ' ἐχρησμολόγει γλυκερῶν κοσμήτορ' ἀοιδῶν,
Μέλλονθ' ἱπποτρόφον ἐς κλέος Ἄργος ἄγειν.
5 Νῦν δέ μ' ἐς ἀθανάτους ἐπαείρειν θυμὸς ἀνώγει
Τοῦτο βάρος, Χαρόλου μάστιγι πληττόμενον.

: IV :

Ad Pamphilum

Mittis vina mihi: mihi, Pamphile, vina supersunt.
  Vis mage quod placeat mittere? Mitte sitim.

Graece

Οἶνόν μοι πέμπεις, τοῦ δ' ἔσθ' ἅλις· εἰ δ' ἔτι μᾶλλον
  Λῆς γε χαρίζεσθαι, πέμφ' ἅμα δίψαν ἐμοί.

: III :

1472, at the age of 18. On Carlo of Brescia[5]

You were still a little boy when Apollo bound your brows with
Corycian[6] wreaths of golden-haired laurel; and he prophesied that
you would be a composer of sweet songs, who would bring fame
to Argos,[7] breeder of horses. But now my heart urges me, goaded   5
on by Carlo's whip, to raise this burden to the immortals.[8]

: IV :

To Panfilo[9]

You send me wine, but I've wine to spare and then some, Panfilo.
Would you like to send me something more pleasing? Send thirst.

In Greek

You send me wine, though I have plenty of it; but if you wish to
do me a greater favor, send me thirst along with it.

: V :

MCCCCLXXII, XVIII anno.

Ad Ioannem Baptistam Bonisignium

Ἤδη τοι πάρα μὲν χειμών, πάρα δ' ἄσπετος ὄμβρος,
Ἀγρονόμοι τε φύγον, μεστὰ δὲ πᾶσα πόλις.
Σὺ μόνος ἀενάους ποταμοὺς καὶ οὔρε' ἄφυλλα
Ποσσὶ περᾷς ἀπαλοῖς, σὺ μόνος ἄντρα νέμῃ,
5   Νῦν μὲν ἄρ' ὠτώεντα λαγών, νῦν δ' ἄγριον αἶγα
Εἰς τὰ λίν' ἐμβάλλων καρχαρόδοντι κυνί.
Νύμφας τ' ἰοφόρους θέλγων πολυδενδρέῳ ὕλῃ,
Γλώττης τ' ἠδὲ λύρης ἄμβροτον ᾆσμα χέεις.
Δεῦρο φίλος, μὴ φεῦγε φίλους, καὶ χάζεο καιρῷ·
10   Πικρὰ ἄνευ γε φίλων ἐστὶ καὶ ἀμβροσίη.

: VI :

MCCCCLXXII. Ad eundem.

Εἰς Σοφίαν παράκλησις

Νῦν γε Νότος πτύει μελανόπτερος ἄσπετον ὄμβρον,
Ἤδη καὶ νιφάδας Θρῇξ Βορέας συνάγει.
Φηγῶν καὶ πτελεῶν ἐμαράνθη φύλλ' ἐπὶ γαίῃ,
Χεῖμα δὲ κερτομέον οὔρεσι κεῖρε κόμας.
5   Πεῦκαι ἄκαρποι ἔασσιν, ἀειθηλεῖς περ ἐοῦσαι,
Ὑψίκομοί τ' ἐλάται, καὶ θανάτοιο φυτόν.

: V :

1472, in his eighteenth year.
To Giovan Battista Buoninsegni[10]

Already winter is here, and with it unending rain; the farm work-
ers have fled, the whole city is full. You alone cross the ever-
flowing rivers and leafless mountains on delicate feet, and you
alone dwell in grottoes, and have your sharp-toothed hound drive
its prey into the nets, now the long-eared hare, now the wild goat.   5
And to charm the huntress Nymphs in the dense forest, you pour
forth an immortal song composed of voice and lyre. Come here,
my friend, do not shun your friends, and give in to the season;
without friends even ambrosia is bitter.   10

: VI :

1472. To the same man.
An exhortation to wisdom

Now the dark-winged south wind spits rain without end, and already Thracian Boreas is gathering snows. The leaves of the
beeches and the elms have withered on the ground, and the sneer-
ing storm has shorn the foliage on the mountains. The pines, ever   5
green though they are, are barren, as are the towering firs and the

Ἀλλὰ καὶ ὡς δάφνή τε καὶ ποικίλον ἔρνος ἐλαίας
Φύλλων καὶ καρπῶν χαίρουσι βριθοσύνῃ·
Πάντα γὰρ ἄλλα χρόνου κρατεροὶ κατέδουσιν ὀδόντες,
10   Ἄφθαρτος δ' ἡμῖν ἐστὶ μόνον Σοφίη.

: VII :

18 aetatis anno. Ad eundem

Ὢ πόποι, ὅσσον ἔχω γε σὲ μείζονα ἠὲ πέπεισμαι·
Πλῆρές τοι Μουσῶν τὸ στόμα καὶ Χαρίτων.
Καὶ σοὶ ἄρ' αὐτομάτως κροτάφους περιέδραμε δάφνη·
Βριθομένη πετάλοις, ἄνθεα λευκὰ χέει.
5   Ἀλλὰ ποῦ εὑρήσω τὰ σὰ ἴχνεα, μαιόμενός περ
Κύματα γῆν αὔρας, νηὶ ποδί πτέρυγι;
Αἰὲν ἐγὼ ποτὶ σὲ γλυκερῷ βεβολημένος οἴστρῳ,
Ὡς βόες ὑλοφάγοι ἔνθα καὶ ἔνθα θέω,
Ῥῖνα μὲν ἐγκλίνων ἐπὶ γῆν, τὰ δ' οὔατ' ἀείρων,
10   Ὄμμασι παπταίνων, πλαζόμενος δὲ ποσί.
Γούνατε δὴ καμέτην· ποῖ γοῦν ἀλαόν σε διώξω;
Ποῖ δ' οὕτω φεύγεις τὸν φιλέοντα, φίλος;
Ἀνδρὶ ἄτερ γε φίλου δνοφερή τ' ἠώς ἀνατέλλει,
Πικροὶ δ' οἱ σχαδόνες, πᾶς δ' ὁ βίος θάνατος.
15   Χωρὶς δ' αὖ κείνων, οὐδ' ἀθάνατός γε θέλοιμι
Ἔμμεναι, οὐ δ' αὐτῶν κοίρανος ἀθανάτων.

tree of death.[11] But even so the laurel and the dappled shoot of the
olive rejoice in the weight of leaves and fruits:[12] for the powerful
teeth of time devour all other things, but for us only wisdom is   10
deathless.

: VII :

At the age of 18. To the same man

Oh my, how much more regard I have for you than I had thought:
your mouth is filled with the Muses and the Graces! And the laurel has spontaneously wreathed your brows: it is bristling with
leaves, pouring out white flowers. But where shall I find your   5
footsteps, though I scour the sea, the earth, and the sky, on ship,
by foot, or on wing? Forever driven to you by a sweet frenzy, like
foraging cattle I race here and there, lowering my snout to the
ground, lifting up my ears, searching with my eyes, wandering on   10
my feet. My limbs are exhausted: wherever shall I pursue you in
your wanderings? My friend, where do you thus flee from the one
who loves you? The dawn rises in shadows for the man without a
friend; honeycombs are bitter, the whole of life is death. Without   15
friends I would not wish to be immortal, not even to be king of
the immortals.

: VIII :

XVIII aetatis anno. Ad eundem

Ὅσσον μὲν χαίρουσιν ὑφ᾽ ἀλκυόνων ὀπὶ καλῇ
Ναῦται ποντοπόροι μαλακὸν πλόον ἀγγελεουσῶν,
Ὅσσον δ᾽ ἐχθίστην βασιλεὺς πόλιν ἐξαλαπάξας,
Ὅσσον τὶς χαλεπὴν φεύξας νόσον, ὅσσον ἐραστής
5 Παρθενίοιο φίλης γλυκερὸν λέχος εἰσαναβαίνων,
Τόσσον ἐνὶ[1] στήθεσφιν ἀγάλλεται ἡμέτερον κῆρ,
Σόν τε πρόσωπον ἰδὸν καὶ σεῦ ἐπὶ μῦθον ἀκουον.
Ὦ λευκοῦ λίθακός τε καὶ ᾄσματος ἄξιον ἦμαρ,
Ἦμαρ μνήμης ἄξιον ἐς πολέας λυκάβαντας.
10 Ὦ μέλιτος γλυκίων φίλε, ὦ χαρίεσσα πρόσοψι,
Χαῖρ᾽ αἰεί, καὶ σοὶ Ζεὺς ὄλβια πάντα παρέξοι.
Τήρησον δ᾽ ἐπάλληλον ἐπὶ στήθεσφιν ἔρωτα.

: IX :

18 aetatis anno. Προσευχὴ πρὸς τὸν Θεόν

Ὦ πάτηρ ἡμέτερε, χρυσόθρονε, αἰθέρι ναίων,
Ὦ πάντων βασιλεῦ, Θεὸς ἄφθιτε, αἰθέριε Ζάν,[2]
Πάντα ἰδὼν καὶ πάντα κινῶν καὶ πάντα κατασχών,
Πρεσβύτερός τε χρόνου, πάντων ἀρχή τε τέλος τε·
5 Παμμακάρων δάπεδον, καὶ οὐρανίων σέλας ἄστρων,
Σύ, πάτερ, ἠέλιόν τε μέγαν λαμπράν τε σελήνην
Πηγὰς καὶ ποταμοὺς καὶ γῆν καὶ πόντον ἔτευξας,

∶ VIII ∶

At the age of eighteen. To the same man

As much as seafaring sailors rejoice at the lovely voice of the halcyons when they report a calm voyage, or a king after sacking a city of the enemy, or a man who has escaped a grave malady, or a 5
lover upon entering the sweet bed of a beloved maiden, so much does the heart in my breast exult upon seeing your face and hearing your voice. Oh what a day, worthy of song and the white stone,[13] a day worth remembering for many years. Oh my friend, 10
sweeter than honey, oh dear apparition, long life to you, and may Zeus bestow upon you all good things. And guard in your heart the love we feel for each other.

∶ IX ∶

At the age of 18. A Prayer to God

Our father, enthroned in gold, that dwells in heaven, O king of all, God immortal, celestial Zeus, who sees all things, and moves all things, and holds all things, older than time, the beginning and end of all; the seat of the angels and the gleam of the stars in 5
heaven, you created, father, and the great sun and the resplendent moon, the springs and the rivers and the earth and the sea,

Πάντα ζωογονῶν, σῷ πάντα πνεύματι πληρῶν·
Οὐράνιοι χθόνιοί τε καὶ οἱ ὑπένερθε καμόντες
10 Πάντες ὑποχθόνιοι σὴν ἐκτελέουσιν ἐφετμήν.
Νῦν δὴ κικλήσκω σὲ τεὴ κτίσις ἔνθα χαμευνάς,
Ἄθλιος ὠκύμορος, Θεέ, γήϊνος ἀνθρωπίσκος,
Ἀλγῶν ὧν ἥμαρτόν σοι καὶ δάκρυα χεύων.
Εἰ δ' ἄγε, μοι, λίτομαι, πάτερ ἄφθιτε, ἵλαος ἴσθι,
15 Κἀξ ἐμέθεν δὴ κόσμου θελξινόοιο ἔρωτα
Δαίμονος ἠδ' ἀπάτας καὶ ἀτάσθαλον ὕβριν ἔλαυνε·
Δεῦε δ' ἐμὴν κραδίην σέο πνεύματος ἀσπέτῳ ὄμβρῳ,
Ὥστε ἀεί σε μόνον στέργειν, ὕπατε κρειόντων.

: X :

18 anno. Ad Iuvianum Monopoliten⟨sem⟩

Τί στάχυας Δήμητρι, τί κύματα δοῦν' ἐθέλεις με
Πρωτεῖ ποντοπόρῳ, Νυκτελίῳ τε βότρυν;
Σὺ μόνος ἐκ γλώττης γλυκερὸν μέλι, σὺ μόνος αὐδήν
Ἀμβροσίην στόματος ἐκ λιγυροῖο χέεις·
5 Τήν μὲν καὶ σκόπελοι καὶ οὔρεα μάκρ' ἐφέπονται,
Ὡς πόκα Θρηϊκίης ἄμβροτον ᾆσμα λύρης.
Εἰ δέ μοι ὠκυπέτης Ἐριούνιος οὔνομα θῆκεν
Ὥστ' ἐπὶ Ῥωμαίους θεῖον Ὅμηρον ἄγειν,
Σὺ δ' ἄρ' ἔχεις μεγάλου Διὸς οὔνομα παμβασιλῆος,
10 Ὥστε σ' ἄνακτα πάσῃ ἔμμεναι ἐν σοφίῃ.
Σὸν γὰρ νεκταρέοιο γάλακτος λαιμὸν ἐπλήρουν
Ἐννέα δὴ θύγατρες Μνημοσύνης καὶ Διός·

bringing all things to life, filling all things with your spirit: the
creatures of heaven and earth, and all the dead below in the Un- 10
derworld fulfill your command. Now then I call upon you, God, I,
your creation here on earth, wretched and ephemeral, a pitiful
human fashioned of clay, suffering for the sins I have committed
against you and pouring out my tears. But come now, immortal
father, I pray you, be gracious unto me, and drive from me my 15
passion for the bewitching world, the deceits of the demon and
wicked pride. Bathe my heart with the boundless rain of your
spirit that I may love you alone forever, O lord over the mighty.

: X :

At the age of 18. To Gioviano da Monopoli[14]

Why do you want me to give ears of grain to Demeter, ocean
waves to Proteus, who plies the sea, and bunches of grapes to Dionysus?[15] You alone pour sweet honey from your tongue, you alone
pour forth an ambrosial voice from your sweet-sounding mouth,
which the rocks and the tall mountains follow, as once they did the 5
immortal song of the Thracian lyre.[16] If the swift-flying messenger
god has granted me his name,[17] so that I might bring back divine
Homer to the Romans, yet you have the name of great Jupiter, the
universal king, so that you might be sovereign in all wisdom. For 10
your throat has been filled with milky nectar by the nine daughters of Memory and Zeus;[18] luxuriant ivy spreads spontaneously

Αὐτόματος δὲ τεὴν περιπέπταται ἀμφὶ ἔθειραν
Κισσὸς τηλεθάων ἄνθεα πολλὰ χέων.
15 Ὦ μάκαρ, ἀθανάτοισι βροτῶν ὦ φίλτατε πάντων,
Χρυσοκόμων θεράπων ὄλβιε Πιερίδων,
Ὦ, χαῖρ', ἱερὴ κεφαλή, λιγύφωνος ἀοιδέ,
Τήρει δ' ἡμέτερον αἰὲν ἔρωτα, φίλος.

: XI :

19 aetatis anno. Ad Ioannem Argyropulum, Dorice

Ὅσσον διψάων ἔλαφος κράνᾳ μελανύδρῳ
Ἄδεται, ὅσσον ὄις θέρεος μέσῳ εὐσκίῳ ἄλσει,
Ὅσσον ἄλῳ μύρμαξ, ὅσσον κάποισι μέλισσα,
Ὅσσον δενδρέῳ τέττιγες, ὅσσον δ' ἁ ὀλολυγών,
5 Ὅσσον δ' ἁ λαλιά τε χελιδονὶς εἴαρι πράτῳ,
Τόσσον νῦν πάντες μουσάων εὔφρανθεν ὀπαδοί
Χ' ἄμμες δ' ἐν πράτοις, ὅτε τεῦ ἀγγέλλετο νόστος
Τᾶς ἱερᾶς κεφαλᾶς, σοφίας πρόμος Ἀργυρόπουλε.
Κοὐδ' οὕτω Βορέω χρυσοπτέρυγας πόκα κούρως
10 Φινέα φαντὶ ποθεῖν, ὥσθ' Ἁρπυίας ἀπέλαυνεν,
Ὡς τό γε πάντες νῦν σοφίας μαιήτορες ὅσσοι
Ἀθανάτω πελόμεσθ' ὁμοθυμαδὸν ὧδε ποθεῦμες
Ὥστε νόῳ βλεφάρων ἀχλὺν ἴλιγγάς τ' ἀποβάλλεν.
Νῦν γὰρ φεῦ σχέτλιοι λοξῇσι πλανώμεθ' ἀταρποῖς,
15 Κοὐ χ' οἷόν τε τυφλὼς εὑρεῖν εὐκαμπέα οἴμαν
Ὀρθοπόρω βιότοιο, καὶ ἐξυπαλύξαι βάραθρον
Ἀνδρομέας ἀνοίας πολύφλοισβόν τε κυδοιμόν,

round your hair, scattering many flowers. O blessed man, of all 15
mortals most dear to the gods, fortunate servant of the golden-
haired Muses, O holy man, hail, sweet-voiced singer, and preserve
for ever our love for each other, my friend.

: XI :

At the age of 19. To John Argyropoulos,[19] *in Doric*[20]

As much as a thirsty deer delights in a spring of dark water, as
much as a sheep delights in a grove of dark shade in the midst of
summer, as much as the ant delights in the threshing floor, the bee
in the gardens, the cicadas and the owl in the trees, and as much 5
as the chattering swallow delights in the onset of spring, so much
now were all the attendants of the Muses gladdened, and I most
of all, when your return was announced, Argyropoulos, our holy
man, chief in wisdom. And not even did Phineus,[21] as the myth
goes, once long for the golden-winged sons of Boreas to drive away 10
the Harpies as much as all of us who are seekers of immortal wisdom long for this with one accord, so that you may drive the darkness and turmoil from our eyes with your mind. For as it is now,
alas, we wander miserably on crooked paths, and in our blindness 15
we cannot find the straight path that leads to the upright life, nor
can we avoid the abyss of human folly and resounding confusion,

Εἰ μὴ χεῖρα λαβὼν σύ γε νῦν, πάτερ, ἄμμιν ὁδαγοῖς,
Πυρσὼς ἀτρεκέων ὑποθημοσυνάων ἅψας.
20 Ἀλλὰ τί οὐ σπεύδεις ἐνθών; τί δ' ἄρ' οὐχ' ὑπακούεις;
Πάντες κοινᾷ κοινὸν ὀπὶ κληίζομες αἰὲν
Ἐνθεῖν, οἷα βρέφη ποθ' ἑὸν κνυζῶντα τιθηνόν.
Πάντων δ' αὖ πέρι αὐτὸς ἐπ' ἐλπίδι τάκομαι ὥς τις
Πιδακόεσσα λιβὰς σέλας ἁλίῳ ἁνίκα φρύγῃ.
25 Ἦ μὰν καὶ λευκῶ λίθακος καὶ ἄσματος ἔσται
Τῆνο τὸ ἆμαρ ἐμοὶ πάνυ ἄξιον, ὁππόκα κέν τυ
Ἂψ' ἀπονοστήσαντα φίλαν ὁράοιμι πρόσοψιν.

: XII :

19 aetatis anno. Ad eundem

Ἁ μὲν ἐν ἀθανάτοισι φατίζεται πότνια Ἥβα
    Νέκταρ χρυσείοις οἰνοχοεῖν δέπασιν·
Σοὶ δ' ἄρ' ἐν ἀνθρώποισι Θεὸς πόρεν, Ἀργυρόπουλε,
    Χρυσέω ἐκ στόματος πῶμα χέειν σοφίας.
5 Ἅδε βίον μὲν ἀγήραον ἀθανάτοισι φυλάττει,
    Τὺ δ' ἄρα κὰκ θνατῶν ἐξελάεις θάνατον.

if you do not take our hands now, father, and guide us, by lighting
the torches of true teaching. But why do you not hasten to come   20
here? Why do you not hear us? We are always calling you in chorus with one voice to come, like babes whimpering for their foster
father. More than all of them, I dissolve with hope, like a trickle of
water from a spring when parched by the gleam of the sun. Truly   25
for me that day will be entirely deserving to be marked by a white
stone and by song, whenever it may be that I shall see your dear
face come home again.

: XII :

At the age of 19. To the same man

It is said that among the immortals queenly Hebe[22] mixes nectar
in cups of gold; but among humans, Argyropoulos, God has
granted it to you to pour drafts of wisdom from your golden
mouth. She safeguards the ageless life of the immortals, while you   5
keep mortality away from mortals too.

: XIII :

21 aetatis anno. Εἰς Θεόδωρον τὸν Γαζῆ

Κεῖτο μέγας ποτ' ἀγὼν Γαζῆ Θεοδώροιο ἄμφι
Μούσαις τ' Αὐσονίαις ἠδ' Ἑλικωνιάσι.
Ταῖς μὲν γὰρ γενεήν, ταῖς δ' αὖ θρεπτήρι' ὄφειλεν·
Ἑλλὰς γὰρ τέκε τόν γ', Αὐσονίη δ' ἔτραφεν.
5   Ἴσον δ' ἀμφοτέρων σοφίῃ γλώττῃ τ' ἐκέκαστο.
Τὸν δ' οὔτ' αὐτὸς ζῶν, οὔτ' ἄρ' ἔκρινε θανών·
Ἀλλὰ καὶ Ἰταλίας μεγάλῃ ἐπὶ Ἑλλάδι κεῖσθαι
Εἵλετο, ὄφρα κλέος ξυνὸν ᾗ ἀμφοτέρης.

: XIV :

Μονόστιχον εἰς τὴν σελήνην

Νυκτορινοὺς ἀκτῖνας ἐς ἡμᾶς πέμπε, σελήνη.

: XV :

Εἰς Θεόδωρον τὸν Γαζῆ

Ἑλλὰς μὲν, Θεόδωρε, σὲ μᾶλλον κλαῦσε θανόντα
Τύρκιον ἢ ὅτέ μιν ἐξαλάπαξε γένος·
Καὶ γάρ ἑ τὸ σκῆπτρον τόθ'³ ὁ βάρβαρος εἷλε τύραννος,
Νῦν δὲ κλέος γλώττης κλέψατο μοῖρ' ὀλοή.
5   Ἀλλά νυ καὶ Ῥώμης ὕπο πρὶν πολέμῳ δεδάμασται,
Πρῶτον δ' αὖ γλώττης πτῶμα τόδ' οἱ συνέβη.

: XIII :

At the age of 21. To Theodore Gaza[23]

Once there was a great contest over Theodore Gaza between the
Muses of Ausonia[24] and of Helicon. For to the one group he owed
his lineage, to the other his upbringing; for Greece gave birth to
him, but Ausonia reared him. He excelled equally in the wisdom   5
and language of both. Neither in life nor in death did he settle this
contest; instead he chose to be buried in Italy, in Magna Graecia,[25]
so that his glory would be shared by both.

: XIV :

A one-liner to the moon

O moon, send to us your nocturnal rays.

: XV :

To Theodore Gaza

Greece grieved at your death, Theodore, more than when she was
destroyed by the Turkish people;[26] for then the barbarian tyrant
but seized her scepter, while now a deadly fate has stolen the glory
of her language. Moreover, while she had already been conquered   5
previously in war by Rome, this was the first disaster for her language.

: XVI :

Εἰς τὸν αὐτον

Τῆνο τὸ Καλλιόπας ἱερὸν στόμα ἠνίδε σιγᾷ,
Τὸ κλέος Ἑλλήνων φεῦ πόκα, νῦν δὲ γόος,
Ἀδνεπὴς Θεόδωρος, ὃς ἐν κραδίῃ ἔχε πάντα,
Τοὔνεκα καὶ πάντων κεῖται ἐνὶ κραδίης·
5 Τοῦδε καὶ ἐν στόματι πρὶν γ' ἔμφρονα πάντα διάνθει,
Ἔμφροσι νῦν κηὐτὸς πᾶσι διὰ στομάτων.
Ἀλλὰ τίνα κραδίαν; τί φάμην στόμα; τοῦδε θανόντος,
Πᾶν στόμα φεῦ βύεται, πᾶσ' ἀπορεῖ κραδία.

: XVII :

Εἰς Δημήτριον μέτρον φαλαίκιον

Ἐξ οὗ δὴ Θεόδωρος οὐρανόνδε
Βῆ, καὶ ὥς γε χελιδόνος νεοσσούς,
Ματρὸς χερσὶ βρεφυλλίου θανούσας,
Ἀπτῆνας λίπεν ὧδ' ὑπὲρ καλιᾶς
5 Μάψ δὴν μάστακα τοῦδε προσδοκῶντας,
Ὦ Δημήτριε, πάντες ἄθλιοί γε
Νῦν γουνούμεθα. σὺ δὲ πρᾶος ἐλθών
Πεινῶσιν, σοφίης ἐδητὺν ἡμῖν
Δός. σὺ νῦν μόνος εἶ γλυκὺς τιθηνός.

: XVI :

To the same man

Look, Calliope's sacred mouth is silent, once the glory of the
Greeks, but now, alas, only a lament, sweet-voiced Theodore, who
had all in his heart, and thus was also in the hearts of all. Upon   5
his lips all wisdom once flowered, now he too is on the lips of all
the wise. But what heart? What lips? Now that he is dead, every
mouth is sealed, alas, every heart is lost.

: XVII :

To Demetrius,[27] in phalaecian meter

Ever since Theodore went to heaven and left us, like a sparrow's
wingless chicks when their mother has died at the hands of an
infant, here in our nest long awaiting his beak in vain, in our mis-   5
ery we all implore you, Demetrius. Come gently and give to us
who are starving the food of wisdom. You are now our only sweet
caregiver.

: XVIII :

Εἰς Κορνήλιον ἰαμβικός

Οὐκ ἐμὰ λέγεις ἔμμεν' ὅσα σοὶ γράφω ἔπη,
Κορνήλι', ἀλλ' ὅμως ἀοιδὸν ἐμὲ καλεῖς.
Σὺ γοῦν βόας τὲ μὴ φύσει κερασφόρους
Λέξεις, ὅμως δὲ βόας καλέσσεις τοὺς βόας.
5 Τοῦτο δ' ἔτυχες λέξας, ἐπεὶ μέτρον οὔπω γράφεις·
Οὕτω βραδύπους ὄνος ἐλάφους ὄντας ταχέας
Ἀρνεῖται, οὕτως ὁ λαγωὸς θρασὺν λύκον.

: XIX :

Εἰς τοὺς σπουδαίους

Φεύγετε Πιερίδων ἀδινοὶ θεράποντες ἄρουραν,
Πᾶς Ἑλικωνιάδων ἦλθε πόλινδε χορός.
Εἰ δέ τις αὖ κείνου θαλάμους καὶ δώματ' ἐρευνᾷ,
Χαλκεοκονδύλου στήθεα ναιετάει.

: XX :

Περὶ τοῦ αὐτοῦ

Σειρήνων ἔφυγεν λιγυρὸν ποτὲ ῥυθμὸν Ὀδυσσεύς,
Ὦ Δημήτριε, σὸν δ' οὐκ ἄν ἔπος γε φύγεν.
Καὶ γὰρ ἐγὼ γλυκεροῖο πότου δόρπου τε χατίζων,
Χθὲς τεὸν οὐδ' ἀέκων ᾆσμ' ἔπιον καὶ φάγον.

: XVIII :

To Cornelius, in iambics[28]

You say that the verses that I write for you aren't mine, Cornelius, and yet you call me "poet" all the same. Why, you would say that oxen are not by nature horned, but nonetheless, oxen, you'll say, are oxen. You happen to have said this because you do not yet   5
write in meter: the slow-footed ass likewise denies that deer are swift, and the hare likewise denies that the wolf is bold.

: XIX :

To the literati

You should leave the countryside in droves, all you servants of the Pierides: the entire chorus of the daughters of Helicon has come to the city. Anyone who inquires after its house and chambers should know that it inhabits the heart of Chalcondyles.[29]

: XX :

On the same person

O Demetrius, once upon a time Odysseus escaped the sweet melody of the Sirens, but he would not have escaped your verse. In fact just yesterday, when I craved something sweet to drink and eat, it was your song that I drank and ate not at all unwillingly.

: XXI :

Δίστιχον περὶ Παύλου καὶ Ξύστου ἀρχιερέων

Ἀρχιερεὺς ἀγαθὸς Παῦλος ποθ᾽ ἦ, ἀλλὰ κακός φώς·
Νῦν δ᾽ ἀγαθὸς Ξύστος φώς, κακὸς ἀρκιερεύς.

: XXII :

Εἰς Παῦλον τὸν ἀστρονόμον

Γῆν μὲν ποσσὶ περᾷ, νῷ δ᾽ οὐρανὸν ἀστερόεντα
Παῦλος καὶ θνητὸς ἐσθ᾽ ἅμα κἀθάνατος.
Ὦ θεοί, ὦ μοῖραι, μὴ κλέπτετε καὶ δότ᾽ ἐπαυρεῖν
Τοῦ μὲν ἐπιχθονίους, τοῦ δ᾽ ἅμ᾽ ἐπουρανίους.

: XXIII :

Ἐρωτικόν δωριστί

Διττὸς ἔρως ἀνιᾷ με· δυοῖν ὑποτάκομαι παίδοιν
Ἴσον τοι χαροποῖν, ἴσον ἐπαφροδίτοιν.
Δριμὺς ὁ μέν γ᾽ ἰταμός θ᾽, ὁ δὲ παρθένῳ ἴκελος ὄψιν·
Ἄμφω ἔρωτας ὁμῶς εἰσπνέετον μαλακώς.
5   Τῷδε κόμαι ἰοειδέες ἐκ καράνοιο τέτανται,
Τῷ δ᾽ ἑτέρῳ ξανθὰ σείεται ἁ πλοκαμίς.
Τὰ πλεῖστ᾽ οὐδὲν ὁμοίω, ἀμειλιχίην δέ θ᾽ ὁμοίω,
Νικᾷ δ᾽ οὔτ᾽ ἄλλος κάλλεϊ καὶ χάρισιν.
Ἄμφω δ᾽ οὐχ᾽ οἷον θ᾽ ὑποτλεῖν, Κύπρι· τὺ δ᾽ ἄρα σύμμοι
10   Βούλευσον ποτέραν ταῖνδε φέροιμμι φλόγα.

204

: XXI :

A couplet on Popes Paul and Sixtus[30]

Once there was Paul, who was a good pope, but a bad man; now there is Sixtus, who is a good man, but a bad pope.

: XXII :

On Paul the astronomer[31]

With his feet Paul treads the earth, with his mind the starry heaven: he is thus at once a mortal and an immortal. O gods, O fates, do not steal him away and grant that terrestrials may enjoy the one, celestials the other!

: XXIII :

An amatory epigram, in Doric

A double passion tortures me: I pine for two boys, both equally splendid, equally alluring. The one is fierce and reckless, the other has a face like a girl: they both inspire sweet loves in equal measure. One of them has dark hair cascading from his head, while a 5 blonde lock waves upon the other. In most respects they are not at all alike, though they are alike in cruelty, but neither beats out the other in beauty and charm. O Cypris,[32] it is not possible to endure them both; advise me, then, which one of these two flames I 10 should bear.

: XXIV :

Ὁμήρου ὑποκριτής

Ἄλλους μέν ῥα σοφούς τε λιγυφθόγγους τε ἀοιδούς,
Τοὺς δ' αὖ ῥητορικῆς ἐρατὸν λειμῶνα δρέποντας,
Τοὺς δ' ἄρ' ἅμ' εἰρήνην κουροτρόφον ἔπρεπ' ἀείδειν
Ἡσυχίην ἀγορήν τε· μόνον δέ με, Φοῖβος Ἀπόλλων,
5 Κηρύττειν πολεμόν τε κακὸν καὶ φύλοπιν αἰνήν.

: XXV :

1480. Ζαμπέτρῳ Ἀρριβαβένῳ, δωριστί

Χείλεα νηπιάχου βάψαι ποτὲ φαντὶ Πλάτωνος
Ξουθὰς Μοψοπίῳ πλησαμένας μέλιτι·
Στεσιχόρου δ' ἤεισεν ἐπὶ στομάτεσσιν ἀηδών·
Δείγματα μειλιχίης ἀμφοτέρου χάριτος.
5 Ἀλλὰ σοὶ οὔτινά γ' ὄρνιν ἐφιζᾶν οὔτι μελίσσας
Πείθομαι, ἀλλ' αὐτάς, Ζάμπετρε, Πιερίδας.
Ἧκ' ἂν δὴ λωτοῖο καὶ αὐτὸς γεύσατ' Ὀδυσσεὺς
Εἰ ὅ γε τοῖος ἔην οἶος ὁ σεῖο λόγος.

: XXIV :

An actor in the role of Homer

It was for other poets, wise and mellifluous, and for those who harvest the lovely field of rhetoric, to sing of the peace that nurtures children, the serenity of civic life; but it was for me alone, Phoebus Apollo, to be the herald of bitter warfare and the dreadful din of battle.   5

: XXV :

1480. To Giampietro Arrivabene,[33] in Doric

Once, they say, the humming bees bathed the lips of Plato when he was a little boy, filling them with honey from Mopsopia;[34] and a nightingale sang upon the mouth of Stesichorus:[35] proofs of the sweet charm of them both. But upon you, Giampietro, no bird has   5
settled, nor bees, I believe, but the very Pierides themselves. Even Odysseus himself would have tasted a little of the lotus, if it had resembled your speech.

: XXVI :

1481. Ἐρωτικὸν περὶ τοῦ Χρυσοκόμου

Βλέψον μ' οὐρανόθεν τὸν ἐμὸν παῖδ' ἀγκὰς ἔχοντα
Καὶ μή, Ζεῦ, φθονέει, κοὔ τιν' ἐγὼ φθονέω.
Στέρξον, Ζεῦ, στέρξον Γανυμήδεϊ, τὸν δ' ἄρα φαιδρὸν
Χρυσόκομόν μοι ἄφες τὸν μέλιτος γλυκίω.
5 Ὄλβιος ὦ τρὶς ἐγὼ καὶ τετράκις· ἦρ' ἐφίλασα
Ἦρ' ἔτι καὶ φιλέω σὸν στόμα, παῖ χαρίει.
Ὦ στόμα, ὦ κόμαι, ὦ μειδίαμα, ὦ φάος ὄσσοιν,
Ὦ θεοί, ἦρά σ' ἔχω, παῖ φίλε, ἦρά σ' ἔχω.
Ἦρά σ' ἔχω τὸν ἐμόν, τὸν ἐρωτίλον· ὄσσα μογήσας,
10 Ὄσσα παθὼν, ὄσσα δρῶν τοῦτο τό' παθλον ἔχω.
Θυμέ, τί νῦν θορυβεῖς ὡς καὶ τὸ πρίν; οὔτις ἔτ' ἔστι
Κίνδυνος, οὐκ ἔτι χρή σε, κραδίη, τρομέειν.
Καὶ γὰρ ὁ ἐκπέρσας ἡμᾶς πόκα καὶ πεφοβηκὼς
Ληφθεὶς ἀγκάλῃς ἠνίδ' ἐμαῖς δέδεται.
15 Τὰν δ' ἄρα τὰν φάσσαν λάβε δή, θεά, τῷ δ' ἐπὶ βωμῷ,
Καὶ τόδ' ἐμοὶ στάσιμον, Κύπρι, τὸ χάρμα δίδοι.
Τὺ δ' ἄγέ μοι μαλακῶς ὄσσον δύνῃ ἔμπνε' ἔρωτας,
Καὶ γλῶτταν γλῶττᾳ, παῖ, περίπλεκτον ἔχε.

: XXVI :

1481. A love poem about Goldenlocks[36]

Look at me from your perch in heaven as I hold my boy in my
arms, and do not envy me, Zeus, as I do not envy you. Content
yourself, Zeus, content yourself with Ganymede, and leave glistening Goldenlocks, who is sweeter than honey, to me. Oh, I am   5
three and four times blessed! I did indeed kiss you, and I kiss your
mouth still, you lovely boy! That mouth, that hair, that smile, the
light in those eyes! O gods, you're really mine, dear boy, you're really mine! You're truly my very own, my darling! After all I've   10
toiled, all I've suffered, all I've done, this is my reward. O spirit,
why are you troubled now as you were before? There is no more
risk, you have no need to tremble still, my heart. For the one who
once conquered me and put me to flight has been captured and,
look, he is bound in my arms! So take this dove then, O goddess,   15
upon this altar and grant me this joy, O Cypris, forever. And you,
my lad, inspire sweet loves in me as much as you can, and keep
your tongue intertwined with mine.

: XXVII :

1490. Latinum nescio cuius Romae adnectam,
quod nos rogatu Ciampolini
Graecum deinde fecimus

Eruta signorum vastis fragmenta ruinis
    Et quae virtutis sunt monumenta tuae,
Roma parens, ignosce brevi si condit hypaethro
    Haec domus et domino sic onerosa suo.
5 Cedere non facile est meritis et tanta videntes
    Haud cupere:[4] in magnis et voluisse sat est.

Graecum Angeli Politiani,
MXD, die XXVIII Iunii in domo Ciampolini insculptum

Εἰκόνας ἡμιτόμους ἅς καὶ γῆς χῶμα κέκευθε
    Μυρίον, ὦ Ῥώμη, λείψανα σῆς ἀρετῆς,
Εἰ μὲν ἐπὶ στεινῷ κρύπτει δόμος οὗτος ὑπαίθρῳ
    Κἂν βαρὺς ὧδε λίαν, ἴλαθι, μῆτερ ἐμή.
5 Εἴκειν δ' οὐ ῥᾴδιον καὶ μὴ ποθέειν τάδ' ὁρῶντας,
    Ἀρκεῖ δ' ἐν μεγάλοις καὶ τὸ θέλημα μόνον.

: XXVII :

1490. I shall attach an anonymous Latin epigram from Rome,
which I subsequently turned into Greek
at the request of Ciampolini[37]

These fragments of statues excavated from your vast ruins, which
are monuments to your virtue, mother Rome, forgive us if this
house stores them in a little courtyard and is thus a burden to its
owner. It is not easy to show proper deference to their merits and   5
those who view their magnitude did not wish it, but in great matters even goodwill suffices.

The Greek version by Angelo Poliziano,
carved on the 28th of June, 1490, at the house of Ciampolini

These broken statues that were hidden by a vast pile of earth, O
Rome, the remnants of your virtue, if this house now conceals
them in a narrow courtyard, and should thus be too burdened,
forgive us, my mother. It is not easy to draw back and not feel   5
longing upon seeing these things, but in great matters goodwill
suffices on its own.[38]

: XXVIII :

MVIID. Εἰς Ἀλεξάνδραν τὴν ποιήτριαν

Ἠλέκτρην ὑπέκριν' ὁπότ' ἄζυξ ἄζυγα κούρην
Κούρῃ Ἀλεξάνδρῃ τήν γε Σοφοκλείην,
Θαμβέομεν πάντες πῶς εὐαμαρὲς Ἀτθίδα γλῶτταν
Ἦπυεν ἀπταίστως, Αὐσονὶς οὖσα γένος,
5 Πῶς δέ γε μιμηλὴν προΐει καὶ ἐτήτυμον αὐδήν,
Τἀκριβὲς ἐντέχνου τήρεε πῶς θυμέλης,
Πῶς ἦθος δ' ἐφύλαττεν ἀκήρατον, ὄμματα γαίῃ
Πήξασ' οὐδ' ὁρμῆς ἤμβροτεν οὐ βάσεως·
Οὐδ' ἀσκημόνεεν φωνὴν βαρύδακρυν ἱεῖσα,
10 Βλέμματι μυδαλέῳ σὺν δ' ἔχεεν θεατάς.
Πάντες ἄρ' ἐξεπλάγημεν· ἐμὲ ζῆλος δ' ὑπένυξεν,
Ὡς τὸν ὅμαιμον ἑῆς εἶδον ἐν ἀγκαλίσιν.

: XXIX :

Εἰς τὸν παῖδα

Μή με πολυστροφάλιγξι κατάφλεγε νεύσεσι, κοῦρε,
Ἄχρι φίλης αἰεὶ πυρσοβολῶν κραδίης.
Σοῦ γὰρ Ἔρως γελάοντος ἐν ὄμμασι δᾷδας ἀνάπτει,
Ὢ ἐμὲ δοὺς ἐς ὅλας ζῶντ' ἔτι πυρκαιάς.

: XXVIII :

1493. On Alessandra, the poetess[39]

When Alessandra played the part of Sophocles' Electra,[40] an unwed maiden in the role of an unwed maiden, we were all amazed
at how easily she pronounced the Attic tongue without mistakes,
and she an Ausonian by race. How true to life and authentic the   5
voice she projected! How she observed the smallest detail of theat-
rical technique! How she maintained the purity of her character,
while fixing her eyes upon the ground and making no mistakes in
movement or in step! Nor did she cut a poor figure by letting
loose a lamentatious howl; rather, she overwhelmed the audience   10
with her teary gaze. And so we were all astonished; and I was
stung with jealousy when I saw her brother in her arms.

: XIX :

To his boyfriend

Don't set me on fire with your winks and nods, my boy, forever
shooting flames deep within my heart. For when you laugh, Love
lights torches in your eyes, you who cast me into great bonfires
while I am still alive.

: XXX :

MVIID. Εἰς Ἀλεξάνδραν τὴν ποιήτριαν

Εὕρηχ᾽ εὕρηχ᾽ ἥν θέλον, ἥν ἐξήτεον αἰεί,
῾Ην ἤτουν τὸν Ἔρωθ᾽, ἥν καὶ ὀνειροπόλουν·
Παρθενικήν ἧς κάλλος ἀκήρατον, ἧς ὅγε κόσμος
Οὐκ εἴη τέχνης, ἀλλ᾽ ἀφελοῦς φύσεως·
5 Παρθενικήν γλώττῃσιν ἐπ᾽ ἀμφοτέρῃσι κομῶσαν,
Ἔξοχον ἔν τε χοροῖς, ἔξοχον ἔν τε λύρῃ·
῾Ης πέρι Σωροσύνῃ τ᾽ εἴη Χαρίτεσσί θ᾽ ἄμιλλα,
Τῇ καὶ τῇ ταύτην ἀντιμεθελκομέναις.
Εὕρηκ᾽, οὐδ᾽ ὄφελος· καὶ γὰρ μόλις εἰς ἐνιαυτόν
10 Οἰστροῦντι φλογερῶς ἔστιν ἅπαξ ἰδέειν.

: XXXb :

Alexandrae Scalae responsum[5]

Οὐδὲν ἄρ᾽ ἦν αἴνοιο παρ᾽ ἔμφρονος ἀνδρὸς ἄμεινον,
Κἀκ σέθεν αἶνος ἔμοιγ᾽ οἷον ἄειρε κλέος.
Πολλοὶ θριοβόλοι, παῦροι δέ τε μάντιές εἰσιν.
Εὖρες ἄρ᾽; οὐχ εὗρες γ᾽ οὐδ᾽ ὄναρ ἠντίασας.
5 Φῇ γὰρ ὁ θεῖος ἀοιδός ᾽ἄγει θεός ὡς τὸν ὁμοῖον᾽·
Οὐδὲν Ἀλεξάνδρῃ σοῦ δ᾽ ἀνομοιότερον.
Ὡς σύ γ᾽ ὁποῖα Δανούβιος ἐκ ζόφου ἐς μέσον ἦμαρ
Καὖθις ἐπ᾽ ἀντολίην αἰπὰ ῥέεθρα χέεις.
Φωναῖς δ᾽ ἐν πλείσταις σόν τοι κλέος ἠέρ᾽ ἐλαστρεῖ,
10 Ἑλλάδι, Ῥωμαϊκῇ, Ἑβραϊκῇ, ἰδίῃ.[6]

214

⁚ XXX ⁚

1493. To Alessandra, the poetess

I have found her! I have found the one I wanted, the one I always
looked for, the one I sought from Love, the one I dreamed of too:
a maiden whose beauty is immaculate, whose ornament could not
be the product of art, but of simple nature, a maiden boasting of   5
skill in Greek and Latin, excelling in dance, excelling in the lyre.
Modesty and the Graces would compete over her, tugging at her
this way and that in turn. I have found her, but to no avail, since
scarcely once a year am I permitted to see her, madly though I   10
burn for her.

⁚ XXXb ⁚

Alessandra Scala's reply[41]

Nothing could be better than praise from a wise man, and what
glory your praise has brought me! "There are many fortune-tellers,
but few true seers."[42] So you found her? No, nor did you come
face to face with your dream. For as the divine bard said, "the god   5
brings like to like." And nothing is more unlike Alessandra than
you. Like the Danube, your deep currents flow from North[43] to
South, and then to the East. In many languages your fame rides
through the air, in Greek, in Latin, in Hebrew,[44] and in your own.   10

Ἄστρα, φύσις, ἀριθμοί, ποιήματα, κύρβις, ἰατροὶ
Ἡρακλῆν καλέουσ'[7] ἀντιμεθελκόμενα.
    Τἀμὰ δὲ παρθενικῆς σπουδάσματα παίγνιά τ' αἰνῶς,
Βόκχορις εἰ κρίναις,[8] ἄνθεα καὶ δρόσος ὥς.
15 Τοιγὰρ μήτ' ἐλέφαντος ἐναντία βόμβον ἀείρω
Αἴλουρον Παλλὰς καὶ σύ γ' ὑπερφρονέεις.

: XXXI :

Εἰς Ἀλεξάνδραν τὴν ποιήτριαν

Τίπτε μοι ὠχρὸν ἴον πέμπεις; ἦ οὐχ ἅλις ὠχρός,
Ξάνρα, τοῦ καὶ ἅπαν αἷμα πέπωκεν Ἔρος;

: XXXII :

Εἰς τὴν αὐτην

Καρπὸν ἐμοὶ ποθέοντι σὺ δ' ἄνθεα φῦλλά τε μοῦνον
Δωρῇ, σημαίνουσ' ὅττι μάτην πονέω.

: XXXIII :

Εἰς τὴν αὐτην

Φύλλα διδοῦσ' ἐράοντι καὶ ἄνθεα, ἦρος ἀπαρχάς,
Αὐτὸ ἐπαγγέλλῃ σῆς ἔαρ ἡλικίης.

Astronomy, natural philosophy, mathematics, poetry, law, medicine, they all call you Heracles, tugging you this way and that.[45] But my interests are those of a girl and terribly childish, like flowers and dew, as Bocchoris would say.[46] No, I'll not make a buzzing 15 sound opposite an elephant, and you, and Athena, will look down your nose at a cat.[47]

: XXXI :

To Alessandra, the poetess

Why do you send me a pale violet? Sandra, is the man whose blood Love has completely drained not pale enough for you?

: XXXII :

To the same woman

Though I long for the fruit, you give me only the flowers and leaves, signaling that I toil in vain.

: XXXIII :

To the same woman

When you give your lover leaves and flowers, the first fruits of spring, you are actually promising the very spring of your womanhood.

: XXXIV :

Aedem Reparatae inambulans amicis stipatus haec composui extempore

Ἔσχε Σιμωνίδεω οἶκος δύο λάρνακας ἔνδον·
Τὴν μέν τοι μισθοῦ, τὴν δ' ἑτέραν χαρίτων.
Ἦν δ' ἡ μὲν χαρίτων κενεή, πλέα δ' ἥ γ' ἐπίμισθος·
Σὺ γοῦν δὴ πάντων, ξεῖνε, λάβῃς ἔρανον.

: XXXV :

Αὐτοσχέδιον καὶ τοῦτο

Ἦν ποτέ τις πολίτης ἀγαθὸς καλαῖς ἐν Ἀθήναις,
Ὃν σὺ Κόθορνον ἔφης, Ἀττικὲ Ξεινοφόων.
Οὗτος ἀριστήεσσι καὶ αὐτῷ ἐφήρμοσε δήμῳ·
Τοὔνεκα κεἰς θάνατον προὔδοθ' ὑπὸ Κριτίου.

: XXXVI :

1493. Αὐτοσχέδια ἐν τῷ περιπατεῖν

Μὴ κύε μ', οὐροπότα· τὰ γὰρ εὔοδμα χείλεα κούρων
Εἰωθὼς φιλέειν τὰ σά γ' ἀποστρέφομαι.

: XXXIV :

While walking into Santa Reparata[48] in the company of friends, I composed these verses extemporaneously

The house of Simonides[49] contained within it two chests, the one for payments, the other for thanks. The one for thanks was empty, but the one for payments was full. Well then, stranger, you should accept everyone's contributions.

: XXXV :

Another improvisation

Once upon a time in the beautiful city of Athens there was a good citizen whom you called "Cothurnus," O Xenophon of Attica.[50] This man accommodated both the aristocrats and the common people: for that reason he was put to death by Critias.

: XXXVI :

1493. Improvisations[51] while taking a walk

Don't kiss me, you piss-tippler: for since I have become accustomed to kissing the perfumed lips of boys, I say no to yours.

: XXXVII :

Ἐις ὄργανα

Οὐκ ἀΐεις δονάκων μέλος ἄσπετον; ἦρα γε τήναις
Τὰν ὄπα τὶς κύκνων μυριὰς ἐνσταλάει.

: XXXVIII :

a) Προτρεπτικόν

Ὀθνείην διάλεκτον ἀεὶ φυγέειν δοκέουσαν
Εἰ δράξαι σπεύδεις, Ἄγγελε, τεῖνε δρόμον.

b) Ἀπόκρισις

Τείνω κοὐ δράττω· τότε γὰρ καὶ μᾶλλον ὀλισθεῖ,
Ὁππόθ᾽ ἑλεῖν δοκέω, ἴκελος ἐγχέλυϊ.

c) Προτρεπτικόν

Οὕτως ὀτρύνωμεν ἀμοιβαδίς, ὅττι μαχαίρας,
Φῆ λόγος ἀρχαίων, ἔστι μάχαιρ᾽ ἀκόνη.

∶ XXXVII ∶

On pipe organs

Do you not hear the endless music of the pipes? Surely a myriad of swans instills in them their voice.

∶ XXXVIII ∶

a) *Exhortation*

A foreign language always seems to flee: if you want to grasp it, Angelo,[52] pick up your pace.

b) *Response*

I am speeding up, but I'm not grasping it: in fact, it slips further away whenever I think I've got it, just like an eel.

c) *Exhortation*

Let's urge ourselves on by turns, because, as a saying of the ancients goes, one knife acts as another's whetstone.[53]

: XXXIX :

Εἰς Ἄγγελον τὸν πρεσβύτερον

Ὅσσον ἐμοὶ φίλος ἐστὶν ὁ Ἄγγελος, ἠνὶ τὸ δεῖγμα·
Καὶ πηλὸν πατέειν εἵνεκ' ἐμοῖο θέλει.

: XL :

Allusio ad antiquum Graecum epigramma

Ἐκπροφυγόντα μάχας τὸν ἑὸν παῖδ' ὡς ἐνόησεν
Σπαρτιάτις μάτηρ φασγάνῳ ἀντίασεν,
Καὶ κτάνε τὸν δύστανον, ὃν ἔτρεφεν, ὃν τέκεν αὐτά·
Ταῦτα δ' ἐκερτόμεεν λόξ' ἐπιδερκομένα·
5 Εἰ τοῖον σ' ἐδόκουν, οὐκ ἂν τέκον· ἔρρε Λακαίνας
Ὡς πάϊς, οὐκ ἐθέλων ὡς Λακεδαιμόνιος.'

: XLI :

Alludit ad Graecum epigramma

Τυφλὸς ἄπους τ' ἤτην ἀλλήλοιϊν θεράποντες·
Τυφλὸς ὁδηγεῖτο, νωτοφορεῖτο δ' ἄπους.

ː XXXIX ː

On Angelo the priest

Here is the proof of what a great friend Angelo is to me: he is even willing to tramp through mud for my sake.

ː XL ː

A play upon an ancient Greek epigram[54]

When a Spartan mother saw her son running away from the battle, she confronted him with a dagger, and killed the poor fellow, whom she had borne and raised herself. Looking at him askance, she sneered, "Had I thought that you'd turn out so, I would never have given birth to you. Die then, like the son of a Spartan 5 woman, since you would not die like a Spartan man."

ː XLI ː

A play upon a Greek epigram[55]

A blind man and an amputee were helping each other: the blind man was given directions, the amputee rode on his back.

: XLII :

Εἰς τοὺς τέσσαρας ἀγῶνας

Ζηνὸς Ὀλύμπια νικῶντες φέρον ἀγριέλαιον,
  Μῆλα δ' Ἀπόλλωνος Πυθικὸς ἦρεν ἀγών,
Ἰσθμιακὴν δὲ πίτυν πόρεν Ἰνῷος Μελικέρτας,
  Σὺ δὲ σέλιν' ἐτίθεις, Ἀρχέμορ', ἐν Νεμέᾳ.

: XLIII :

Germanici epigramma

Thrax puer astricto glacie dum ludit in Hebro
  Frigore concretas pondere rupit aquas.
Dumque imae partes rapido traherentur ab amne
  Abscidit tenerum lubrica testa caput.
5 Orba quod inventum mater dum conderet urna:
  'Hoc peperi flammis, cetera,' dixit, 'aquis.'

Politiani epigramma

Παῖς Ἕβρῳ ἐπέθρωσκε πεπηγότι τυτθὸς ἀθύρων·
  Κρυστάλλου δ' ἐάγη μαρμαρόεν δάπεδον,
Χ' ᾧ μὲν ὀλισθαίνων πέσεν εἰς βυθόν, ἀλλ' ἀδιάντου
  Κρατὸς ἔκερσε δέρην ὀστρακόεις παγετός·

224

∶ XLII ∶

On the four Games[56]

Victors in Zeus' Olympic Games wore the wild olive; Apollo's
Pythian Games offered apples to the winners; Melicertes, son of
Ino,[57] supplied pine from the Isthmus; and you, Archemorus,[58]
established celery as the prize at Nemea.

∶ XLIII ∶

An epigram by Germanicus[59]

While a Thracian lad was playing on the Ebro's frozen ice, his
weight caused the frozen waters to break. And as his lower limbs
were pulled by the swift current, the smooth sheet of ice sliced off
his tender head. When his bereaved mother found it, she placed it   5
in an urn and said, "I gave birth to this for the flames, the rest for
the waters."

Poliziano's epigram

A little boy leaped about playfully upon the frozen Ebro, but the
sparkling surface of ice broke. He slipped and fell into the depths,
but the ice, hard as a potsherd, sliced his head from his neck

5 Σκῆνος ἄρ᾽ ἐνδόμυχον ῥοθίου ταχὺς ἔσπασεν ὁλκός,
   Τῷ πυρὶ δ᾽ ἡ μήτηρ μοῦνον ἔδωκε κάρη.
   Εἶπε δ᾽ ἐπιστενάχουσα· ᾽τί δύσμορος υἱὸν ἔτεξα;
   ᾽Αρ᾽ ὡς στοιχείοιν βρῶμα γένοιτο δυοῖν;᾽

: XLIV :

Antiquum contra illud Graecum

Ἀμφοτέρους ἀδικεῖς, καὶ Πλουτέα καὶ Φαέθοντα,
Τὸν μὲν ἔτ᾽ εἰσορόων, τοῦ δ᾽ ἀπολειπόμενος.

Politiani Graecum epigramma

Οὐδετέρους ἀδικῶ· τὸ γὰρ ἄπνοον οὐκ ἔτι λεύσσει
῞Ηλιον, ἔμπνου γ᾽ αὖ Πλουτέϊ κοὐδὲ μέλει.

: XLV :

1493. Allusio ad Graecum epigramma

Παιδὶ Λάκαινα σάκος πολεμησείοντι διδοῦσα·
῾Παῖ,᾽ ἔφη, ᾽ἢ σὺν τῷδ᾽ ἢ ἐπὶ τῷδε νέου.᾽

without wetting it. The swift current of the waves then swept his 5
body off into the depths, so his mother could give only his head to
the pyre. As she lamented, she said, "Why in my misfortune did I
give birth to a son? So that he might end up as fodder for two of
the elements?"

: XLIV :

An ancient epigram responding to that Greek one[60]

You wrong both Pluto and Phaethon,[61] the latter by still looking
upon him, the former by failing to go to him.

Poliziano's Greek epigram

I wrong neither of them: my lifeless half no longer looks upon the
sun, and Pluto has no business with the living half.

: XLV :

1493. A play upon a Greek epigram[62]

Said the Spartan woman as she gave a shield to her warlike son,
"Son, either come back with this, or upon it."

: XLVI :

Πατρόκλου ὑποκριτής

Μὴ μέμφοισθ' ἐπὶ δουρί· τὸ γάρ τοι κού σθένεν Ἕκτωρ
Ἀντία οὐδ' ἐσιδεῖν, μὴ ὅτι καὶ φορέειν.

: XLVII :

Εἰς Βαρῖνον τὸν Καμηρτέα γραμματικόν

Ἑλλάδι τοῖς ἰδίοις πεπλανημένῃ ἐν λαβυρίνθοις
Οὐ μίτον ἀλλὰ βίβλον προὔθετο δαιδάλεον
Οὐχ Ἕλλην, Ἰταλὸς δὲ Βαρῖνος· κούτι γε θαῦμα
Εἴ γε νέοι τὴν γραῦν ἀντιπελαργέομεν.

: XLVIII :

Εἰς Ἀλεξάνδραν τὴν ποιήτριαν

Ἂν μηδ' εἰσαθρεῖν, ἂν μηδ' ἔξεστιν ἀκούειν,
Ἆρ' οὐδὲ γραπτῆς τεύξομ' ἀποκρίσεως;

228

: XLVI :

An actor in the role of Patroclus

Do not criticize me because of the spear, for Hector could not even bear to look at it, let alone carry it.[63]

: XLVII :

On Guarino Camerte, the grammarian[64]

Greece, wandering aimlessly in her own labyrinths, was not offered a thread, but an ingenious book, and not by a Greek, but by the Italian Guarino. There's no reason to be surprised if we young men return a favor to our aged mother.[65]

: XLVIII :

To Alessandra, the poetess

If I am not allowed to see you, nor even to hear your voice, shall I not at least have from you a written reply?

: XLIX :

Εἰς τὸν Πῖκον Μιρανδουλέα

Καὶ τοῦτ᾽ ἀστρολόγοις ἐπιμέμφομαι ἠερολέσχαις,
Ὅττι σοφοὺς Πίκου μοι φθονέουσ᾽ ὀάρους.
Καὶ γὰρ ὁ ἐνδυκέως τούτων τὸν λῆρον ἐλέγχων
Μουνάζει ἐν ἀγρῷ δηρὸν ἑκὰς πόλεως.
5 Πῖκε, τί σοὶ καὶ τούτοις; οὔ σ᾽ ἐπέοικεν ἀγύρταις
Ἀντᾶραι τὴν σὴν εὐτυχέα γραφίδα.

: L :

Εἰς Ἀλεξάνδραν τὴν ποιήτριαν

Δέξο τὸν ἐξ ὀστοῦ, δάμαλι, κτένα, τὸν τριχοτάκτην,
Δὸς δὲ τὸν ἐκ σαρκός, τόν γε τριχωτὸν ἐμοί.

: LI :

Εἰς τὸ ὄργανον

Χάλκειον δονάκων ὁρόω στίχον· ἀλλὰ τίς αὐτῷ
Τεχνᾶται κρύβδην τὸν πολύθρουν κέλαδον;'
Οὗτος ὁ τοῖς πλαγκτῆρσιν εὔτροχα[9] δάκτυλα παλμοῖς
Δινεύων, τρομεράς τ᾽ ἀμφισοβῶν σελίδας.'
5 Ἀλλὰ πολυσπερέων πόθεν οἱ τόσος ἑσμὸς ἀητῶν;'
Οὐκ ἀθρεῖς ἀσκοὺς διχθαδίους ὄπιθεν;'

: XLIX :

To Pico della Mirandola[66]

I hold this, too, against those bloviating astronomers, that they
keep me from scholarly conversations with Pico. And in fact, while
steadfastly refuting their drivel, he is off by himself in the country
for a long time, far from the city. Pico, why do you bother with 5
them? It is unbecoming for you to raise your otherwise felicitous
pen against charlatans.

: L :

To Alessandra, the poetess

Accept this comb, my little filly, made of bone to tidy your hair;
and give me yours, which is made of flesh and hairy.[67]

: LI :

On a pipe organ[68]

"I see a row of bronze pipes, but who is it that secretly draws from
it this complex sound?" "It is this man, the one whirling his fingers
easily in wandering pulses and flipping about the trembling pages."
"But what's the source of this great swarm of wide-ranging winds?" 5
"Do you not see the double bellows in back?"

: LII :

Versus hos pone scripsi
in libro ducis Urbinatis
cum mihi commodatum remitterem

῍Ηδε βίβλος τίνος ἐστί; ῾Νέου τινός, ὃς καλὸς ὄψιν,
Σῶμα δὲ ῥωμαλέος· καὶ γὰρ τέχνῃ τε βίῃ τε
Ἀθλεύων πάντεσσι μεταπρέπει ἠϊθέοισιν·
Ἱπποσύνῃ καὶ ὅπλοισι μέγ' ἔξοχος, οὐκ ἀμελῶν δὲ
5   Οὐδὲ βίβλων, σοφίην ἀσκῶν διδυμάονι γλώττῃ.
Πρᾶος, ἐλευθέριος, γλυκύς, οὐκ ἀπροσήγορος, εὔφρων.'
Εἰπὲ τύχην.'Βασιλεύς.'Ἀρκεῖ τάδε· τὸν Γοΐδωνα
Εἶπας, ἀνικήτοιο πατρὸς γόνον, ἡγεμονῆα
Οὐρβίνου μεγάλοιο, θεοῖς ἐναλίγκιον ἄνδρα.'

: LIII :

Εἰς τὸν Πῖκον

Πολλάκι τοξευθεὶς φλεχθείς θ' ὑπὸ Πῖκος Ἐρώτων
Οὐκ ἔτλη προτέρω, πάντα δ' ἀφείλεθ' ὅπλα,
Τόξα, βέλη, φαρέτρας, καὶ νηήσας τάδε πάντα
῟Ηψεν ὁμοῦ σωρὸν λαμπάσι ληϊδίοις.
5   Σὺν δ' αὐτοὺς μάρψας, ἀμενηνὰ χερύδρια δῆσεν
Ταῖς νευραῖς, μέσσῃ δ' ἔμβαλε πυρκαϊᾷ·
Καὶ πυρὶ φλέξε τὸ πῦρ. τί δ' ὦ ἄφρονες αὐτόν, Ἔρωτες,
Τὸν Πῖκον Μουσῶν εἰσεποτᾶσθε πρόμον;

232

: LII :

I wrote these verses in the back of a book belonging to the
Duke of Urbino[69] *when I sent it back to him*
after he had loaned it to me

"Whose book is this?" "Some young man's, with a nice face and a
solid build; indeed, he distinguishes himself in skill and strength
when he competes with all the young lads. He excels in horseman-
ship and swordplay, but he does not neglect his books, perfecting   5
his knowledge in both languages. He is gentle, open, sweet-
tempered, not unapproachable, and kind." "Tell me his rank." "A
king." "That's all I need: you are speaking of Guido, son of an in-
vincible father, lord of great Urbino, a man most like the gods."

: LIII :

On Pico[70]

After being shot many times and set aflame by Loves, Pico bore it
no longer, and took away all their weapons — bows, arrows, quiv-
ers. And after he had piled all that up, he set fire to the heap with
the torches he had also stolen. Then he rounded them all up, tied   5
their feeble little hands with strings, and tossed them into the
midst of the pyre. In so doing, he burned fire with fire. You crazy
Loves, why did you make an aerial assault on Pico, Prince of the
Muses?

: LIV :

Κύπρις ἀναδυομένη

Κύπριν Ἀπελλείας ἔργον χερός, ὡς ἴδον, ἔσταν
Δαρὸν θαμβαλέος, τὰν ἀναδυομέναν.
Τᾶς ἄτε παρθενικᾶς, ἄτε καὶ φιλοπαίγμονος αἰδὼς
Τὰν ὄψιν μίγδαν ἔλλαχεν ἠδὲ γέλως.
5 Καὶ τᾷ μὲν ῥαθάμιγγας ἁλιβρέκτοιο καράνου
Δεξιτερᾷ θλίβεν καὶ κελάρυζεν ἀφρός·
Ἦν δ' ἄρα τᾶς νοτίδος τὶς ἐμοὶ φόβος, ἁ δέ γε λαιὰ
Ἔσκεπε τὰν ἄβαν τὰν ἔθ' ὑποβρύχιον
(Καὶ γὰρ ἕως λαγόνων ὕψαλος πέλε), καί τις ἔτι φρὶξ
10 Ματρὸς ἀπ' ὠδίνων ὄμφακα μαστὸν ἕλεν.
Εἰ τοίαν πόκ' Ἄρης ἔχε δέσμιος, οὐκ ἀποδῦναι
Οὐδ' Ἀφαιστείας ἤθελ' ἀλυκτοπέδας.

: LV :

Εἰς Ἀφροδίτην ὡπλισμένην

Ἐς τί σάκος κρατέεις, Παφία, λόγχαν τε τινάσσεις
Καὶ θώρακ' ἐνέδυς καὶ κόρυν ἀμφίφαλον;
Μέμνασ' ὄττ' οὐ σοὶ δέδοται πολεμήϊα ἔργα
Τᾷ τρυφερᾷ, διέπεις δ' ἱμερόεντα γάμον.'
5 Ἀλλ' οὐκ ἐς δᾶριν θωρήσσομαι, ὅπλα δ' Ἄρηος
Ἐνδύομ' ὡς κ' Ἄρης ἐκλελάσθοιτο μάχας.
Ἐν γὰρ ἐμοὶ μῶνᾳ καὶ τεύχεα καὶ Κύπριν εὑρών,
Οὔποκ' ἐμῶν θαλάμων ἔσσετ' ἀπαυλόσυνος.'

: LIV :

Venus Anadyomene[71]

When I laid eyes upon the Venus Anadyomene, Apelles' handi-
work, I stood in amazement for a long time. Her face was all
modesty and smiles, like that of a maiden and one who delights in
play. With her right hand she wiped away the drops of water from 5
her sea-drenched head, and the foam was splashing about her —
indeed I was almost afraid of the spray. Her left hand covered her
maidenhead which was still below the waves, since she was under
water up to her hips, and her unripe breasts still trembled from 10
the birth pangs of her mother. If she had looked like this once
when Ares was chained and held her in his arms, he would not
have wanted to slip free of Hephaestus' bonds.

: LV :

On Aphrodite in armor[72]

"Why are you wielding a shield, O goddess of Paphos, and shaking a spear? Why are you wearing a coat of mail and a double-
crested helmet? Bear in mind that the works of war are not your
concern, delicate lady; you administer the charms of matrimony."
"But I am not arming for combat; rather, I don the arms of Ares 5
so that Ares himself may forget about battle. For when he finds
both his arms and Cypris in me alone, he will never slip away from
my bed."

: LVI :

Latinum epigramma Pulicis antiqui poetae Graecum feci.
Id tale est:

Cum mea me genetrix gravida gestaret in alvo,
    Quid pareret fertur consuluisse deos.
'Mas est' Phoebus ait, Mars 'femina' Iunoque 'neutrum';
    Cumque forem natus, hermaphroditus eram.
5 Quaerenti letum, dea sic ait: 'Occidet armis,'
    Mars 'cruce,' Phoebus, 'aquis'; sors rata quaeque fuit.
Arbor obumbrat aquas; ascendo, decidit ensis
    Quem tuleram, casu labor et ipse super.
Pes haesit ramis, caput incidit amne, tulique
10   Femina vir neutrum, flumina tela cruces.

Graecum Politiani, in quo ut de tertia persona
de Hermaphrodito narratur. 1494

Ἔγκυος οὖσα γυνὴ τέκεος πέρι Φοῖβον, Ἄρηα,
    Ἥρην, τοὺς ἅμα τρεῖς ἐξερέεινε θεούς.
Ἄρσενα Φοῖβος, Ἄρης θῆλυν φάτο, κοὐδέτερον δὲ
    Ἥρη, πάνθ᾽ ὑγιῶς· ἀνδρόγυνος γὰρ ἔφυ.
5 Εἰρομένῃ δὲ μόρον ᾽μόρος οἱ ξίφος᾽ ἔχραεν Ἥρη.
    ᾽Σταυρός᾽ Ἄρης, Φοῖβος ᾽κύματα᾽· πάντ᾽ ἀπέβη.
Δένδρῳ ἐφειστήκει, πέσε δ᾽ οἱ ξίφος, αὐτὸς ἐπ᾽ αὐτῷ
    Ἥριπεν εἰς ποταμὸν κύμβαχος, ἐκ δὲ ποδοῖν
Ἥρθη ἀπ᾽ ἀκρεμόνων. θάνε γοῦν θῆλυς τὲ καὶ ἄρρην
10   Κοὐδέτερον, σταυρῷ, κύμασι καὶ ξίφεϊ.

: LVI :

I have turned into Greek a Latin epigram by the ancient poet
Pulex.[73] *It goes like this:*

When my mother was carrying me in her pregnant womb, it is
said that she asked the gods what she would give birth to. "It's a
male," said Phoebus; "a female," said Mars; and "neither," said Juno.
And when I was born, I was a hermaphrodite. To her inquiry   5
about the manner of my death, the goddess said "he'll die in
arms;" "on the cross," said Mars; "by water," said Phoebus, and
each prediction was true. There was a tree shading the waters: I
climbed it, the sword that I carried fell, and I accidentally slipped
on top of it. My foot got caught in the branches, my head fell into
the river, and I — female, male, and neither — endured water, arms,   10
and cross.

Poliziano's Greek epigram, in which the story of the
Hermaphrodite is told in the third person. 1494

A pregnant woman made inquiries about her offspring to Phoebus, Ares, Hera, all three gods at once. Phoebus said that it would
be male, Ares female, and Hera neither, all of them correctly, for
he was born androgyne. To her inquiry about the manner of his   5
death, Hera prophesied, "the sword"; "the cross," said Ares; "water,"
said Phoebus: and all came to pass. When he had climbed into a
tree, his sword dropped from him and he fell upon it, tumbling
into a river headfirst, while he hung from the branches by his feet.
And so indeed he died — female and male and neither — by the   10
cross, the water, and the sword.

: LVII :

1493. Εἰς τοὺς κώνωπας

Τοὺς κώνωπας ἐρᾶν μᾶλλον πρέπει ἤέπερ ἄνδρας,
Φύντας τῶν γονίμων ὡς Κύπρις ἐξ ὑδάτων,
Καὶ μιμησαμένους ἀερσιπότητον Ἔρωτα
Εἰρεσίῃ¹⁰ πτερύγων τῷ τ᾽ ἔμεν᾽ αἱμοπότας,
5 Τὸν κῶμον τ᾽ ᾄδοντας ἐγερσιγύναικα πλανήτην,
Αἰνῶς ὑπναπατῶν ἱεμένους ὀάρων,
Ἐς λέχος ἐμπταίοντας, ἐπ᾽ αὐτοὺς πολλάκι μαστούς,
Κἀμφαφόωντας ὅλης ἄψεα θηλυτέρης,
Ψαύοντας χειλῶν τε καὶ ἐκμυζῶντας ὀπωπῆς
10 Μαρμαρυγάς, γλώσσης τ᾽ ἠρέμα γευομένους,¹¹
Ἀγρύπνους, ἰταμούς, σκοτοδερκέας· ἆρά τις ἀνδρῶν
Ὅσσα γε κώνωπες δείγματ᾽ ἔρωτος ἔχει;

: LVII :

1493. On mosquitoes[74]

Mosquitoes ought to experience love more than men, since, like Cypris, they are born from the fertile waves and they imitate Eros who flies upon the airs by rowing their wings and drinking blood, singing their wandering revel to wake the ladies, longing desper-   5 ately for close encounters that cheat sleep, descending upon their beds, often upon their very breasts, and feeling all around all the woman's limbs, touching her lips and sucking out the beauty of her face, and softly tasting her tongue—sleepless, vigorous,   10 equipped with night vision. Can there be any man who exhibits as many signs of love as mosquitoes?

AD BARTHOLOMAEUM FONTIUM

Clara licet summo Federicum gloria caelo
　　Et nitidis certet tollere sideribus,
Vel quia munitam castris inducere fossam
　　Obstrusumque hosti claudere novit iter,
5　Novit et armigeras dictis incendere turmas
　　Et fera magnanimos vertere in arma duces,
Deicit et celsas ignitis molibus urbes,
　　Occultas aperit militibusque vias;
Vel quod, equum fusis impellere doctus habenis,
10　　Qua ruit hostili sanguine tingit humum,
Quantus Bistonio Gradivus in axe coruscat,
　　Cum rapit ardentes in fera bella Getas;
Vel magis argutos placida quod fronte poetas
　　Allicit effusis undique muneribus,
15　Laurigerasque petit posita modo cuspide nymphas,
　　Implicat et ternis bracchia nexa choris;
Et licet Eridanum, Phaethontis flebile bustum,
　　Qui regit et Mutinae tecta superba premit,
Aut rex Oebalii qui temperat ora Galaesi
20　　Teque, olim Musis incluta Parthenope,
Materiam sacris valeant praebere poetis,
　　Sive illi pacem, proelia sive gerant,
Quid tamen externo iuvat indulgere labori,
　　Quid iuvat externos concinuisse duces?
25　Non libet admoto[1] fauces perfundere vino,
　　Cum propior valeat tollere lympha sitim.[2]
Nonne magis referam Petrum patriaeque parentem
　　Cosmum, non Medicae pignora bina domus?
Temperet ut cives tanta Laurentius arte,
30　　Stelligeros quanta Iuppiter ipse polos?

TO BARTOLOMEO FONZIO[1]

Even though brilliant glory vies to raise Federico[2] to the summit of
heaven and the glittering stars, whether because he knows how to
surround his camp with a fortified ditch and bar his enemy's access by making it impassable, and he knows how to fire up his   5
armed troops with his words and direct his brave captains against
the enemy's weapons, and he takes down lofty citadels with fiery
engines, and opens secret paths for his soldiers;[3] or because, with
his skill in giving his horse the reins to charge, he stains the   10
ground with enemy blood wherever he rushes, as resplendent as
Gradivus in his Bistonian chariot, when he sweeps the raging Getae into savage wars;[4] or rather because he attracts tuneful poets
with his benevolent brow, lavishing gifts upon them from every
direction, and no sooner has he laid aside his spear than he seeks   15
out the laureate nymphs, and wraps them in his arms, entwined in
dances three at once;[5] and even though the one who rules by the
river Po, Phaethon's sad resting place, and keeps the proud houses
of Modena in check,[6] or the king who governs the shores of the
Oebalian river Galaesus, as well as you, Parthenope, once famed   20
for its Muses,[7] even though all these could offer subject matter for
sacred poets, whether it be peace or war that they wage, what use
is it in any case to devote oneself to foreign ventures, what use is it
to sing of foreign lords? There's no pleasure in drenching one's gul- 25
let with imported wine, when the local water can quench your
thirst. Shall I not rather tell of Piero and the Father of his Country, Cosimo, the two pillars of the House of Medici? Of how Lorenzo guides the citizenry with as much skill as Jupiter himself   30

241

Ut tumidum conata iugo subducere collum
    Protendit victas iam Volaterra manus?
Ut modo Palladiae Pisis cedetis Athenae
    Otiaque antiquae dulcia Parthenopes?
35 Nonne magis referam ludicrae munera pugnae,
    Verinus quamvis dixerit illa meus?
Paene puer iuvenes valido Laurentius ictu
    Deiecit forti conspiciendus equo;
Paene puer terrae galeas devolvit inanes,
40   Stravit cornipedes, arma virosque simul:
Has ego non humili complectar carmine laudes,
    Virtutis referens munera prima suae.
Paene puer fudit patris Laurentius hostes,
    Compulit et proprios deseruisse lares.
45 Armatos cives armis circumdatus ipse
    Duxit, et infidas expulit urbe manus.
Territus effugit patriis Detisalvus ab oris,
    Nunc terit in longa tempora pauperie.
Haec mea Musa canet, nostro haec sunt ore canenda,
50   Et meus hoc tantum pulvere sudet equus.
His mihi descriptis, libeat quoque forsan ad illos
    Flectere converso protinus axe rotas.
Ante pharetratos cecinit Landinus amores,
    Ante celebrata est carmine Xandra suo;
55 At postquam Medicas illam transmisit in aedes
    Et Petro meritum praestitit officium,
Lectitat hunc sacris Ferraria culta poetis
    Miraturque animae iam monumenta suae.
Sic ubi iam Medicae solvisti debita genti,
60   Carliadem vexas nunc, Ugoline, tuam:
Carliadem, qua non Latio praestantius ullum,
    Quod videam, nostro tempore surgit opus.

steers the starry heavens? Of how, after she arrogantly attempted
to withdraw her neck from the yoke, Volterra now extends her
hands in defeat? Of how Pallas Athena's city of Athens shall soon
give way to Pisa, as shall the sweet pursuits of ancient Parthenope?[8] Shall I not rather relate the public games of mock combat,   35
even though my friend Verinus has told of them? While practically a boy, Lorenzo, a vision to behold on his bold steed, dis-
lodged the other youths with a powerful blow; while practically a
boy, he sent empty helmets rolling on the ground, laid low horses,   40
men, and arms at once:[9] it is these praises that I shall encompass
in verse not humble, as I recount the first fruits of his virtue.
While practically a boy, Lorenzo routed the enemies of his father,
and compelled them to abandon their own homes. Himself sur-   45
rounded by arms, he led the citizens in arms and drove the bands
of traitors from the city. Dietisalvi fled in terror from his native
lands, and now spends his life in tedious poverty.[10] This my Muse
shall sing, this is the song that must come from my mouth, and   50
only in this arena shall my steed toil. When I have told of all this,
perhaps it might be pleasing, too, to turn my chariot and steer
straightaway toward those others.

Landino first sang of the loves sent him from Cupid's quiver;
Sandra was first celebrated in his poetry; but afterward he trans-   55
ferred her to the House of Medici and offered Piero his well-
deserved allegiance, and Ferrara, a city cultivated by sacred poets,
reads him avidly and now marvels at the monuments of his soul.[11]
So too, now that you have paid your debts to the Medici family,
Ugolino, you hammer away at your *Carlias*, the *Carlias*, than which   60
no more splendid work, so far as I can see, arises in Latium in our

Ipse Cleonaeum liber contunde leonem
 Alcidaeque gravi subice colla polo;
65 Ipse et Erythaeos iam nunc molire iuvencos
 Pacatumque nemus, o Erymanthe, tuum;
Ipse refer praeversa levis vestigia cervae,
 Thermodontiacas ipse referque manus:
Me iuvat in Medicam versus connectere gentem,
70 O animae, Fonti, portio magna meae!
Et tibi, Laurenti, noster praeludat Homerus,
 Molimur forti dum tua gesta pede.
Hactenus haec. Sed iam tacito tibi pectore, Fonti,
 Saevus Amor rapidas ventilat usque faces.
75 Ast ego mirabar: 'Graciles quid protinus artus
 Vexat? Cur tenero pallor in ore sedet?'
Permessi quoties laticem, cum decolor esses,
 Culpavi et Phoebi Pieridumque choros!
At quondam nostros, demens, lusisse furores
80 Te memini et vario corripuisse ioco.
Ridebas gelidae tolerantem frigora noctis,
 Cum tegeret madidas cana pruina comas;
Ridebas, Fonti, dominae fastidia nostrae,
 Esset cum misero ianua clausa mihi;
85 Ridebas, scopulo cum surdior illa Sicano
 Temneret in duro limine pervigilem;
Nec te paenituit lacrimas ridere cadentes
 Turgidulasque novo semper ab imbre genas.
I nunc, sacrorum, Fonti, derisor amantum,
90 I, temne aligeri iura superba dei!
Quam magis optares Ephyraei dura tyranni
 Supplicia, et poenam, Tantale saeve, tuam!
Quam magis Atraciamque rotam tortosque dracones
 Et Tityi volucres tergeminumque canem!

time.[12] Now that you are free, go on and batter the lion of Cleonae
and set the neck of Hercules under the weight of heaven; now you   65
can get to work on the young bulls of Erythea and on your grove,
Erymanthus, which has now been made safe; tell of how the swift
hind's tracks were outstripped and tell of the armed bands of
Thermodon:[13] what gives me pleasure is to string together verses
in honor of the Medici family, O Fonzio, you who are a great part   70
of my soul! And for you, Lorenzo, may my Homer serve as pre-
lude,[14] while I prepare to sing of your deeds in heroic meter.

Enough of this! But now within your silent breast, Fonzio, savage Love constantly fans his fiery torches. And in astonishment I   75
asked, "What is it that constantly tortures your slender limbs?
Why this pallor on your delicate cheek?" How often I blamed the
water of Permessus and the choruses of Phoebus and the Pierides
when you were pale! And yet I recall that once, you madman, you   80
made fun of my mad passions and pounced upon me with various
jests. You used to laugh at me when I put up with the cold air of a
chilly night, while the white frost covered the damp leaves; you
used to laugh at the contempt my mistress showed me, Fonzio,
when her door was shut against me in my misery; you used to   85
laugh, when she scorned me, deafer than a cliff in Sicily, as I lay
awake on her stone threshold; and you showed no regret, laughing
at my tears as they fell and my cheeks always a bit swollen from
recent weeping. Go now, Fonzio, ridiculer of hallowed lovers,
go on and scorn the lofty laws of the winged god! How much   90
more would you prefer the harsh torments inflicted by the
tyrant of Ephyra and your punishment, cruel Tantalus! How
much more would you prefer Atracian wheel with its entwined
serpents and the birds of Tityos and the three-headed hound![15]

95 Nil tibi Socraticis sapientia condita libris
       Proderit, aut Samium consuluisse senem;
    Nil tibi contulerit sacri monumenta Maronis
       Aut Tulli varios edidicisse locos;
    Frustra Hieronymum[3] sublimia dicta tonantem,
100   Frustra Augustini scripta severa leges;
    Frustra Nasonem, lepidi vel culta Tibulli
       Carmina, vel qui te, Cynthia sola, canit.
    A, miser, in sterili sulcum producis harena!
       Diligit Aonios nulla puella modos,
105 Sed magis aurato gaudent procedere limbo
       Sidonioque graves murice ferre sinus;
    Semper Erythraeo poscunt de litore gemmas,
       Ut lapis in tereti splendeat articulo.
    A, ego quos cecini versus ad limen amicae!
110   Sed nebulae et tepidi diripuere Noti.
    Postibus, a, quoties elegeia nostra pependit!
       Nec tamen excussa ianua aperta sera est.
    Iactabam, memini, Pheobum nostramque poesin;
       Divitis illa tamen maluit usque torum.
115 Auro flectuntur pueri facilesque puellae,
       Corrumpunt iustos aurea dona senes.
    Inclusam Danaen munibat aenea turris,
       Perviaque aurato est tegula facta Iovi.
    Quare, si sapias, aurum viridesque smaragdos,
120   I, lege, quae Venerem conciliare queant.
    Crede procellosis turgentia lintea ventis,
       Ut dominae gravida classe parentur opes.
    Nec te, si madidus nimbis consurgit, Orion
       Terreat, aut si quas ingerit Haedus aquas,
125 Sive Therapnaeae sidus pluviale maritae
       Ingruit, et pueri stella proterva Phrygis.

The wisdom stored in Socratic texts will do you no good at all,   95
nor will it help you to consult the old man of Samos;[16] there will
be no benefit for you in having learned by heart the monuments of
sacred Vergil or various passages of Cicero. In vain will you read
Jerome thundering out his lofty phrases, in vain the severe writings   100
of Augustine; in vain will you read Ovid, or the sophisticated poems of charming Tibullus, or he who sings of you alone, Cyn-
thia.[17] Ah, poor man, you are tracing your furrow in barren sand!
No girl is in love with Aonian measures; instead they take pleasure   105
in making an entrance in gold embroidery and in wearing gowns
loaded with the purple dye of Sidon. Always they ask for gems
from the shore of the Red Sea so that they can have a gleaming
stone upon their smooth fingers. Ah, what verses I have sung
upon the threshold of my girlfriend! But they were scattered by   110
the mists and the warm south winds. Ah, how many times an elegy by me hung upon her door posts! And yet that door did not
slide the bolt and open. I used to boast of Phoebus, as I recall, and
my poetry; however, she continued to prefer a rich man's bed.
Boys and girls are easily swayed by gold, gifts of gold corrupt vir-   115
tuous old men. When Danae was locked up, a tower of bronze
protected her, and yet the roof proved pervious to Jupiter in a
shower of gold. And so, if you have any sense, go now and gather   120
the gold and green emeralds that can win over Venus. Entrust
your swelling sails to the storm-filled winds, so that you may load
your fleet with wealth acquired for your mistress. And if Orion
rises soaked in storm clouds, don't let that frighten you, or if the
Kid brings some rains, or if the rainy constellation of the bride of   125
Therapne impends and the shameless star of the Phrygian lad.[18]

Nil habet in sacros tempestas iuris amantes
    Cognatasque undas temperat alma Venus.
Sed quando in misero quae tempora ducis amore
130   Scripsisti, et vitae munera cuncta tuae,
Nunc simul et nostro, Fonti, sermone vicissim
    Disce aliquid vitae de ratione meae.
Libera iam tuto ratis est mihi condita portu,
    Nec metuit si quas increpat aura minas.
135 Quare ego Maeonii divina poemata vatis,
    Ut coepi, in Latios vertere tendo modos.
Sed quoniam variae delectant fercula mensae,
    Dulcius et vario gramina flore nitent,
Saepe mihi numeris ficti referuntur amores
140   Et canitur gracili mollis amica pede.
Nunc me contractis epigrammata ludere velis,
    Nunc iuvat ad mollem flectere dicta lyram.
Saepius eloquium magni Ciceronis adoro:
    Hic quoque succedunt verba soluta mihi.
145 Nam modo me, Fonti, vel epistula blanda moratur,
    Actio vel multis plurima ficta locis;
Et modo me retinent calamo praecepta quieto
    Tradita, pacatis et pia verba notis.
At cum Pieria taedet pallere sub umbra,
150   Egredior thalami conscia tecta mei.
Protinus inde peto Matthaei limina Franci:
    Ille mihi lepidos ingerit usque iocos,
Suscitat ille meo languentes pectore vires,
    Et mentem a taetro vindicat ille situ.
155 Hinc me digressum Marsilius excipit ingens,
    Non minus ingenio qui favet usque meo.
Hic aperit quanto currunt vaga sidera lapsu,
    Altus agit quali tramite Phoebus equos;

Storms have no power over blessed lovers and kindly Venus tempers the waves, her kin.

But since you have written to me of the time you pass in unhappy love, Fonzio, and all the occupations of your life, now you   130
must likewise listen to what I say and in turn learn something
about the way that I live. My ship has now freely taken refuge in a
safe harbor, and it does not fear what threats the wind roars. And   135
so, as I have begun to do, I attempt to turn the divine poems of
the Maeonian bard[19] into Latin measures. But since the dishes of
a varied table are pleasing, and grasses gleam more sweetly when
mixed with flowers, I often tell of fictitious love affairs in my poems, and the subject of my song is a tender girl in slight verse. At   140
one moment I take pleasure in pulling in my sails and playing at
epigrams, at another it pleases me to tune my words to the gentle
lyre. More often I pay homage to the eloquence of great Cicero: in
this endeavor words come to me also in prose. For sometimes I   145
busy myself with his charming correspondence, Fonzio, or his
numerous orations composed on many subjects; at other times his
precepts delivered in the middle style occupy me, and pious words
expressed in peaceful notes.

But when I grow weary of turning pale in the shade of the
Muses, I leave the shelter of my privy chamber. From there I head   150
straight for the house of Matteo Franco:[20] he always unloads a
string of clever jokes on me, he rouses the failing forces in my
heart, and frees my mind from its abominable torpor. When I   155
depart from here, great Marsilio, who also always takes an interest
in my talent, receives me.[21] He reveals to me the vastness of the
course run by the wandering stars, and the nature of the path
along which Phoebus drives his horses on high; he teaches me

Hic docet undeni resecant ut sidera circi,
160   Cur nitido tantum lacteus orbe patet;
  Ut cum patre Venus miseris mortalibus aequa est,
    Cur saepe obscuris Luna laborat equis;
  Aurea cur celso pendentia vincula mundo
    Maeonii finxit Musa beata senis;
165 Cur saepe aerii luctantur in aequore venti,
    Cur glacie et saeva grandine terra riget
  Atque eadem Icario cur mox perrumpitur aestu;
    Cur pluvius madidas combibit arcus aquas;
  Quae causa est vernum laxari fulmine caelum,
170   An ruat e puro stella serena polo.
  Et modo pallentes humano corpore morbos
    Qua valeam medica pellere monstrat ope;
  Impia non sani turbat modo dicta Lucreti,
    Imminet erratis nunc, Epicure, tuis.
175 Ille Iovis quinto solium conscendere passu
    Edocet, et celsi lucida signa poli:
  Namque agere ostendit pigrae nil corpora molis,
    Mox imperfecte, cum loca forma super;
  Hinc anima exseritur divinae conscia mentis,
180   Contiguus summo est angelus inde Iovi.
  Saepe graves pellit docta testudine curas,
    Et vocem argutis suggerit articulis;
  Qualis Apollinei modulator carminis Orpheus
    Dicitur Odrysias allicuisse feras,
185 Marmaricos posset cantu mulcere leones
    Quasque niger tigres semper Amanus habet,
  Caucaseo traheret duras e vertice cautes
    Saxaque Sicaniis condita gurgitibus.
  Hinc, ubi conticuit, Musarum concitus oestro
190   Deferor ad solitos protinus ipse lares,

how eleven circles divide the constellations; why the Milky Way 160
extends so far and wide in the gleaming orb; how Venus is propitious to poor mortals, as is her father; why the Moon often labors
when her steeds have been darkened; why the fertile Muse of the
old man of Maeonia imagined that there are golden chains hanging in the vault of heaven;[22] why the winds of the air often wrestle 165
each other on the sea; why the earth freezes with ice and savage
hailstones and why then it also cracks open from the heat of the
Dog Star; why the rainbow imbibes the wet waters; what causes
the sky to be ripped open by thunder in springtime, or an un- 170
clouded star to fall out of the pure firmament. And now he is
showing me by what medical skill I might drive pallid diseases
from the human body; now he's confounding the words of mad
Lucretius; now, Epicurus, he's attacking your errors. He teaches 175
me how to ascend on the fifth step to the throne of Jupiter and the
bright stars of heaven's vault: for he shows us that bodies consist-
ing of inert matter do not function at all, and that they then function imperfectly when form is added to their parts; from this the
soul, which participates in the divine mind, extricates itself and
from that point on is an angel next to Jupiter.[23] He often dispels 180
the weight of my cares with his learned lyre, and adds his voice to
accompany his nimble fingers. Like Orpheus, who composed
songs worthy of Apollo and is said to have attracted the wild
beasts of Thrace, he could charm the lions of Marmarica with his 185
song, and the tigers that always inhabit dark Mt. Amanus, and he
could attract hard crags from the summit of the Caucasus, and
rocks hidden in the seas of Sicily.[24]

Then, when he has finished, aroused by passion for the Muses,
I return straight to my usual abode and, challenging Apollo, I 190

Atque iterum meditor numeros Phoebumque lacesso
    Attonitusque sacram pectine plango chelyn.
Rursus in Andronici doctum me confero ludum,
    Qui tumidi nodos laxat Aristotelis
195 Smyrnaeique docet iucunda poemata vatis:
    Iam populat Graias Dardana flamma rates.
Fulminei posthac aperit Demosthenis artem,
    Aequiparat nostri quem Ciceronis opus.
Hic Verinus adest, hic sacri templa Lucardi
200   Qui regit, Aoniis pectora nota choris.
Carolus hic patrias certat superare Camenas,
    Et Marsupinam tollere ad astra domum:
Carolus ille, inquam, Musarum dulcis alumnus,
    Quo nullus toto est gratior orbe mihi.
205 Nec minor egregia surgit virtute Ioannes
    Baptista, Etrusci gloria certa soli;
Et quos longa mora est tenui comprendere versu
    Excipiunt socii Dorica verba mei.
Nec secus hinc reliquum teritur mihi temporis, et me
210   Bibliotheca tenet, Vespasiane, tua,
Cui tantum Graiae debent Latiaeque Camenae,
    Smyrnaeo quantum Dorica terra seni.
Namque deus veluti Cressis Epidaurius herbis
    Extinctum patri reddidit Androgeon,
215 Sic tu quos rapuit nobis cariosa vetustas
    Restituis Latio, Vespasiane, viros;
Per te Lethaeos iam spernit Graecia fluctus,
    Nec metuit Stygium Romula lingua deum.
Felix, cui liceat revocare in lumina vitae
220   Mortua priscorum tot monumenta virum!
Felix, cui liceat sanctorum nomina vatum
    Perdita flammatis eripuisse rogis!

compose verses again; inspired, I pluck the sacred lyre with my
plectrum. Again I go to the learned school of Andronicus,[25] who
unties the knots of Aristotle's obscurities, and instructs me in the   195
sweet poems of Smyrna's bard: already he has reached the part
where the Trojans destroy the Greek ships with flame. Afterward
he expounds upon the brilliant technique of Demosthenes, for
whom the works of our very own Cicero are a match. Verino is
here, the one who directs the church of San Lucardo, a heart well   200
known to the choruses of Aonia. Here Carlo is engaged in compe-
tition to surpass the Muses of his father, and to elevate the house
of the Marsuppini to the stars, that celebrated Carlo, I say, sweet
protégé of the Muses, the man I like best in all the world. No less   205
eminent in the distinction of his qualities is Giovanni Battista,
true glory of Etruscan land;[26] and others — it would take too long
to include them all in my slender verse — listen to what my friend
says in the Doric tongue. The rest of my time after this is spent in
the same way, and your library also receives me, Vespasiano,[27] to   210
whom both the Greek and Latin Muses owe as much as the land of
Greece owes to the old man of Smyrna. For just as the god of Epidaurus used Cretan herbs to restore Androgeos to his father after
his death,[28] so too, Vespasiano, you restore to Latium the men   215
whom the decay of antiquity has taken away. Thanks to you Greece
now scorns the streams of Lethe, and the language of Romulus
does not fear the Stygian god. Fortunate the one who can recall to
the light of life so many of the dead monuments of ancient men!   220
Fortunate the one who can rescue from the flames of the pyre the

Hunc prope consisto donec Cythereius ignis
    Advocat exorta lucida signa face.
225 Sic ego labentis produco tempora lucis
    Inter Hyantei munera grata chori.
At cum festa dies suadet cessisse labori,
    Quae subeant animum gaudia disce meum.
Attonita geminos vestigo mente poetas,
230 Ut referat numeros ille vel ille suos.
Sic Aganippei Michlotius incola fontis
    Pierio blandos ingerit ore modos;
Sic arguta refers nobis epigrammata, Bracci,
    Qui Marsi lepidam vincis Amazoniam.
235 Par est ambobus studium, par vita, nec illis
    Ingrata est Musae pars quotacumque meae.
Nam licet et Marsi vincant et scripta Catulli
    Augustique iocos exuperare queant,
Et licet his cedat culti Gaetulicus oris,
240 Vel Pedo, vel celebris Musa benigna Coci,
Attamen esse aliquid faciunt mea carmina, vates
    Esse aliquid nugas censet uterque meas.
Scilicet alterni vos copula fallit amoris,
    O socii, mentis vincla benigna piae!
245 Offundit tenebras ac veri lumina tollit
    Sanctum iucundae foedus amicitiae.
His ego suffixus totam vagor usque per urbem,
    Atteritur pedibus et via longa meis,
Donec flammigeras prono Phaethonte quadrigas
250 Lucidus Hesperio Cynthius amne lavat.
Haec tibi suscepto pro munere munera reddo,
    Haec pro susceptis carmina carminibus.
Ergo vale, Fonti, et memori nos mente reconde
    Mutuaque alternus pectora servet amor.

lost names of sacred poets! I linger by him until the star of Cythera[29] raises its torch to call forth the bright stars. This is how I   225
prolong the hours of the day as it slips away among the pleasant
gifts of the Hyantean chorus.[30]

But you should hear what pleasures creep into my mind when a
holiday leads me to set aside work. My mind inspired, I go in
search of two poets, so that one or the other of them might read   230
me his verses. And so Michelozzi, who dwells by the spring of
Aganippe, pours forth sweet measures with a voice worthy of the
Muses;[31] and so, Braccesi, you recite to me your clever epigrams,
surpassing the delightful *Amazonia* of Marsus.[32] Both have the   235
same calling, the same kind of life, nor is any portion of my Muse,
however small, displeasing to them. For although they surpass the
writings of Marsus and Catullus, and they can do better than the
jokes of Augustus, and although Gaetulicus' cultivated style takes
second place to them, as does Pedo and the generous Muse of the   240
famous Cook,[33] still they maintain that my poetry amounts to
something, and both poets rate my trifles as of some worth. Evidently, my friends, the ties our mutual love, the generous bond of
a faithful heart, deceive you. The sacred pact of a sweet friendship   245
clouds your judgment and removes the light of truth. Fixed upon
these thoughts, I wander throughout the whole city, and it's a long
road that's worn by my feet, until Phaethon sets and the bright   250
Cynthian bathes his flaming chariot in the river of the West.[34]
This is the gift I give to you in exchange for a gift received, these
verses in exchange for verses received. And so farewell, Fonzio, remember me and keep me in your heart, and may our mutual love
preserve the hearts we share.

SYLVA IN SCABIEM

Quae tam foeda lues, graciles delapsa per artus,
Ambustos lacerat nervos? quae tam impia diris
Vis inimica mali populatur viscera flammis
Marcentesque bibit venas avidoque, pavendum,
5   Igne liquefactas sorbet furiosa medullas?
An mihi Tartareum misera in praecordia virus
Eumenides Stygiamque facem et, crudele, virentes
Oris Cerberei spumas rabiemque Chimaerae
Afflarunt? Totum videor gestare sub alvo
10 Vesbion aut fessos Volcani incude caminos
Et Phlegethonteae glomerata incendia ripae.
     Cor salit, ardentes strident sub pectore fibrae,
Aret hiulca sitis, putridum vesana cruorem
Est rabies, siccoque in gutture febris anhelat
15 Exesas depasta genas, suffectaque tabo
Gliscit laxa cutis. Rubor igneus excitat orbes
Sanguineos, fugiunt oculi, squalentia pallor
Ora vorat, titubant gressus, genua aegra fatiscunt
Ossaque, me miserum, vix summam tabida pellem
20 Informant. Pro saeve dolor metuendaque pestis,
Pro facies infanda mali! maculosa cruentis
Horrent membra notis; umeros, colla, ora, lacertos,
Pectus, terga, latus, clunes, ventrem, inguina, suras
Occupat una lues; totum est in vulnere corpus,
25 Corpore de toto sanies fluit albida, crassus
Stillat ubique cruor: requies non ulla laborum.
     Non medicae fomenta manus, non tristia prosunt
Pocula et epoti numeroso e gramine succi,
Unguinaque et lacrimae terebynthi et sulpura viva,
30 Argenti spumae cinerisque immixtus acervo

A SILVA ON SCABIES

What is this disgusting disease that descends into my scrawny limbs, scorching and tearing at the sinews? What is this accursed and malignant force of evil that devastates my entrails with dreadful flames, imbibes my failing arteries, and — the horror! — madly 5 swallows up the liquefied marrow in insatiable fire? Could it be that the Eumenides have breathed into my poor heart this hellish poison, a Stygian torch, and — a cruel touch — the greenish slobber from the mouth of Cerberus and the madness of the Chimera?[1] I feel as if I am carrying in my belly the whole of Vesuvius or the 10 anvil-wearied forges of Vulcan and the fires heaped upon the banks of Phlegethon.[2]

My heart is pounding, my entrails burn and rattle in my breast, a gaping thirst is drying me up, a raging frenzy is consuming my putrid blood, and a fever gasps in my parched throat, devouring 15 my hollowed-out cheeks; and my flaccid skin is swollen and suffused with pus. A fiery redness kindles my bloody orbs, my eyes disappear, a pallor devours my filthy face, my footsteps falter, my knees droop weakly and, wretched me, my decaying bones barely give shape to my skin. Oh, the savage pain and the terrifying pes- 20 tilence, oh, the unspeakable aspect of this evil! My limbs shiver, stained with bloody marks: shoulders, neck, face, arms, breast, back, side, buttocks, belly, groin, calves — a single plague overruns them all. My body is entirely a wound, a whitish matter flows 25 from my entire body, congealed blood drips all over: there is no respite from the pains.

The poultices applied by a doctor's hand don't help, nor do bitter drafts or drinking potions made from countless herbs, or ointments or tears of terebinth or fresh sulfur, litharge of silver or 30

Conspersusque ⟨in⟩ membra latex fluviive propinqui
Lympha natata diu, nepetae malvaeque virentes,
Et fumus terrae et gelido sal fusus aceto
Milleque iam fessis medicamina condita aenis.

35 Ipsa Machaoniae trepidant ad munera curae,
Ipse mihi Chiron genitusque Amythaone vates,
Ipse mihi, artis inops, Epidaurius astupet anguis
Coryciaque pater qui fatum mugit in umbra
Claraque Paeoniae titubat solertia dextrae.

40 Seu nox astrigero caelum subtexit amictu,
Sive diem retegit Nabataeo a litore Titan,
Consumpta irriguis exundant fletibus ora
Semper et assiduo singultant ilia pulsu:
Non licet in dulcem summittere lumina somnum.

45 Pocula non sapiunt, non si mihi nectaris imbrem
Sangarius puer aut Iunonia porrigat Hebe.
Si mihi Mopsopias amor est exsugere ceras
Coryciumve favum aut quem florea parturit Hyble,
Omnia Cyrneas spirant alvearia taxos;

50 Siquis harundineos quot habet pastoria Zancle
Apponat sucos, haeret sapor omnibus idem,
Habrotanosque graves et dira absynthia credas.

    Iam vero quae tum facies, cum personat intus
Ignis edax? furor est artus laniare cruentis

55 Unguibus aut rabidos torquere in viscera morsus:
Sanguineas putrido divellit corpore crustas
Unca manus penitusque artus scrutatur hiantes
Exuviasque rapit nervorum et detegit ossa.
Tum sanies obscena natat, rigat uvida marcens

60 Membra fluor, scabros tabes crudeliter ungues
Polluit, illotus scatet atro in corpore sudor.
Quin etiam ad numeros (pro scaevum et grande doloris
Ingenium!), ad numeros iuvat asprum avellere corpus

water mixed with a heap of ash and sprinkled on my limbs, or
long swims in the water of a nearby river, not catmint or green
mallows, not steam from the ground or salt infused in cold vine-
gar, not the thousand medications stored in now exhausted vessels.
Machaon's remedies tremble at the very prospect of helping, Chi-   35
ron himself is dumbfounded at my case, as is the seer born of
Amythaon, and the serpent of Epidaurus, bereft of his skill, and
the father who bellows out prophecies in the dark Corycian cave,
and the celebrated skill of Paeon's hand falters.³ Whether the night   40
is veiling the sky in her starry cloak, or the Titan Sun is coming
from the Arabian shore to uncover the day, my exhausted face is
always overflowing with copious tears and my abdomen rattles
with continuous throbbing: it's not possible to close my eyes in
sweet sleep. Beverages have no taste, not if the boy from the river   45
Sagaris or Juno's daughter Hebe should offer me a shower of nec-
tar.⁴ If I have a craving to suck out a beehive from Attica or a
honeycomb from Cilicia or one produced by blossoming Hybla,
every hive has for me the aroma of Corsican yew trees; if anyone   50
were to serve me all the juices produced by the sugar canes of pastoral Messina, the same taste would inhere in all of them, and you
would think that they were intense habrotanum or dreadful ab-
sinth.⁵

What then will you do, when the consuming flame crackles
within? It is madness to rend your limbs with bloody nails or to   55
take wild wrenching bites from your flesh: yet my hand like a claw
tears bloody morsels from my putrid body and probes deep within
my gaping limbs, pulling out what is left of the sinews and expos-
ing the bone. Then a foul pus flows out, a withering flux pours   60
over my damp limbs, the ooze cruelly pollutes my mangy fingernails, and a filthy sweat breaks out over my blackened body. And
furthermore, it even gives me pleasure (oh, the perverse and abundant genius of pain!), it gives me pleasure to pick at my coarse

Et spoliare artus penitusque immergere venis
65 Crudeles digitos. Tum dirum murmur et atrox
Prosequitur fremor, ac rabie confusa voluptas
Concordem digitis gemitum laniantibus effert.
Tum laxas nares, tum dentem dente videres
Attritum exacui pressasque infrendere malas
70 Suspendique genas ac nasum cogere rugas
Liventem et totam demitti in lumina frontem,
Sardonioque putes risu deducere rictum.
Non secus, Icarii quotiens iuba fulgurat astri,
Cernimus in triviis villosum saepe Molossum
75 Nunc pede, nunc rostro, tremulae nunc verbere caudae
Pellentem obscenas furiali murmure muscas
Aut pulicis dentem aut praegnantem sanguine taetro
Tabanum et morsus frustra intentare crepantes.
Si tamen arentes vulnus conduxerit oras
80 Spemque animo dederit sacrum expugnare veternum,
Nulla fides: nostro subeunt in corpore obusto
Continuo ardentes papulae recidivaque pestis
Pullulat heredemque sibi moribunda cicatrix
Parturit. Ampulant foedae per marcida bullae
85 Membra, putri sanie distentae et sanguine crasso
Proluviem expletae ventris. Perit impia mater
Suppliciis fecunda meis semperque novatur
Pestis acerba. Mali misero finisque doloris
Ultimus aerumnae gradus est et origo futurae:[1]
90 Qualis Oronteo phoenix longaevus in orbe,
Dura renascentis repetens cunabula vitae,
Ut casiae gramen nardique accendit aristas
Cinnamaque et costi segetem glaebasque Sabaeum
Ac myrrhae lacrimas et divitis uber amomi,
95 Incubat ipsa super flammis viridemque iuventam
Morte sua redimit seque ipsa reseminat ales.

body rhythmically, pillaging my own limbs and cruelly plunging
my fingers deep into my veins. A dire murmur and a horrible rum-   65
bling follow then and a sense of pleasure mixed with frenzy elicits
a moan in harmony with my lacerating fingers. Then you would be
able to see my nostrils flare, my teeth sharpened by grinding upon
themselves, my clenched jaws gnashing, my cheeks slackened, my   70
livid nose contracting wrinkles, and my forehead sunk entirely into
my eyes, and you'd think that I was clenching my jaws to a sar-
donic smile. In just this same way, whenever the mane of the star
of Icarius gleams,[6] we often see a shaggy Molossian hound in the
crossroads, now with its paw, now with its snout, and now with   75
the beat of its tremulous tail trying to drive off the disgusting
mosquitoes with their mad buzzing or the biting fleas or the gad-
flies swollen with noisome blood, pointlessly aiming its whining
bites at them. If, however, the wound has closed its dried-out
edges and offered your heart hope that this cursed torpor can be   80
defeated, don't believe it: dry pustules immediately break out on
my burned body and the recurrent pestilence spreads and as the
scar fades away it generates its own successor. Grotesque blisters
swell over my decaying limbs, distended with putrid matter and   85
filling my stomach's discharge with congealed blood. The unholy,
but fertile mother of my torments passes away and the repulsive
pestilence is continually renewed. And for me in my misery the
final end of this terrible pain is a step toward further tribulation
and a new start. Thus does the long-lived phoenix in the region of 90
the Orontes return to the harsh cradle where its life is reborn, and
when it has set fire to slivers of cassia, spikes of nard, cinnamon, a
crop of costum, and lumps of incense,[7] teardrops of myrrh and a
cluster of precious amomum, the bird settles upon the flames and   95
by its own death repurchases the freshness of youth and by itself

Verum ubi iam lentus papulae maturuit umor,
Protinus ulcus hiat fluidoque infecta veneno
Squalentem tunicam, foedum et miserabile visu,
100 Sorbet hiulca cutis membrisque affixa cruentis,
Qua trahitur parcente manu, secum illita vestis
Viscera tota trahit, totos rapit impia nervos
Et tenui omento crepitantia dedolat ossa.
Hic vero non iam gemitus, non murmure mixtae
105 Proveniunt lacrimae: pavidas it stridor ad auras
Terrificus totosque alto clamore penates
Efferus incendit dolor et furialis anhelo
Vox pulmone sonat. Tum quo vocat impetus, illuc
Auferor ac memet fugiens nemora avia lustro,
110 Fortior ad rabiem, rapto velut enthea thyrso
Thyias, ubi Ismarius trieterida suscitat Euan,
Rupibus Edoniis furit aeternumque nivalem
Othryn et arctois Pangaea exusta pruinis
Perlegit ac Getico sulcatum Strymona plaustro,
115 Nebride picta sinus Boreaeque frementis hiatu
Indociles dispersa comas, simul 'Euhion, euhoe!,'
'Euhion!' ingeminat tortoque effulgurat angui.
       Quin etiam horrendum ac dictu mirabile monstrum
Ingenerat cutis, humanus cui pabula sanguis,
120 Cui latebrae perfossus homo, tepidumque cruorem
Innatat et vivo depascier hospite gaudet.
Pellegenam appellant: non ille aut prodigus artus
Aut faciem ferus aut crassam porrectus in alvum,
Sed spatii exiguus. Liceat vix pelle latentem
125 Tangere acu, vix pugnaci deprendere visu
Carnificem immersum tabo vitiataque morsu
Frusta eruptantem et saniem rabido ore vomentem.
Quantaque ad aestivi passim spiracula solis
Ludere lascivo temeraria corpora motu

begets itself again. But when the viscous fluid of the pustule has fully developed, the sore immediately opens and my parched skin is infected with the liquid poison and absorbs my filthy tunic — a disgusting and miserable thing to behold — and now that it is 100 stuck to my bloody limbs, wherever the smeared cloth is pulled by my cautious hand, it pulls along whole pieces of flesh, remorselessly tearing whole nerves and hewing away from their delicate membrane my rattling bones. At this point no longer do any moans well up, no tears mixed with murmurs: instead a terrifying 105 hissing sound rises to the trembling airs and a savage pain sets the whole household on fire with a piercing cry and my voice resonates madly as my lungs gasp for air. Then I am carried away to wherever the impulse calls me, and I range the pathless forests in an attempt to escape myself, more strongly disposed to madness, like 110 a divinely inspired Bacchant who seizes hold of a thyrsus when Ismarian Bacchus rouses the triennial festival and rages on the Thracian crags, scanning ever-snowy Mt. Othrys and Mt. Pangaeus, consumed by arctic frosts and the river Strymon which is furrowed by carts of the Getae, her breast adorned with a fawn 115 skin and her unkempt hair scattered by the blast of the roaring North Wind, at the same time crying out continually "Euhoe Bacchus!" and brandishing serpents like thunderbolts.[8]

It is indeed a horrible and incredible monster that is generated in the skin, one whose nourishment is human blood, whose lair is 120 the human body transfixed, which swims into the warm bloodstream and happily feeds upon its living host. They call it the "skinborn": it is not large of limb or fierce in appearance or extending into an ample belly, but tiny in size. You could barely touch it 125 with the point of a needle when it is hiding in the skin; if you were to focus your vision stubbornly, you could barely detect this executioner, immersed in gore, belching morsels tainted by its bite and vomiting bloody matter from its rabid mouth. And the bodies that you often see skipping all about, moving randomly against the

130 Saepe vides, aut quanta sui fert semina mundi
Ridiculus per inane senex, qui mente capaci
Innumeros perimit reparatque ab origine soles
Et putat infantem semper consurgere Phoebum,
Tantus membra patet, tanta est mensura superbi
135 Hostis. At in magno vix umquam larga nocendi
Corpore tam saevam rabiem natura locavit.
Siquem accensa siti dipsas calcata momordit
Aut seps tabificus crescensve in guttura prester
Marmaricive furor iaculi atque haemorrois ingens,
140 Siquem Cinyphia stravit basiliscus harena
Purpureo horrificam rutilans diademate frontem,
Non tamen improprie truncant immitia Parcae
Vellera, non gemitum surda Mors exigit aure,
Non lacrimas ridet, sed Fatum in vulnera praeceps
145 Succidit virides properanti falce dolores.
Hic ferus exiguo parcit vitalia dente
Carpere, non tacito temerat praecordia rictu,
Non arcem invadit cerebri cordisve recessus
Pertemptat, sed prima ferox in viscera lentum
150 Serpit et infando terebrat conamine pellem.
Quacumque ingreditur, morsu, exitiale, cruento
Perfurit et rutilum describit sanguine campum,
Defodit in summo latebrosa cubilia dente,
Itque reditque frequens scatebris longumque cavernas
155 Perforat ac rubro distinguit pectora sulco.
Sic Tartessiaci scrutator pallidus auri,
Sponte diem fugiens ac picti sidera mundi,
Reptat harenivago terrena in viscera lapsu,
Arcanis inhians opibus, causasque malorum
160 Elicit ad superos. Tacito sic tramite novit
Haud expectatos inferre cuniculus hostes
Aggeribus tutis turritae aut moenibus urbis.

glimmer of a summer's sun, or the atomic particles of the universe   130
which that amusing old man says are scattered through the void —
that old man who with his capacious intellect says that countless
suns are destroyed and recreated from scratch and believes that
Phoebus always arises as an infant[9] — they are the same size, the
same measure as the body of my proud foe. But nature, although   135
she is generous in doing harm, has hardly ever placed such savage
frenzy in a large body. Whenever a *dipsas*, burning with thirst, is
stepped upon and bites someone, or a *seps* that causes its victim to
waste away. or a *prester* with its swollen gullet, or a furious *iaculus*
from Marmarica, or an enormous *haemorrois*; whenever a *basilisk*   140
has laid someone low in the sands of Libya, its horrifying forehead
glowing red with a violet diadem,[10] the Parcae still do not cut the
cruel threads of life improperly, nor Death turn a deaf ear to the
moan it exacts or laugh at your tears; instead, Fate is swift to
pounce upon the wounds and cuts short fresh pains with his swift   145
scythe. This beast refrains from biting the vital parts with its tiny
teeth, nor does it defile the diaphragm with its silent jaws, nor
does it invade the citadel of the brain or attack the recesses of the
heart, but first it ferociously winds its slow way into the flesh and   150
with an unnatural effort bores into the skin. Wherever it enters —
and this is fatal! — it rampages with its bloody bite and traces out
a red plain of blood as it excavates secret lairs at the point of its
teeth. It comes and it goes gushing constantly and for a long time
it carves out hollow spaces, making a distinctive red track on the   155
chest. It is like a man who's grown pale prospecting for Tartessian
gold, voluntarily shunning the daylight as well as the stars of the
painted sky, crawling along a sandy shaft into the earth's entrails
out of longing for secret riches, the causes of evil which he brings   160
out to the world above. It is as when a tunnel succeeds in unex-
pectedly introducing the enemy along a silent path into the secure
ramparts and walls of a turreted city. It is as when a porcupine, its

Sic umeros iaculis bicoloribus horridus hystrix
Callidaque invalidis metuens vulpecula natis
165 Multicavas fodere domos aut scrupea subter
Saxa aut praecipiti sub rupe, ubi maxima quercus
Rugosis alte radicibus hispida findit
Terga iugi ramisque errantibus implicat umbras;
Atque adeo exigui quamquam patet orbita passus,
170 Haud tamen est oculo vestigia certa sequaci
Prendere; sic tecta fallax ambage retexit
Errabundus iter diversosque impedit orbes
Callidus et caeco confundit tramite sulcos,
Ut labyrintheum, Minoia limina, tectum
175 Fraude loci dubia tacitisque anfractibus olim
Cecropiae struxere manus, flexuque recurvo
Multifidum seclusit iter Discordia, gyris
Confundens spatia, atque insertos orbibus orbes
Implicuit Dolus et inextricabilis Error.
180   Si vero infandae numeros aut nomina gentis
Percensere velis, vix tantus vere rubenti
Muscarum quondam populus mulctraria circum
Involitat stabulis, tenuique proboscide grandes
Diripiunt guttas ac lactea murmure rauco
185 Obscenae volucres huc illuc pocula raptant;
Vix, ubi flaventes iam surrigit area messes,
Tam multae erumpunt caveis sudataque longum
Formicae ancipiti populantur forcipe farra;
Iamque attrita diu crebro pede gramina signans,
190 Terrigena ingreditur legio, repetitaque genti
Graniferae innumero describitur orbita passu;
Instat nigra cohors operi: pars dura fatigat
Agmina, pars tremulis adnutans cornibus ultro
Itque reditque frequens; haec magnum versat acervum
195 Praedatrix, haec immodico sub pectore sudat,

266

back bristling with two-colored spines, and the cunning fox, fear-
ing for its still frail offspring, dig lairs of many hollows either be-   165
neath jagged rocks or below a steep cliff, where a great oak splits
the prickly slopes of the mountain with its deeply wrinkled roots,
casting an enveloping shadow with its wandering branches; and
though the track made by its tiny footstep is open to view, it is still   170
not possible to perceive its certain imprint with your eager eye.
This is how a swindler alters his route, moving on a secret, round-
about way, cunningly entangling his rounds in different directions
and confounding his tracks on an invisible path; just like the house
of the labyrinth, the home of Minos, with that place's uncertain   175
delusion and silent bends, which Athenian hands constructed long
ago, whose manifold paths Discord sundered with a crooked maze,
throwing the space into confusion with spirals, whose rings within
rings were entangled by Deceit and inextricable Error.

If in fact you should want to tally the numbers or names of this   180
unspeakable race, their population is scarcely equaled by the number of flies that sometimes swarms around the milk pails in the
stables at the first blush of spring, stealing away great globules
with their tiny snouts and plundering the milky goblets as the   185
filthy creatures fly here and there, buzzing noisily. When the
golden harvest piles up on the threshing floor, scarcely do as many
ants erupt from their holes and with their double pincers pillage
the grain won with such hard labor; and making their imprint
now on the grass worn down for so long by a multitude of feet, the   190
earthborn legion advances, with countless steps tracing the track
repeatedly taken by this nation of grain gatherers — the black co-
hort eagerly takes on the task, some of them urging on the tough-
ened ranks, others coming and going ahead continually, nodding
as their antennae quiver; one of them rummages through a great
heap to pillage it, another one works up a sweat upon its outsized   195

267

Astruit illa domi fruges atque horrea complet.
Hunc Stygiae numerum gentis rabiemque feracis
Exstimulat populi foedo rex impius ore
Lichobrotus, quo non sordentem gnavior alter
200   Expleri ingluviem aut obscenum lambere lingua
Mucorem; miserumque nefas Cocytia quondam
Helcomedusa fero peperit regina Cybistae.
Non illo quiquam fuit atrum innare cruorem
Doctior aut illa contractum extendere morsu
205   Ulceris os, sed enim furias praegressa parentum,
Impietas nati tantum scelere imminet illis,
Pelea magnanimus quantum superabat Achilles.
At regem, insanae feritatis laude superbus,
Consequitur, vivas haud segnis rodere carnes,
210   Sarcophagus, semperque cavis habitare sub antris
Audax Troglodytes, exturbatorque soporis
Hypnophobus, teretes et Dactylotrogus² acuto
Dente cavans digitos, cumque illis sanguine largo
Ebrius Haemopion, nec non Cheroglyphus omnem
215   Consuetus terebrare manum, capitisque nigrescens
Texta Melancoryphus, residemque immobilis alvum
Scalpta manu rabida Lichenor vulnera lingens.
Dipsada quid memorem? quid Oryctona Leucochroonque
Apodaque et Phlebem, cumque Helcodamante Philagon,
220   Bdellamque Ulonomonque, Palirroon Eurybatemque,
Quotque alii nostro pinguescunt sanguine fratres?
Promptius expediam Boreas quot frigore frondes
Decutit arboribus, quot se formosior annus
Induit in flores, refugo quot lambit harenas
225   Oceanus ponto lunaribus incrementis.
    Ergo ego tot Stygio portenta excita barathro
Corpore fixa gero, necdum puro aethere cassus,
Diripienda feris trado mea viscera monstris

breast, still another piles up the produce at the nest and fills up
the granaries. The foul mouth of their impious king, *Bloodlicker*,[11]
rouses this troop of the Stygian race and stirs the fury of this
abundant people. There is none more energetic than him when it
comes to filling his filthy maw or in licking disgusting mucus with   200
his tongue. *Ulcerqueen*, mistress of the Cocytus, long ago birthed
this wretched abomination to *Diver* the Ferocious. No one has
been more skilled than he at swimming into black blood, nor has
any been more skilled than she at enlarging the mouth of a wound   205
with her bite, but the impiety of the son exceeds even the madness
of his parents, posing a threat to their criminality to the same degree that greathearted Achilles surpassed Peleus. But the king is
followed by *Flesh-eater*, who is puffed up by the praise for his deranged cruelty and ever eager to gnaw on living tissue; and *Hole-*   210
creeper, who dares to dwell in deep-channeled caverns; and *Sleep-*
chaser who drives away sleep; and *Fingergnawer* who hollows out
smooth fingers with his sharp teeth; and along with them *Blood-*
sucker, drunk on copious amounts of blood, and *Hand-carver*, too,
who has a knack for boring through the whole hand; and *Blacktop*,   215
who wears a black headband, and *Manlicker*, who lies motionless
on his lazy belly, licking the wounds he scratched out with his rabid hand. Need I mention *Thirster?* What about *Earthdigger* and
Whiteskin and *Footless* and *Bloodvessel*, *Polluter* and *Woundlord*, and 220
Leech and *Scardealer*, *Reflux* and *Broadstep*, and all their brethren
who grow fat on our blood? I could sooner provide an account of
how many leaves Boreas shakes off the trees when the weather
turns cold, or how many flowers the lovelier season of the year
dons as apparel, or how many grains of sand Ocean laps up into   225
the sea at the waxing of the moon.

And so I carry that many monstrosities summoned from the
Stygian abyss fixed in my body, and though I am not yet deprived
of the pure ether, I resign my flesh to be torn apart by wild

Moturusque hosti lacrimas: en oblita, dirum,
230 Pectora semilacer, totos en pervius artus,
Mille patens plagis, en cunctis hospita morbis
Membra trahens, aegris obtundens questibus auras,
Invisus superis, vitam lucemque perosus!
Vivo tamen, nec te pietas, Mors impia, nostri
235 Ulla subit, surdas precibus sic obstruis aures:
Siccine aena mihi duxistis vellera, Parcae?
Vos, o vos fidi quondam et mea turba sodales,
Huc huc adventate, meos exscindite luctus!
Ite, animam invisam, pietas haec maxima, ad umbras
240 Trudite Tartareas Ereboque hoc reddite monstrum.
Heu mihi, quod saevi fugiunt contagia morbi
Egregii comites (sic, o sic, maxime, visum,
Iuppiter!), attactumque pavent et acerba tuentes
Prospiciunt vivum haud secura fronte cadaver.
245   Ille ego sum, o socii, quamquam ora animosque priores
Fortuna eripuit, qui quondam heroa canendo
Proelia et exhaustos Rhoeteo in Marte labores,
Ibam altum spirans; quique olim immania bella
Cosmiadae Etruscis aggressus credere Musis,
250 Cantabam patulo quantum sese aequore ferret
Iulius armipotens, cum suspiratus amanti
(a nimium!) nymphae, ferratos durus in hostes
Ingrueret sublime volans, claususque minaci
Casside et undantem flammis thoraca coruscoque
255 Umbonem Phoebo radiatus, Iapyge campum
Persultarit equo, ac tota cervice superstans,
Arma, viros victor subversaque quadrupedantum
Pectora pulvereis trifida trabe funderet arvis.
Altaque magnanimi vel bello exempla secutus
260 Fratris, Olympiaco iuvenilia tempora ramo
Cinxit et aeternum peperit sibi Marte triumphum.

monsters, an object of tears even for my enemies. Look at me, my   230
chest defiled (an awful sight!), half lacerated! Look at me, pierced
through all my limbs, exposed to a thousand blows! Look at me,
barely dragging my limbs that shelter diseases of every sort, beat-
ing the airs with pitiful complaints, hated by the gods, hating light
and life! And yet I am alive, but no pity for me wells up within
you, pitiless Death, so thoroughly do you stop up your ears, deaf   235
to my entreaties: Fates, is this how you spun the bronze threads of
my destiny? You, O you who were once my faithful comrades and
my retinue, come here, come here and tear away my afflictions! Go
on and drive this life I hate down to the shades of Tartarus and   240
restore this monster to Hell: this would be the greatest act of piety! Woe is me, for these excellent friends of mine flee from con-
tact with this savage disease (this then, oh this must be the will of
great Jupiter!). They are afraid of my touch and gazing bitterly at
me, their brows far from untroubled, they see a living corpse.

    My friends, though Fortune has stolen my voice and my former   245
spirit, I am still the one who once used to proceed in lofty spirit,
singing of heroic battles and of the struggles endured in the Trojan
War;[12] who undertook to entrust the fierce wars of Cosimo's scion
to the Tuscan Muses and sang of how grandly Giuliano bore him-   250
self in arms on the open plain,[13] while, amid the sighs of the girl
who loved him all too well, flying on high, he rushed hard against
his armored opponents; and how, arrayed in a menacing helmet,
agleam in his corselet swelling with flames and his shield with   255
flashing sunlight, he bounded through the field on his Apulian
horse and, towering over all by a whole head, with his victorious
trident he routed arms, men, and greathearted steeds overthrown
on the dusty fields. Following the lofty example of his high-
spirited brother even in war, he girded his youthful brow with an   260
Olympic wreath and by his valor acquired an immortal triumph.

Haec quondam memorata mihi, nunc dira canenti
Pallida Tartareis metuendum assibilat hydris
Eumenis, umbriferique allatrat ianitor antri.
265 Guttura triste sonant, numeri ferale gemiscunt;
Ipsa, meis stupefacta malis, lacrimabile carmen
Dat chelys et dominum delamentatur ademptum.
Sponte sua nexae circum mea tempora vittae
Puniceum Stygia variant ferrugine textum,
270 Sponte cadunt lauri ac spoliatum frontis honorem,
Coniferae subeunt, feralia serta, cupressi.
Ipse altum attolli nostro quoque carmine nomen
Passus et ambabus gaudens consurgere linguis,
Cessantem torvo me lumine terret Achilles,
275 Impendique suis cupiens solacia damnis
Et vaga Romuleo subniti ad sidera cantu,
Troia pios iterat questus residemque canendi
Vexat et Ausonium reddi sibi poscit Homerum.
Stant circum attonitae, vatum pia numina, Musae:
280 Haec longas neglecta comas, haec pectine vincta
Inter se digitos genibus, caput illa silenti
Fulta lyra, palmis haec ora excepta supinis,
Semianimemque pavent oculis agnoscere alumnum,
Nec digitis nec voce mei solacia luctus
285 Intempesta canunt. Quid enim modulamina surdis
Auribus aut rigido studeant detrudere cordi?
Ocius Euripi refluum mare Carpathiasque
Pacarent hiemes tremefactaque litora denso
Verbere, raucisonis qua fluctibus adsilit Aegon.
290 Somniferam prius octipedis sub sidere Cancri
Aspida et orbatam mulcerent carmine tigrem.
Neve super miseri quisquam sit sanguinis insons,
Tu quoque te nostro, sic Parcae stamina versant,
Subtrahis aspectu, requies o sola laborum,

Once these events were told by me, but now, as I sing of terrors, a
pale Fury hisses alarmingly at me with her hellish serpents and the
doorkeeper of the cavern of the shades barks at me.[14] My throat   265
sounds grimly, my verses are a funeral lament; my lyre itself,
stunned at my pains, produces a tearful song and bewails the loss
of its owner. Of their own accord the ribbons wound round my
temples change their purple texture to a dark-red hellish hue; of   270
their own accord my laurels fall away and on my brow, now de-
spoiled of honor, are replaced by funeral garlands of coniferous
cypress. Achilles himself, who allowed his name to be elevated on
high in my song and was pleased that it was ennobled in both
languages, gives me a terrifyingly stern look because I am slacking
off,[15] and Troy, desiring some compassion as compensation for its   275
losses and the support of a Latin song to reach the wandering
stars, repeatedly makes respectful complaints, pestering me for my
poetic inactivity and insisting that her Italian Homer be restored
to her. The Muses, the poets' loyal divinities, stand around in dis-
may: one has neglected her long hair, another wraps her fingers   280
around her plectrum upon her knees, another leans her head on
her silent lyre, while still another rests her face weakly upon her
palms, and they are all afraid to glance at their half-dead protégé,
and neither by playing nor by singing do they perform any inop-   285
portune consolation for my sorrow. Why indeed should they wish
to squeeze out melodies for ears that are deaf or a heart that is
hardened? Sooner could they calm the ebbing strait of the Euripus
or the storms of the Carpathian Sea or the coasts that are shaken
by repeated pounding where the Aegean dashes against them with
its roaring waves.[16] They could sooner soothe with song the death-   290
dealing viper that dwells beneath the constellation of eight-legged
Cancer, or a tigress that has lost her cubs.

And just to make sure that no one is blameless in this miserable
bloodshed, you too pull back from the sight of me (thus the Fates
spin their threads), you, the only respite from my travails,

295 O mihi plus superis dilecte, o magne, virentis
     Spes una Etruriae, Laurens, quo florida tellus
     Et nato genitrix et filia patre superbit,
     Pectore qui dubium validis ne potentior armis,
     Palladiam praefers gladio Mavortis olivam,
300 Iusque piumque refers, vix undis cedere passus
     Apeninigenam cognati Thybridis Arnum,
     Aeternumque nova titulum virtute propagas
     Riphaeum ad Boream Libyae sitientis ab Austro,
     Qua fessum Titana fovet Maurusia Tethys
305 Gurgite Atlanteo, nitidae qua praevia luci
     Roscida nocturnos abigit Pallantias ignes.
     Nempe tuos vultus, genitor, tuaque ora videndo,
     Ipse ego Caucaseas seducta mente catenas
     Iapetionidae intrepidus, colloque minantem
310 Tantaleo silicem atque Ephyraei immania regis
     Pondera, quemque ferox flammato pectore montem
     Concutit Alcyoneus Phlegraeaque fulgura ferrem.
     Utque, Paraethonio sinuosum attollitur Austro
     Cum mare caeruleum ac torta vertigine fluctus
315 Saxa subesa ferit spumisque sonantibus albens
     Aestuat et bibulas aspergine tingit harenas,
     Si placidum ponto caput exserat aequoreus rex,
     Mox rauci cadit ira freti cumulique minaces
     Sternuntur, pulsae nubesque hiemesque recedunt
320 Et pavefacta silent animosi murmura venti:
     Sic, ubi turbineo luctusque dolorque furorque
     Pectore bacchantur totoque in corde superbit
     Tempestas effrena animi, si cominus adsis
     Sidereo radians vultu, procul exulat omnis
325 Tristitia ac tumidam mulcent placida otia mentem.
     Quare, age, seu doctas, Neleia moenia, Pisas
     Pandis Hyanteis, pater o dulcissime, nymphis,

you whom I have loved more than the gods above, O Lorenzo the   295
Magnificent, the one hope for Tuscany's prosperity, in whom the
blooming land takes pride, as a mother does in her son or as a
daughter does in her father—you of all people, about whom one
might question whether your greater strength lies in intellect or
military might, you who prefer the olive of Pallas Athena to the
sword of Mars, you who restore justice and piety, scarcely allowing   300
the Arno, born in the Apennines, to give way to waters of her kin,
the Tiber,[17] you who by new acts of valor extend your undying
fame from the South Wind of parched Libya to the North Wind
of Scythia, to where the Moroccan Sea cradles the weary Sun in   305
the swells of the Atlantic, and to where the dewy daughter of Pallas drives away the nighttime stars, paving the way for the bright
light of day.[18] Certainly when I see your face, father, and your expression, I could endure the chains of Iapetus' son on the Caucasus without fear and with calm reflection, as well as the rock that   310
threatens the neck of Tantalus, and the enormous burdens of the
king of Corinth, and the mountain that Alcyoneus rattles ferociously with fires from his breast, and the lightning flashes of the
Phlegraean fields.[19] And just as when the azure sea is lifted in
curls by the South Wind from Paraetonium and the waves, twist-
ing and churning, batter the worn rocks, surging white in booming   315
foam and bathing the thirsty sands with its spray, if the King of
the Ocean raises his calm head from the spray, then the anger of
the roaring sea subsides and the menacing white caps are leveled,
the clouds and the squalls are driven out of the sky and recede,
and the rumblings of the violent wind fall silent in terror; just so,   320
when grief and pain and madness are raving in my dizzy breast
and an unrestrained soul storm revels in my entire heart, if you are
close at hand, your celestial visage radiating, all my sadness is banished far away and my restless mind is soothed by a gentle peace.   325
And so, come then, my sweetest father, whether you are opening
the Nelean walls of learned Pisa to the Boeotian nymphs, or laying

Sive triumphatas Volaterrae substruis arces
Indocilemque diu populum obluctantia cogis
330 subdere colla iugo atque animos contundere inanes;
Seu mage te gelidi subter querceta Mugelli
Dulcia Bistonio modulantem carmina plectro
Populifer Sevis et Garsae piscosa fluenta
Mirantur tacite; seu te Florentia laeto,
335 Undique purpurei turba coeunte senatus,
Ore videt reducem caligantesque serenat,
Adventu grata, oculos praeductaque fronti
Nubila dispellit natumque patremque salutat.
Quicquid agis, quocumque solo pulcherrimus alta
340 Maiestate nites, si non tamen excidit omnis
Cura mei, siqua est priscae pietatis imago,
Si meritis haud digna fero, per sidera caeli,
Per faciles superos, per spes florentis alumni
Successusque tuos, oro: miserere laborum
345 Tantorum, pelle agrestis hoc pectore morbos,
Ac praesens me redde mihi vitamque labantem
Suscipe et eiectam sancto refer ore salutem.
Arbiter ipse deum, tonitru qui concutit orbem,
Quem caelum, quem terra tremunt, quem pontus et aurae,
350 Qui lucem noctemque regit, contraria torquet
Sidera sideribus, volucresque hominesque ferasque
Et genus aequoreum dias in lumina oras
Evocat, omnipotens et numine cuncta gubernans
Plena suo, si sollicitas fors attigit aures
355 Unius vox maesta viri, qui dulcia vota
Nuncupet imploretque Iovem, non ardua rerum
Impediunt mundique vices, quin obvius ille
Supplicibus veniat, placidusque optata secundet.

276

the foundations of the defeated citadel of Volterra, compelling its
long disobedient population to submit their obstinate necks to the
yoke and crushing their pointless arrogance;[20] or if the Sieve,   330
whose banks abound with poplars, and the streams of the Carza,
which teem with fish, silently gaze at you in astonishment beneath
the cool oak groves of Mugello, while you play sweet songs on the
Thracian lyre;[21] or if Florence, with senators dressed in purple   335
crowding all about, looks upon your return with a happy expression and, heartened by your arrival, clears the mists from her eyes,
dispelling the clouds spread across her brow and hailing you as
both son and father. Whatever it is that you are doing, in whatever
land your glory shines in lofty majesty, if care for me has not yet   340
slipped utterly away from you, if any trace remains of your former
regard for me, if I suffer worse than my good deeds deserve, by the
stars of heaven, by the indulgent gods above, by our hopes for my
flourishing pupil,[22] and by your own triumphs, I beseech you: take
pity on these great pains of mine, drive this wild malady from my   345
heart, and by your presence restore me to myself, sustain my failing life and with your blessed visage bring back my lost health.
The arbiter of the gods himself, who shakes the world with thunder, by whom the heaven, earth, sea and sky are made to tremble,
who governs day and night, rotating the stars in motions opposite   350
to each other, who calls birds, humans, beasts, and creatures of the
sea into the divine borders of light, all powerful and governing all
things filled with his godhead, if by chance the melancholy voice   355
of one man reaches his busy ears, a man who publicly offers sweet
prayers and calls upon Jupiter's aid, the troubles of the universe
and the world's vicissitudes do not prevent him from attending to
his suppliants and gently indulging their prayers.

: I :

Laurentio Medici mecenati suo[1]

Sum tuus, O Medices; fateor, tuque ipse fateris:
    Sum tuus usque; tui sit tibi cura, precor.
Heu pereo! Heu lacerant gemini mea corda leones!
    Eripe me a rabidis, spes mea sola, feris.

: II :

Angeli Politiani ad Laurentium Medicem Petri Francisci
Filium hendecasyllabi[2]

Quaeris quid mihi de tuo Marullo,
Laurenti, videatur? Est poeta
Unus qui referat suum Catullum,
Aut si quid tenerum magis Catullo est.
5   Nil argutius elegantiusque
Isto quem tibi dedicat libello.
Nec tot prata coloribus novum ver
Pingit, lassula cum reversa hirundo,
Quam carmen varium tui Marulli est:
10 Cuius delicias, facetiasque,
Lusus, nequitias, sales, lepores
Nuper Roma legens superba, dixit:
Quo iam se mihi comparent Athenae?

ADDITIONAL POEMS

: I :

For Lorenzo de' Medici, his patron

I am yours, Medici. I declare it, and you declare it yourself. I am yours utterly: take care of your own, I pray. Alas, I am lost! Alas, twin lions tear at my heart![1] O my one and only hope, save me from the raging beasts!

: II :

Hendecasyllabics addressed to Lorenzo de' Medici,
son of Pierfrancesco[2]

You ask me, Lorenzo, what I think about your friend, Marullus?[3] He is a poet, the only one who reminds us of his favorite, Catullus, or if there could be anything more refined than Catullus. There is nothing more clever or elegant than that little book he 5 dedicates to you. The start of spring, when the tired little swallow has returned, does not paint the meadows with as many colors as mark the poetry of your friend Marullus. Its delights and cle- 10 verness, playfulness, naughtiness, wit, and charm recently provoked Rome to say proudly as she read it, "How could Athens compare herself to me now?"

: III :

Idem ad eundem

Quod plane Venerem tuus Marullus,
Laurenti, referat novo libello,
Miraris, video, rogasque causam.
Scis ut bella gerat colatque Martem:
5   Mars ergo Venerem suo clienti
Ostendit modo, quam statim Marullus
Pictam rettulit in novo libello.

: IV :

Iulio Medici[3]

A te deceptam, Iuli crudelis, amantem
    Dispeream, versu dicere ni cupio!
Temptantem revocat fallacis cura puellae,
    Quae me, quae pactam fallit acerba fidem.
5   Deceptam atque tuam cupio celebrare puellam,
    Fallentem atque meam flectere discupio.

: III :

The same author to the same man

Your friend Marullus is clearly representing Venus in his new little
book, Lorenzo, a fact that surprises you and so you ask the cause.
You know how he wages war and cultivates Mars: so Mars has just   5
shown Venus to his client, and Marullus wasted no time in relating a portrait of her in his new little book.

: IV :

For Giuliano de' Medici[4]

Damned if I don't desire to tell in verse of the lover who was deceived by you, cruel Giuliano! Whenever I try, I am recalled from
the effort by my love for an unfaithful girl, who cheated on me and
cruelly broke her promised pledge. Your girl who was cheated I   5
long to celebrate, my girl who cheats I desperately want to win
over.

: V :

In Chrysocomum Angeli Politiani

Aspicis ut fulvo radiat coma pressa galero,
    Ut nitido Phoebi sidere pura micat.
Tam bene Callaicis liquidum fornacibus aurum,
    Tam bene nec fusis fulget Apollo comis.
5 Sed quid ago? En crinem[4] penitus vultumque retexit
    Chrysocomus, iam non invidet hora mihi.
O ego ter felix! ergo haec [. . . .][5] mihi fas est
    Cernere! Sunt, sunt haec sidera non oculi.
Nil me fallis, Amor; clausum hoc te lumine cerno
10   Inicere arcanas in mea corda faces.

: VI :

In eundem, ad Maronem Vergilium

Mitteris ad puerum nostri, Maro, pignus amoris.
    Videris hunc, dices: 'Noster Alexi, vale!'
Viderit hunc tecum, supplex clamabit Alexis,
    'Do tibi me, Corydon; da mihi Chrysocomum!'

: V :

On Goldenlocks⁵ by Angelo Poliziano

You see how his hair gleams beneath his yellow cap, how purely it
glistens in the bright light of Phoebus. Liquid gold from the forges
of Galicia does not shine so well; Apollo does not shine so well
when he lets down his hair. But what am I to do? Look, Golden- 5
locks has completely uncovered his hair and face—now time isn't
jealous of me. Oh, I am triply happy! Now then I have the privi-
lege to see this! These are stars, not mere eyes. You don't fool me,
Love, I see that it's you who are enclosed in that eye, tossing your 10
secret torches into my heart.

: VI :

On the same person, addressed to Vergil⁶

You are being sent to the boy as a token of my love, Vergil. When
you see him, you are to say, "Farewell, my Alexis." When he sees
him with you, Alexis will cry out submissively, "Corydon, I give
myself to you, but give me Goldenlocks."

: VII :

In Iudaeum qui ferro petiit statuam Virginis orti Sancti Michaelis Angeli Politiani

Hanc ferro effigiem petiit Iudaeus, et index
    Ipse sui vulgo dilaniatus obit.

: VIII :

Angeli Politiani in Gallam meretricem[6]

Dum futuo Gallam nexisque amplexibus haerent
    Inguina, dum quatitur sollicitata Venus,
Nescio quid medias sensi mihi lambere pugas,
    Nec mora, succusso dissilui femore.
5 Inspicio cunnum: cunno intestina fluebant.
    Extabat cunni margine coliculus,
Qualis farta rubet teneris lucanica ofellis,
    Continuoque amens mentula facta mea est.
Mercedem poscis? Mercedem, Galla, reposco;
10   Nam pedicasti, Galla, ego non futui.

⁝ VII ⁝

On a Jew, who used a knife to attack a statue of the Virgin in Orsanmichele, by Angelo Poliziano

A Jew attacked this portrait with a knife, then turned witness against himself and perished, torn to pieces by the mob.

⁝ VIII ⁝

By Angelo Poliziano on Galla, the prostitute

While I was fucking Galla and our loins were locked together in clinging embraces, while Venus was aroused and quivering, I felt something licking the middle of my ass, and immediately I leaped away, shaking my thigh. I inspect her cunt: her cunt was all moist 5
inside. From the edge of her cunt the clit was standing out, all red like a sausage stuffed with tender bits of meat, and my cock immediately went crazy. You ask for payment? Galla, I demand payment in return: for you buggered me, Galla, I didn't fuck you. 10

: IX :

In Antonium de Organis⁷

Iure novas talem, Florentia, marmore civem;
    Namque diu templi vox fuit ille tui,
Doctus inaequales digitis et flamine cannas
    In vix credendos paene animare modos.
5 Quae non diverso gens huc properabat ab orbe,
    Ut biberet dulcem carminis aure sonum!
Sed licet is numeros omnes impleverit artis,
    Sola tamen summum gratia rara facit.

: X :

Aliud⁸

Pictorem genuit celebrem Florentia Ioctum,
    Quo melior toto nullus in orbe fuit.
Quem si laudati vidissent tempora Apellis,
    Gloria pictoris non minor huius erat.
5 Solus hic ante omnes pictura floruit, a quo
    Posset Alexander pingier ora pati.
Quin etiam magni turris celeberrima templi,
    Aera ubi sacra sonant, hoc duce celsa manet.

: IX :

On Antonio degli Organi[7]

It is right that you should renew such a citizen as this in marble, Florence, since he was for long the voice of your temple, skilled in using his fingers to breath life into pipes of different length to produce tones of unbelievable quality. What nation did not hurry   5 here from every distant part of the world to drink in with their ears the sweet sound of his song! But though he has mastered every measure of his art, his rare grace by itself makes him the best.

: X :

Another one[8] [To Giotto the painter]

Florence gave birth to the celebrated painter Giotto, who had no peer in all the world. If the age of the celebrated Apelles[9] had seen him, the glory of this painter would not have been less. He alone   5 above all flourished in the art of painting, the only one by whom Alexander could allow his likeness to be painted. And furthermore the very famous tower of the great cathedral, where the sacred bells sound, remains aloft under his guidance.

: XI :

Aliud

Ioctus vivacis picturae lumen et auctor
    His saeclis fulsit: patria grata valet.
Vicit Apelleas artes et signa Lysippi,
    Mors illum: vivit gloria, fama, decus.
5 Extruxit turrim quam cernis marmore claram.
    Mirae operum laudes urbis et orbis erunt.

: XII :

Aliud

Daedalea quam sit Ioctus celeberrimus arte
    Marmoreae haec testis fabrica turris erit.
Primus et extinctum picturae Ioctus honorem
    Restituit tabulis, qualis Apellis erat.
5 Neve ingrata foret, posuit memorabile bustum
    Posteritas, quamquam cuncta per ora volat.

: XI :

Another

Giotto shone upon this age, the glorious founder of the art of life-
like painting, to the profound gratitude of his nation. He bettered
Apelles' works and the sculptures of Lysippus,[10] but death got the
better of him, though his glory, fame and grace live on. He built   5
that bright marble tower that you behold. The city and the world
will be filled with admiring praise of his works.

: XII :

Another

That Giotto was most celebrated in the craft of Daedalus[11] the
building of this marble tower will attest. And Giotto was the first
to restore its vanished honor to painting's canvas, such as Apelles'
had been. And that she might not appear ungrateful, Posterity   5
erected this bust in his memory, although his name is on all the
world's lips.[12]

: XIII :

Aliud

Quis fuerit Ioctus picturae gloria cunctis
    Ostendit, nulli qua fuit arte minor.
Huius et inventum mirandae haec fabrica turris;
    Plura quoque ingenii sunt monumenta sui.
5 Grata igitur posuit celebri Florentia templo
    Hoc bustum, quamquam cuncta per ora volat.

: XIV :

Aliud

Qui decus extinctum picturae reddidit orbi,
    Phidiacas potuit qui superare manus,
Cuius opus Romae, variis compacta lapillis,
    Pontificis primi stat ratis ante fores,
5 Qui, prope quam cernis turrim, miracula Memphim
    Et tua te vetuit marmora, Roma, loqui,
Hoc tumulo patrio requiescit munere Ioctus.
    Cetera si cupias nosse, loquetur opus.

: XIII :

Another

The glory of his painting shows to all who Giotto was. In that art
he was second to none. The construction of this wonderful tower
was his invention, too. And there are more monuments to his genius. And so a grateful Florence set up this bust in her celebrated   5
cathedral, although his name is on all the world's lips.

: XIV :

Another

The man who restored the vanished glory of painting to the world,
who could surpass the skilled hands of Phidias,[13] whose work,
compacted of variegated stones,[14] stands before the doors of the
Pope in Rome, who stopped Memphis from boasting of its mar-   5
vels or Rome of her marbles next to this tower that you see, rests
in this tomb by the gift of his nation, Giotto. If you want to know
the rest, his work will speak for him.

: XV :

Epigramma[9] Ad Mulum qui puellam rus devehet

O mule noster, mule quem puto nostrum
Sat esse, quando te utimur velut nostro,
Sed sive noster, mule, sive non noster,
Hunc mihi tamen laborem operamque da, sodes.
5 Meam puellam cum vehes, vehito molli
Tergo gradatim, aut, si volet ipsa, tolutim:
Succusor etenim mulus haud vehit, vexat.
Et si iubebit te ire, mule, subsultim,
Ut est proterva et ludibunda, haec cursim
10 Cave cave faxis; cave tibi quae dico.
Quod si te aget calcaribus flagellisque,
Tamen gradatim perge vel ire tolutim;
Neu tu obstinatus contumaxque cervicem
Intende, neu renitere, neu quassa caput,
15 Neu calce nisi virum feri atque rivalem
Sed sic ut ipsa nec cadat neque se lasset.
Nam si cadet puella sive erit lassa,
Tu, mule, poenas tu dabis, mihi crede.
Memento haec, si me amas, beneque mi velis.

: XVI :

Disticon ad quandam puellae pulcherrimae imaginem[10]

Vidit ut hanc Livor faciem: 'Si carpere non est
Hanc,' ait, 'at fas est carpere ab hac venerem.'

: XV :

An epigram addressed to the mule that will carry
his girlfriend to the country

O mule of mine, mule whom I think of as pretty much belonging
to me, since I use you as my own, but, whether you are mine or
not, mule, please grant me this strenuous service anyway. When 5
you are carrying my girl, see that you carry her gently on your back
at a walk, or, if she wants, a trot: for a jittery mule isn't transport,
it's torment. And, mule, if she orders you to prance, playful and
reckless as she is, don't you dare do this at a gallop, just don't: 10
mind what I say to you. But if she eggs you on with spurs and
whips, you must still go at walk or a trot. And don't be stubborn
and disobediently strain your neck, or struggle against her, or
shake your head, or use your hoof to strike someone unless it be 15
her husband and my rival, but do it in such a way that she doesn't
fall off or wear herself out. For if my girl falls off or is worn out,
you, mule, will pay the penalty, trust me. Remember these things,
if you love me, and do wish me well.

: XVI :

A couplet on a certain painting of a very beautiful girl

When Envy saw this face, he said, "Since it's not possible to get *at*
her, at least it's fair to get sex *from* her."[15]

293

: XVII :

De agello[11]

Non ager hic oleae, non frugum aut fertilis uvae:
    Sola fames in eo nascitur atque sitis.
Diceret hunc cernens tam parvum Epicurus: 'Origo est
    Ex agris, non, ut credideram, ex atomis!'

: XVIII :

Angeli Politiani ad Dinobram[12]

Concubitum, Dinobra, tuum cum nuper adirem,
    Et staret cupido mentula tenta mihi,
Iam resupina toro, iam cunno ad bella parato,
    Mercedem Veneris grandia dona petis.
5 Mens dare suadebat, sed mentula sanior illa
    Demisso vultu protinus obstupuit.
Tu tamen hanc frustra palpas, sed languida perstat,
    Quodque petas curat mentula, non quod agas.
Quam nunc esse tibi dicam, mea mentula, mentem,
10   Quae bene, vel cum mens desipit, ipsa sapis?

: XVII :

On his little farm

This farm doesn't produce olives, or fruits or grapes: only hunger and thirst sprout in it. If Epicurus were to see it, so small as it is, he would say, "Creation comes from farms, not, as I had thought, from atoms!"

: XVIII :

By Angelo Poliziano to Dinobra

Recently, when I was about to have sex with you, Dinobra, and my cock stood stiff, eager as I was, while you were already lying on the bed, your cunt already primed for battle, you asked for some great gifts as payment for sex. My mind was in favor of paying, but my 5 cock was smarter than it and immediately dropped its head in as-tonishment. You, however, stroke it in vain, but it remains limp, and my cock is only concerned with what you're asking, not with what you're doing. How shall I characterize your state of mind, my cock, since you're pretty smart on your own, even when my 10 actual mind is deranged?

: XIX :

Culex[13]

Non sum femina, Scala, nec Latinis
Nec Graecis: ideo placet puella.

: XX :

In Salviatum[14]

'Quid tam, furca, doles, laqueus cum gestiat?' 'Heu, heu,
    Salviatum eripuit celsa fenestra meum.'

: XXI :

In eundem

Salviatus mitrae sceleratus honore superbit,
    Et quemquam caelo credimus esse Deum?
Scilicet hoc[15] scelera, hoc artes meruere nefandae?
    At laqueo en pendet. Estis, io, superi!

: XIX :

The mosquito[16]

I am not feminine, Scala, not for speakers of Latin or Greek: that's why I like girls.

: XX :

On Salviati[17]

Why do you mourn so, Sir Gallows, while the noose exults? "Alas, alack, the high window has snatched away my Salviati!"

: XXI :

On the same man

The criminal Salviati preens himself on the dignity of the miter, and still we are to believe that there is any god in heaven? Apparently this is what his crimes, his nefarious arts have earned him? But, look, he's hanging from the noose! Hurray! You gods do exist!

: XXII :

In eundem

Et laqueum et gestans rutilum Fortuna galerum,
  'Utrum,' inquit, 'mavis, accipe, Salviate.'
Respondit: 'Sat mitra caput decet. Ipsa, quid inde
  Conveniat collo, tu quoque caeca vides.'

: XXIII :

Ad Laurentium commendat praeceptorem
Andronicum Angelus Politianus[16]

Ipse canenda geris, Laurens, nos gesta canemus;
  Ei mihi, sed nostro est parvus in ore sonus!
Exsuperat teneras, Medices, tua gloria vires,
  Nostraque materiam carmine Musa premit.
5 At tenerae crescent vires crescentibus annis,
  Exiguusque meo crescet in ore sonus.
Tum liceat nomen fama tibi ferre per aevum
  Et tua non humili gesta sonare tuba.
Tu tantum Andronicum serves! O quantus ab illo
10 Spiritus in nostri pectoris ima venit!
O quos ille tibi gignit nutritque poetas,
  Dum tonat Argolicis Troica bella modis!
Iam tibi Aristotelem vertit, penitusque retrusas
  Naturae arcano concinit ore vices.
15 Unica materies illi es, spes unica solus;
  Una illi vitam tu dare voce potes.
Parva petit, dare magna soles; da parva petenti:
  Parva tamen nescis si dare, magna dato.

298

∶ XXII ∶

On the same man

Carrying both a noose and a red cap, Fortune said, "Take which-
ever one you would prefer, Salviati." His reply: "The miter suits
my head well enough. What then fits my neck, you will yourself
also see, blind though you are."

∶ XXIII ∶

Angelo Poliziano commends his teacher
Andronicus[18] to Lorenzo

You perform deeds worthy of song, Lorenzo, and I shall sing of
those deeds; but, alas, the sound upon my lips is small! Your glory,
Medici, exceeds my feeble powers, and my Muse shrinks the subject matter in her song. But my feeble powers shall grow with in-   5
creasing years, and the tiny sound upon my lips shall grow too.
Then I might be able to carry your name in fame through the ages
and herald your deeds on a trumpet no longer humble. Only take
care of Andronicus in the meantime! Oh, what inspiration comes   10
from him into the very depths of my heart! Oh, what poets he
brings into the world and nurtures for you, while he intones the
Trojan War in Greek measures![19] Now he is translating Aristotle
for you, harmonizing the deep-hidden condition of Nature upon
his arcane lips.[20] You are his only means of subsistence, you alone   15
his singular hope; you have the power to grant him a livelihood
with but one word. He asks for little, you usually give much; give
him the little he asks for: but if you don't know how to give just a
little, give him a lot.

: XXIV :

Angeli Politiani ad amicum suum[17]

Omnia non semper possunt cognoscere vates,
    Semper et humanum non viget ingenium.
Ut semper tenerae non lucent cornua lunae,
    Nec Phoebus semper mergit in amne rotas;
5 Spicea sic aestas toto non volvitur anno,
    Nec durant pratis arboribusque comae,
Semper et Herculei non urunt terga leonis,
    Cynthius aurata nec sonat usque lyra.
Quis me compulerit pueriles scribere versus
10   Ignotum est, video, culte poeta, tibi.
Credis ut Aonio tecum concurrere gyro
    Ipse velim et vatem vincere carminibus?
Accipe quid contra dicam tibi, docte Ioannes,
    Curque seni ignarus scribere non timui.
15 Iam sol Tyndaridas geminos lustrare quadrigis
    Coeperat, ut tepidum iam promovere diem,
Cum somnus dulci solvit mea membra sopore,
    Curarum domitrix pressit et alta quies.
Ecce ego conspicio venientes ordine Musas!
20   Aut fuit, aut vacuae somnia mentis erant.
Quaeque suos vario velarat flore capillos,
    Cuiusque in manibus laurea virga fuit.
Ut primum thalami tetigerunt limina nostri,
    Lucida ab aethereo est lumine facta domus.
25 Hic dea, Pieridas inter pulcherrima cunctas,
    Incepit roseo sic prior ore loqui:
'Surge, age, Phoebaeos qui vis cognoscere vates,
    Ut tua Gorgoneis ora rigentur aquis.

: XXIV :

By Angelo Poliziano to his friend[21]

Poets cannot always know everything, and the human intellect does not thrive all the time. Just as the horns of the young moon do not shine forever, nor does Phoebus dip his wheels in the stream forever, so too the summer harvest does not roll along the   5 whole year, nor does the foliage last in the meadows and forests, nor does the hide of Hercules' lion roast us forever,[22] nor does the Cynthian[23] forever play upon his gilded lyre. Who it was that compelled me to scribble childish verses is unknown to you, I see,   10 my learned poet. Do you believe that I would willingly compete with you on the Aonian circuit and defeat a true poet with poetry? My learned friend Giovanni, listen to what I have to say to you in response and hear why in my ignorance I was not afraid to write to an old man. The sun in his chariot had just begun to begun to   15 illuminate the twin scions of Tyndarus[24] as they advanced the warmth of the day, when sleep dissolved my limbs in sweet slumber and a profound peace conquered my cares and overwhelmed me. Look, I see the Muses approaching in single file! Either it   20 happened, or they were the dream visions of my idle mind. Each one had veiled her hair with colorful flowers, and a laurel branch was in the hands of each. When first they touched the threshold of my bed chamber, the house was made bright with an ethereal light. At this point the goddess who was the most beautiful among   25 all the Pierides,[25] began to speak first from her rosy lips as follows: "Arise, come, you who wish to know Phoebus' bards, that your lips may be sprinkled with the Gorgon's waters.[26] Go, walk swiftly and

I, Geminiani celeri pete moenia passu,
30   Moenia quae multum Cynthius ipse colit.
Hic vates viridi redimitus tempora lauro
     Ad Phoebum poterit praevius esse tibi.'
Dixit, et ex oculis cunctae fugere sorores,
     Et mea destituit lumina somnus iners.
35 Scis nunc cur numeros misi tibi, docte poeta?
     Ut tangam sacri, te duce, fontis aquas.

: XXV :

Angelus Politianus Alexandro Braccio salutem

Qualis prisca fuit Mimnermi Musa poetae,
     Antimachus quales edidit ore modos;
Et Cyrenaei sunt qualia carmina vatis,
     Qualia vel nostris Umbria culta dedit;
5 Aut quales cecinit facundo pectore versus
     Ingenium cuius Delia pulchra fuit,
Vel sua crudeli qui fodit viscera ferro,
     Quique procul Getico pulsus in orbe canit;
Talia dulcisono modularis carmina plectro,
10   O animae, Bracci, portio magna meae.
Quare, age, si quis erit nigro qui dente lacessat
     Bassum, liventes iniciatque manus,
Ipse tuo fortem clipeum protende sodali.
     Sic faveat semper turba novena tibi,
15 Praebeat et solitum cantus Elegia tenorem,
     Et dominam placida flectere voce queas.

seek out the walls of San Gimignano, the walls that the Cynthian   30
himself highly esteems. Here is a poet, his brows encircled with
verdant laurel, who will be able to lead you to Phoebus." She finished speaking and all the sisters fled from my sight, and restful
sleep abandoned my eyes. Now do you know why I sent my verses   35
to you, learned poet? That I might touch the waters of the sacred
fount with you as my guide.

: XXV :

Angelo Poliziano to Alessandro Braccesi, greetings[27]

Like the ancient Muse of the poet Mimnermus, like the measures
Antimachus produced; and like the songs of the bard of Cyrene or
the ones that cultured Umbria gave us; or like the verses sung by   5
the eloquent heart of he whose inspiration was the beautiful Delia;
or like the one who pierced his own flesh with cruel steel, and the
one who sings in exile far away in the land of the Getae;[28] such are
the songs that you compose upon your sweet-sounding lyre, O   10
Braccesi, the greater part of my soul. Therefore, come, if there be
any who assail Bassus with the tooth of envy and attempt to lay
their jealous hands upon him, and extend your mighty shield to
shelter your friend. Thus may the gang of nine[29] always favor you!
And may Elegy offer you her familiar strain of song, and may you   15
be able to sway your mistress with your pleasing voice.

: XXVI :

Iuveni eruditissimo Thomaso Baldinotto
Angelus Politianus salutem

Si quisquam Hippotaden Boreamque Eurumque prementem[18]
    Flexit Hyantei carminis eloquio,
Aut si floriferae Cyclopa e montibus Hyblae
    Sirenes solitae ducere carminibus,
5 Nempe adamantaeo fuerit si pectore, vel si
    Saxum habeat, vel si ferrea corda gerat,
Saeva Medusaeis videat si colla colubris,
    Qualia Cepheni, qualia vidit Atlas,
Audiat hic si fors tua, dulcis, carmina, Thoma,
10   Optet ab Aegeis currere verticibus,
Optet anhelanti caelum transmittere penna,
    Optet ab extremis currere Gangaridis.
Multos fama trahit, multos tua carmina, quosdam
    Natura aethereo mitis amore trahit.
15 A, ego quantum ausim, liceat si forte sonantis
    Aonio cantus spargere monte chelys!
Non Zetes Calaisque leves, non callidus Argi
    Victor, non Danaes filius aurigena,
Non aurae aut volucres superent. Pro tristia fata!
20   Sic sors mortales imperiosa domat!
Tu tamen Argolicum dum carmine tollis Homerum,
    Quam merito vati munera digna refers!
Perge igitur; mox laurigero sublimior oestro,
    Aggredere Aonia fortia bella tuba.
25 Iamque vale, et nostrum serva sub pectore amorem,
    Ut Capitolino prisca Camena Iovi.

: XXVI :

Angelo Poliziano to Tommaso Baldinotti,[30]
a most learned young man, greetings

If in fact anyone ever swayed Hippotes' son, who restrains both
Boreas and Eurus, with the power of the Muses' song,[31] or if the
Sirens used their songs to draw the Cyclops out of flowery Mt.
Hybla,[32] then beyond question, even if someone has a heart of   5
steel, or of stone, or a soul made out of iron, if he should look
upon Medusa's savage neck of serpents, as the Ethiopians and Atlas did,[33] if by chance this person should hear your sweet poems,
Tommaso, he would wish that he could run here from the eddies   10
of the Aegean, he would wish that he could cross the sky on beat-
ing wings, he would wish that he could hurry from the remotest
Ganges. Many are drawn by fame, many by your songs, some are
drawn by the ethereal love of gentle Nature. Ah, how bold I   15
would be if only my lyre could scatter a ringing song from the
Aonian mount. Neither Zethus nor Calais, both light on the
breezes, nor the clever victor over Argus, nor the golden-born son
of Danaë, nor the winds nor the birds would outstrip it.[34] But, oh,
the fates are bitter! Thus does an imperious destiny tame us mor-   20
tals! And yet, as you extol the Greek poet Homer in song, how
justly you repay that bard with worthy gifts! Continue then, and
next, lifted higher by the spur of winning laurels, begin to tell of
valiant wars on the Aonian trumpet. And now, farewell, and pre-   25
serve your love for me in your heart, like the Muse of old for
Capitoline Jupiter.

: XXVII :

In principio studii de vita Ovidii[19]

Ei[20] iacet Euxinis vates Romanus in oris,
    Romanum vatem barbara terra tegit!
Terra tegit vatem teneros qui lusit amores
    Barbara, quam gelidis alluit Hister aquis.
5 Nec te, Roma, pudet, quae tanto immitis alumno
    Pectora habes ipsis barbariora Getis?
Ecquis, io Musae, Scythicis in finibus aegro
    Taedia qui morbi demeret, ullus erat?
Ecquis frigidulos qui lecto imponeret artus,
10   Aut qui dulciloquo falleret ore diem?
Aut qui temptaret salientis tempora venae,
    Aut fomenta manu qui properata daret,
Conderet aut oculos media iam morte natantes,
    Aut legeret summam qui pius ore animam?
15 Nullus erat, nullus: veteres tu dura sodales,
    Heu, procul a Ponto, Martia Roma, tenes!
Nullus erat: procul, a, coniunx parvique nepotes,
    Nec fueras profugum, nata, secuta patrem!
Scilicet immanes Bessi, flavique Coralli,
20   Aut vos pelliti saxea corda Getae,
Scilicet horribili dederit solamina vultu
    Sarmata ab epoto saepe vehendus equo,
Sarmata cui rigidam demisso in lumina frontem
    Mota pruinoso tempora crine sonant.
25 Sed tamen et Bessi extinctum et flevere Coralli,
    Sarmataque et durus contudit ora Getes.
Extinctum et montes flebant silvaeque feraeque,
    Et flesse in mediis dicitur Ister aquis.

: XXVII :

At the start of his studies on the life of Ovid

Alas, the Roman poet lies dead on the shores of the Black Sea, a
barbarian land covers the Roman poet! A barbarian land, which
the Danube washes with her cold waters, covers the poet who
wrote light verse about tender passions. And yet, Rome, are you   5
not ashamed that by such cruelty to so great a son you have a
heart more barbarous than the Getae themselves?[35] O Muses, was
there not anyone at all in the land of the Scythians to release the
poor man from this wearying malady? Was there no one to lay his
frail cold limbs upon the couch or to while away the day with   10
agreeable conversation? Or to feel the pulse of his throbbing ar-
tery, or speedily to apply a poultice by hand, or to close his eyes
just at that moment when they wavered upon the point of death,
or out of piety to gather in his mouth his last breath? No one,   15
there was no one: alas, Rome, Mars' city, it is cruel for you to keep
his companions of old far from the Black Sea! There was no one:
ah, his wife and little grandchildren were far away, nor had you,
his daughter, followed your father into exile, child! I suppose that
the savage Bessi were there, the blond-haired Coralli, or you hard-   20
hearted Getae dressed in skins; I suppose that consolation was
offered by the grim-faced Sarmatian, who often had to be carried
by the horse he drank from, the Sarmatian, who lowered his stern
brow to his eyes while his forehead rattled when stirred by his
frozen hair. But still, even the Bessi wept at his death, the Coralli   25
too, and the Sarmatian and the hard-hearted Getae bruised their
cheeks. The mountains wept at his death, and the forests and the
beasts, and it is said that the Danube wept in midstream. Indeed,

307

Quin etiam pigro concretum frigore Pontum
30   Nereidum lacrimis intepuisse ferunt.
Accurrere leves Paphia cum matre volucres,
     Arsuroque faces supposuere rogo.
Quem simul absumpsit rapidae violentia flammae,
     Reliquias tecto composuere cado,
35   Impositumque brevi signarunt nomine saxum:
     'Qui iacet hic teneri doctor Amoris erat.'
Ipsa locum late sancto Cytherea liquore
     Irrorat nivea terque quaterque manu.
Vos quoque, Pierides, vati libastis adempto
40   Carmina, sed nostro non referenda sono.

꞉ XXVIII ꞉

Ad Horatium Flaccum Ode[21]

Vates Threicio blandior Orpheo,
Seu malis fidibus sistere lubricos
Amnis, seu tremulo ducere pollice
     Ipsis cum latebris feras;

5 Vates Aeolii pectinis arbiter,
Qui princeps Latiam sollicitas chelyn,
Nec segnis titulos addere noxiis
     Nigro carmine frontibus;

Quis te a barbarica compede vindicat?
10 Quis frontis nebulam dispulit, et situ
Deterso levibus restituit choris
     Curata iuvenem cute?

they say that even the Black Sea, which was frozen solid by the
slow-moving cold, grew warm with the tears of the Nereids. Light-   30
winged Cupids rushed to him with their Paphian mother and lay
their torches under the pyre to cremate him. And when the force
of devouring flame had consumed him, they composed his remains in a covered urn. They set a stone upon it which they   35
marked with a brief inscription: "He who lies here was once tender Love's professor." With her snow-white hand, the goddess of
Cythera herself sprinkled the spot, three times, four times with
holy water. You too, maidens of Pieria, performed libations of
song for your dead poet, but of a kind that cannot be repeated in   40
my voice.

: XXVIII :

An Ode to Horace

Poet more seductive than Thrace's Orpheus, whether you choose
to stop the flowing rivers with your lyre, or with your tremulous
thumb to lead the beasts along with their very lairs; poet, arbiter   5
of the Aeolian song, you who were the first to stir the Latin
lyre, and were not remiss in using dark verse to pin labels to
guilty brows;[36] who is it that frees you from the barbarian's
shackles? Who is it that dispels the cloud from your brow, and   10
wipes away the dust to restore you to the light-footed choruses in

O quam nuper eras nubilus et malo
Obductus senio! Quam nitidos ades
15 Nunc vultus referens, docta fragrantibus
        Cinctus tempora floribus!

Talem purpureis reddere solibus
Laetum pube nova, post gelidas nives,
Serpentem, positis exuviis solet
20   Verni temperies poli.

Talem te choreis reddidit et lyrae
Landinus veterum laudibus aemulus,
Qualis tu solitus Tibur ad uvidum
        Blandam tendere barbiton.

25 Nunc te deliciis nunc decet et levi
Lascivire ioco; nunc puerilibus
Insertum thyasis aut fide garrula
        Inter ludere virgines.

: XXIX :

*In Ioannem Picum comitem Mirandulanum*²²

Dulcis Nobilitas, pudens Iuventus,
Maiestas hilaris, decora Virtus,
Mores, Gratia, Forma, Musa, Candor,
Qui qua sint facie requirit, unum
5 Picum si videat, videbit omnes.

well-trimmed, youthful vigor? O how recently it was that you were in shadow and covered with vile decay! Now you are here and how bright is the visage that you bring back, girding your 15 learned brow with fragrant flowers! You are like a serpent, which is regularly returned to the brilliant sunshine by the warmth of a spring sky, delighting in the freshness of youth, its old skin now shed after cold winter snows. Emulating the praises of the an- 20 cients, Landino has restored you to the choruses and the lyre just as you were when you used to play the soothing lute by the waters of Tivoli. Now it is finally fitting for you to indulge in pleasure and 25 lighthearted games; now it is fitting for you to join the young boys' revels or to play upon the garrulous lyre among the young girls.

: XXIX :

On Giovanni Pico, his friend from Mirandola

Sweet Nobility, modest Youth, cheerful Majesty, decorous Virtue, Character, Grace, Beauty, Poetry, Sincerity — anybody wanting to discover what they look like will see them all, if they look at Pico 5 alone.

: I :

Sic fluit occulte, sic multos decipit aetas,
    Sic venit ad finem quidquid in orbe manet.
Heu, heu, praeteritum non est revocabile tempus!
    Heu propius tacito mors venit ipsa pede!

: II :

Ab. Sacrum pingue dabo, non macrum sacrificabo.
    Ca. Sacrificabo macrum, non dabo pingue sacrum.

: III :

In viridi teneras exurit flamma medullas.

: IV :

In Ciccam fabrum[1]

Fabrum magister, Cicca, natus oppidis
Vel obsidendis vel tuendis, hic iacet.

DUBIA

: I :

Time flows so secretly, deceives so many, everything in the world comes to an end in this way. Alas, alas, time once passed cannot be recalled! Alas, death comes closer of its own accord on silent foot.[1]

: II :

Abel: I will give a rich sacrifice, I'll not make a meager one. Cain: I will make a meager sacrifice, I'll not give a rich one.[2]

: III :

In green wood the flame consumes the delicate marrow.[3]

: IV :

On Cecca the engineer[4]

The master of engineers, il Cecca, born for besieging or defending towns, lies here.

313

Note on the Text

❧❧❧

Poliziano published relatively little of his poetry in his lifetime: only the *Silvae* appeared in editions prepared by the author; a few other pieces circulated in print, and these only because they had been included in other works, such as the *Miscellanea*. But Poliziano was plainly in the process of remedying this deficit when death overtook him in late September of 1494, and then, only two months later, the French king Charles VIII entered Florence with his troops, putting an end to the Medici regime that had nurtured Poliziano's brand of humanism (see Introduction). In a letter to an absent Piero de' Medici sent earlier that year, Poliziano reported that he had completed his book of *Letters* and intended to see to their publication upon Piero's return.[1] That publication never happened, nor did any of the other projects that occupied Poliziano during the last months of his life.

A collection of his Latin epigrams was also in the works, as we learn from a letter that was eventually included in the publication of Poliziano's Latin correspondence. In the summer of 1494 Poliziano wrote to Antonio Zeno (about whom next to nothing is known) in response to his energetic requests for Poliziano's poetry (*Epist.* 7.14). He attached his youthful translation of the Ἔρως δραπέτης (*Love the Runaway*, *Epigr. Lat.* 132) of Moschus and also his own Latin elegy *In uiolas* (*Epigr. Lat.* 72), but he did not gratify all of Zeno's requests, who had apparently asked also for at least some of Poliziano's epigrams in Latin. For in the closing sentence of the letter, he adds, "I'm not sending you the epigrams, since I think they'll soon be published together with the Greek ones" (*epigrammata tibi non mitto, quod ea simul cum Graecis publicare statim cogito*). This plan was never brought to fruition by Poliziano, whose death came later in the autumn, before he was able to organize his Latin epigrams into a collection. That he was able to do so for his Greek epigrams we learn from a letter to Antonio Codro Urceo of the same summer (*Epist.* 5.7).[2] For the text of the Greek and Latin epigrams, the principal source

315

is the collected edition of his works, which appeared from the Venetian press of Aldus Manutius in July 1498.[3]

During the four years that intervened between Poliziano's death and the publication of the Aldine edition, many of his books and papers were dispersed, and we know little about how any of them were reassembled to provide the basis for that edition. In his preface to the collected edition, Manutius reports that it was Poliziano's friends, chiefly Alessandro Sarti, who had prepared his works for publication (*scito non esse haec edita ab ipso, sed ab amicis, et praecipue ab Alexandro Sartio Bononiensi, litteratis omnibus pergrato viro*). Among those other anonymous friends, scholars have included one of Poliziano's last and most devoted students, Pietro Crinito, who preserved many of his teacher's papers after his death.[4] But, as Manutius suspected, many of Poliziano's papers had been irretrievably dispersed, and did not form part of the edition that he published in 1498. The extent of Crinito's (or others') editorial interventions in the published works is contested by scholars, but for most of the Greek and Latin poetry contained in this edition, the Aldine provides our only evidence, however unsatisfactory, of Poliziano's intended publication.[5]

AN ELEGY FOR ALBIERA DEGLI ALBIZZI

The elegy was composed for the anthology of testimonials to the memory of Albiera degli Albizzi prepared by her intended husband, Sigismondo della Stufa (see Introduction). The collection is preserved in two manuscripts, which contain Poliziano's long poem along with his shorter epitaphs on the subject (*Epigr. Lat.* 41–46). One is an early copy by Tommaso Baldinotti, who had succeeded Poliziano as secretary to Sigismondo's father, Agnolo della Stufa, made before Poliziano had presented a corrected version for the anthology.[6] The other is the anthology as it was presumably meant to be distributed when Sigismondo dedicated the collection to Annalena Malatesta, who had founded the monastery of San Vincenzo, where Albiera had been educated.[7] Poliziano subsequently made corrections and alterations in his elegy, as is evident from the version that Crinito and Sarti included in the Aldine edition, presumably drawing on an autograph copy found among Poliziano's papers. These corrections perhaps reflected an intention to publish the poem separately, perhaps as part of his intended collection of Latin epigrams, but there is no way to ascertain that. Unless otherwise noted, the text presented here follows the editions of Francesco Bausi,[8] with some alterations of orthography and punctuation, and the elegy appears before the *Book of Epigrams* as it does in the original Aldine edition. The notes are also indebted to Bausi's edition.

THE BOOK OF EPIGRAMS

In the Aldine edition, the first of Poliziano's Latin epigrams is printed immediately following the last line of the *Elegy on Albiera*, with no indication of a change of title. The pages that follow bear the header *Liber Epigrammatum*. It is impossible to determine whether the collection of Latin poems transmitted under this title bears any resemblance to the publication intended by Poliziano himself. The titles provided in the Aldine all refer to him in the third person, one of several indications that the ordering is the work of his editors, although they surely relied on autograph copies found among Poliziano's papers. The text of this edition restores the order of the original collection in the Aldine, which was not followed in the only modern edition of the poems, by Isidore Del Lungo. In his edition of 1867, the Latin poems are disaggregated from the Aldine collection and rearranged in generic categories as epigrams, elegies, odes, hymns, and a prologue.[9] The poetic collection that Crinito and Sarti assembled more closely resembles earlier humanistic miscellanies, such as Giovanni Antonio Campano's (1429–77) book of epigrams, published as part of his collected works in 1495, or the book of epigrams by Poliziano's rival Michael Marullus, which was published in its first edition between 1483 and 1490.[10] This was the format in which Poliziano's works were disseminated and read in subsequent editions until the nineteenth century, and the restored order has at least the sanction of a long history of reception. But since most modern scholarship on Poliziano's epigrams refers to the Del Lungo edition, a concordance to the ordering of poems in that edition is provided at the end of this volume for the convenience of scholars.

Many of the Latin poems included by Crinito and Sarti in the *Book of Epigrams* are found in manuscripts copied by friends, associates, and students, but the Aldine edition remains the basis for any modern edition.[11] In most cases it is not possible to decide whether the text of the Aldine represents Poliziano's own corrections or intervention by the editors.[12] And given the circumstances of the publication of most humanist collections, the distinction is not of great importance to most readers. The text printed here is based on the Aldine, with the more significant corrections signaled in the accompanying notes. The text and notes of Del Lungo and modern studies, particularly those of Alessandro Perosa, have been consulted as well. Orthography and punctuation have been modernized.

THE BOOK OF GREEK EPIGRAMS

The Greek epigrams appear at the end of the Aldine edition and are the only poems that we can be certain have undergone the scrutiny of the author. As with the Latin poems in the *Book of Epigrams*, many of the Greek epigrams can be found in manuscripts of the fifteenth and sixteenth centuries,[13] but the assumption that the versions in the Aldine represent Poliziano's last thoughts is inescapable. In the preface to the collection by Poliziano's former student Zanobi Acciaiuoli, it is reported that the collection appears just as the author had left it. It is highly unlikely that Acciaiuoli abstained completely from the kind of silent editorial intervention that was characteristic of his contemporaries, but it is reasonable to accept that the text and the arrangement of the poems are as Poliziano would have had them. The text here follows that of Filippomaria Pontani (2002) unless otherwise noted, and my notes are indebted to his. Some punctuation has been modified.

TO BARTOLOMEO FONZIO

The long elegy addressed to Fonzio does not appear in the Aldine or any subsequent editions, nor is it transmitted in any manuscripts. The sole source for the text is a late sixteenth-century edition of the works of the Hungarian humanist Janus Pannonius (1434–72), to whom it was wrongly attributed by his editor, Johannes Sambucus.[14] It is likely that Sambucus acquired a manuscript of the elegy, now lost, during a visit to Florence in 1567, when he also retrieved works by Pannonius.[15] Poliziano's authorship was not recognized until two centuries later. The identification is confirmed by the coincidence of lines 27 to 52 of the elegy with a fragment attributed to Poliziano in a manuscript that once belonged to Tommaso Baldinotti.[16] The text presented here follows that of the two recent editions by Bausi, *Due poemetti* (2003) and *Poesie* (2006), with only minor changes in orthography and punctuation, unless otherwise noted.

A SILVA ON SCABIES

The poem survives in only one manuscript, which was discovered by the great Renaissance scholar Paul Oskar Kristeller in 1952 in the Biblioteca Governativa in Parma.[17] The text of this edition follows the first edition by Perosa (1954) with updated punctuation and orthography, unless otherwise noted.

ADDITIONAL POEMS AND DUBIA

The Aldine edition of 1498 omits a number of poems, several of which were surely available to its editors. They include poems of a pederastic (*Additional Poems* 5 and 6) or otherwise obscene nature (8 and 18), but also poems that praise Poliziano's bitter enemy Michael Marullus (2 and 3). And there is reason to believe that Crinito and Sarti deliberately edited out of their collection unflattering references to Marullus and others as well, which would not have set Poliziano in a favorable light with the new Republic of Florence or its patron, the king of France (Perosa, *Studi*, 1:44–45). A number of these poems were collected for his edition by Del Lungo, and several more were added by Alessandro Perosa in 1956.[18] They are included in this section. Except where otherwise noted, the text presented here in the main follows these printed editions, with some changes in punctuation and orthography. Further information on the manuscripts can be found in Maïer, *Les manuscrits d'Ange Politien*. The printed sources for these poems are as follows:

Additional Poems
1   Del Lungo, *Epigr. Lat.* 29
2   Del Lungo, *Epigr. Lat.* 30
3   Del Lungo, *Epigr. Lat.* 31

4   Del Lungo, *Epigr. Lat.* 56
5   Del Lungo, *Epigr. Lat.* 62
6   Del Lungo, *Epigr. Lat.* 63
7   Del Lungo, *Epigr. Lat.* III
8   Perosa, *Studi,* 1:52
9   Del Lungo, *Epigr. Lat.* 85
10   Del Lungo, *Epigr. Lat.* 87
11   Del Lungo, *Epigr. Lat.* 88
12   Del Lungo, *Epigr. Lat.* 89
13   Del Lungo, *Epigr. Lat.* 90
14   Del Lungo, *Epigr. Lat.* 91
15   Del Lungo, Appendix, Addenda 60b
16   Perosa, *Studi,* 1:31
17   Ibid.
18   Perosa, *Studi,* 1:49–50
19   Del Lungo, Appendix, Addenda 54b
20   *Coniurationis commentarium,* ed. Celati, 70
21   Ibid.
22   Ibid.
23   Del Lungo, *Elegiae* 1
24   Del Lungo, *Elegiae* 2
25   Del Lungo, *Elegiae* 3
26   Del Lungo, *Elegiae* 4
27   Del Lungo, *Elegiae* 13
28   Del Lungo, *Odae* 3
29   Perosa, *Sylva in scabiem,* p. 55

Dubia

1   Del Lungo, 102
2   Del Lungo, 103
3   Del Lungo, 104
4   Del Lungo, 168–69

NOTES

1. For the letter, dated May 23, 1494, see Del Lungo, 84–85.

2. Above, p. xvi.

3. Abbreviated in the notes as *Ald.* The preface to this edition may be found with an English translation in Manutius, *Humanism and the Latin Classics,* ed. Grant, 182–87.

4. On Crinito (Pietro del Riccio Baldi), see *DBI* 38 (1990), s.v.

5. On the genesis of the Aldine and its consequent impact on subsequent editions, see Perosa, "Contributi e proposte."

6. The manuscript is Rome, Biblioteca Corsiniana, MS 45 C 17.

7. The manuscript is Turin, Accademia delle Scienze, MS NN V 7, on which see Patetta, "Una raccolta manoscritta."

8. See Bausi's editions, *Due poemetti* (2003) and *Poesie* (2006); my account is indebted to his discussions of the transmission in the prefaces to both editions.

9. Del Lungo, xxiv–xxv. Perosa, "Studi sulla tradizione," 540, also believes that Crinito and Sarti found an essentially completed collection of epigrams compiled by Poliziano, into which they randomly inserted longer elegies, hymns, etc. Yet it hardly seems plausible that they would have taken such a casual approach to Poliziano's legacy.

10. Marullus' *Poems* were edited by Charles Fantazzi in this I Tatti Renaissance Library (2012).

11. For information on the manuscripts in which the Latin epigrams are transmitted, Maïer, *Les manuscripts d'Ange Politien*, is fundamental.

12. On this problem, see Perosa, "Studi sulla tradizione," 558–62.

13. For these manuscripts, see Pontani, xlix–lxx.

14. Ianus Pannonius, *Opera,* ed. Sambucus (1569), ff. xii^v–xvii^v.

15. See Perosa, "Studi sulla tradizione," 546.

16. Rome, Biblioteca Corsiniana, MS Cors. 582; see Picotti, "Tra il poeta e il lauro," 271, note 2.

17. MS Pal. 555; see the edition by Perosa (1954).

18. Perosa, "Studi sulla tradizione."

Notes to the Text

ॐ§?ॐ

AN ELEGY FOR ALBIERA DEGLI ALBIZZI

1. Either Poliziano mistakenly scanned the final syllable as short, or we may correct to *impetis*.

THE BOOK OF EPIGRAMS

1. aetati *Ald.*

2. asseruit *Ald.*

3. obstrusas *Ald., correxi.*

4. tuae *Ald.*

5. tibi *Ald.*

6. Eidem *Ald.* This suggests that at one point a different ordering of the epigrams had been contemplated, or that another epigram to Bembo has dropped out of the text, or that the poem was transcribed from a codex containing other poems about Bembo.

7. Timadem *Ald.*

8. Timades *Ald.*

9. esse *Ald., correxi.* In the text of Planudes' epigram, probably read ἵμεν.

10. The final short syllable is lengthened before the caesura, as it was occasionally in ancient elegiacs (e.g., Propertius 2.8.8) or hexameters (e.g., Vergil, *Eclogues* 3.97).

11. Either Poliziano has mistaken the quantity of the penultimate syllable or the text is corrupt.

12. horridus caprimulgus *Ald.*

13. mendicantum *Ald.*

14. Poliziano has made an error in scansion by treating the first syllable as long.

15. Lamia *Ald.*

16. Quicquid *Ald.*

17. Atque *Ald.*

18. Contrary to classical practice, Poliziano scans the first syllable as long here and at *Scab.* 296.

19. *post* 22 nigris sodalem muribus *Ald.*

20. dicam nivem cum purpura / fusam, rosam cum lilio *Riccardianus 771*

21. lucretio *Ald.*

22. This line is absent in *Ald.* and other editions; it is found only in Florence, Biblioteca Medicea Laurenziana, Plut. 90.39, of the sixteenth century.

23. Here, as well as in lines 22, 31, and 33, Poliziano breaks with classical norms by allowing a trochee in the third foot.

24. qui tuum *Ald., corr. Wilson*

25. fides *Ald.*

26. In *Ald.* the poem is followed by a performance note: 'Quis dabit *et cetera. Et repetitur usque ad versiculum* O dolor, dolor *et cetera.*'

27. Poliziano included this poem in a letter to Antonio Zeno (*Epist.* 7.14), describing it as a work of his youth that he had delayed sending because there were passages that he was dissatisfied with. It seems likely that the differences between the text of the letter and *Ald.* are due to Poliziano's second thoughts, so the text printed here follows that of the letter, with variants reported in the notes. See Pontani, xxiv.

28. simplex *Ald.*

29. at totam agnosce figuram *Ald.*

30. corpore non niueus *Ald.*

31. tum mens illi effera *Ald.*

32. more citans pinnas, nunc hos nunc aduolat illos *Ald.*

33. super *Ald.*

34. sed et ipsum Hyperiona vincit *Ald.*

35. *From line 27 Ald. reads* et oscula si fors / Ferre volet, fugito: sunt noxia et oscula in ipsis / Suntque venena labris.

36. Nequicquam attigeris *Ald.*

37. namque *Ald.*

THE BOOK OF GREEK EPIGRAMS

1. ἐπὶ *Ald., corr. Pontani ad loc.*

2. Πάν *Ald.*, against the meter, corrected by Lavagnini, as reported in Ardizzoni's 1951 edition

3. ποθ' *Ald., corr. Wilson*

4. opere *Ald.*

5. The version of the poem that is preserved in an autograph manuscript of Giano Lascaris (Vatican City, Biblioteca Apostolica Vaticana, Vat. Gr. 1412) probably represents a later revision by Alessandra or perhaps Lascaris. This text follows Pontani in reproducing the later version. Some of the more significant variants are cited below, *exempli gratia*.

6. Λυδίῃ *Ald.*

7. Ἀλκείδην καλέει σ' *Ald.*

8. ἐξείποι *Ald.*

9. τροχαλοῖς ἑτερότροπα *Epist.*

10. εἰρεσίους *Epist.*

11. 9–10 *om. Ald.*

TO BARTOLOMEO FONZIO

1. amoto *Ald. correxi.*

2. Lines 27 to 51 were excerpted in Rome, Biblioteca Corsiniana, MS Cors. 582, with the heading *Eiusdem Angeli* [sc. *Politiani*] *ad Laurentium Medicen* and printed by Del Lungo as *Elegia 8.*

3. Poliziano scans the name correctly at *Epigr.* 9.19, but treats the penultimate syllable as long here.

A SILVA ON SCABIES

1. futura *MS, corr. Wilson.*

2. Dactylotrocus *MS, correxi.*

ADDITIONAL POEMS

1. The only source for this epigram is Florence, Biblioteca Nazionale Centrale, MS Naz. II II 62 (formerly Magl. VII, 725).

2. The only source for this epigram and the following one is Florence, Biblioteca Riccardiana, MS 971.

3. The source for this and the following four epigrams is Florence, Biblioteca Medicea Laurenziana, Plut. 90 sup. 37.

4. crimen *MS*

5. *Perhaps supply* iterum.

6. See Florence, Biblioteca Medicea Laurenziana, Plut. 90 sup. 37 (Perosa, *Studi*, 1:13).

7. The principal witness to this epigram is Florence, Biblioteca Medicea Laurenziana, MS Mediceo-Palatini 87. See Del Lungo, 155–56, note.

8. The only witness to this and the following four epitaphs for Giotto is Florence, Biblioteca Nazionale Centrale, Autogr. Palat. II, 57. The title for *Epigr. Lat.* 130 above (= Del Lungo, *Epigr. Lat.* 86), also included in this MS, is *Epitaphium Jocti pictoris florentini;* hence each of the five epitaphs, introduced with the heading *Aliud,* "Another one," also refers to Giotto.

9. As published in Del Lungo, Addenda to the *Epigrammata Latina,* 60b (pp. 556–57). The source for this epigram is Florence, Biblioteca Nazionale Centrale, Magl. VII, 628 (see Perosa 2000, 1: 29). The meter is choliambic, like Catullus 44, of which there are several verbal echoes.

10. As published in Perosa, *Studi*, 1:31, from Oxford, Bodleian Library, MS Lat. Misc. C. 62.

11. As published in Perosa, *Studi*, from the same Bodleian MS.

12. The principal source for this epigram is Florence, Biblioteca Riccardiana 924; it was first published by Perosa, *Studi*, 1:49–50.

13. Poliziano includes this epigram in a letter (*Epist.* 12.8) to Bartolomeo Scala (see *Epigr. Gr.* 57) on the gender of the Latin noun *culex*.

14. These three epigrams were first published in the second redaction of Poliziano's *Coniurationis commentarium*, on the Pazzi conspiracy, in 1480 in Rome with the printer Johannes Bulle; the texts are also transmitted in another edition by Bulle, as well as in the 1553 Basel edition of Poliziano's works and in several manuscripts copied from the printed editions. See Celati, "La seconda redazione," 287. We thank Dr. Celati for supplying this information.

15. haec *Basel 1553*

16. Preserved in Florence, Biblioteca Medicea Laurenziana, Plut. 90 sup. 37.

17. This and the following two poems are transmitted in a manuscript that once belonged to Tommaso Baldinotti, now Rome, Biblioteca Corsiniana, MS Cors. 582.

18. prementem *Perosa*: frementum *MS*

19. The poem was not included in the Aldine edition, but Crinito printed it in his *Libri de poetis latinis* (Florence, 1505), and the title is included in Modesti's list in Florence, Biblioteca Medicea Laurenziana, Plut. 90 sup. 37; see Perosa, *Studi*, 1:28.

20. et *edd.*, corr. *Wilson*

21. Prefixed to the edition and commentary on Horace published by Cristoforo Landino in 1482.

22. This short tribute to Pico della Mirandola in hendecasyllabics follows *Scab.* in Parma, Biblioteca Palatina, MS Pal. 555, p. 697. The poem was first published in Perosa's edition of *Scab.* (1954), 55.

DUBIA

1. The title is found in the list in Laur. 90 sup. 37, ff. 108r–9r, but the epitaph is preserved only in Vasari's brief biography. Its opening sentence can be scanned as two iambic senarii (which may have misled viewers), but the remainder of the text given by Vasari is in prose. The church of San Piero a Scheraggio, where Cecca was buried, was destroyed in the sixteenth century, so the original inscription cannot be consulted.

Notes to the Translation

᠅

Add.	Additional Poems
Alb.	*An Elegy for Albiera degli Albizzi*
Ald.	[Politiani opera], ed. A. Sarti (Venice: Aldus Manutius, 1498)
Anth. Pal.	*Anthologia Palatina*
Anth. Plan.	*Anthologia Planudea*
DBI	*Dizionario biografico degli italiani* (Rome, 1960–), online at Treccani.it
Del Lungo	*Prose volgari inedite e poesie latine e greche . . . di . . . Poliziano*, ed. I. Del Lungo (Florence, 1867)
Epigr. Gr.	*The Book of Greek Epigrams*
Epigr. Lat.	*The Book of Epigrams*
Font.	*To Bartolomeo Fonzio*
Perosa, *Studi*	A. Perosa, *Studi di filologia umanistica*, ed. P. Viti, 3 vols. (Rome, 2000)
Pontani	*Angeli Politiani liber epigrammatum graecorum*, ed. F. Pontani (Rome, 2002)
Scab.	*A Silva on Scabies*

AN ELEGY FOR ALBIERA DEGLI ALBIZZI

1. The daughter of Maso di Luca degli Albizzi and Caterina di Tommaso Soderini, who died at the age of fifteen on July 14, 1473, and was buried in San Pier Maggiore.

2. Sigismondo della Stufa (1454–1525), a close friend and political ally of Lorenzo de' Medici.

3. The phrase is construed by inferring a subjunctive form such as *posset* from *temperet*, the verb of the coordinate clause, a fairly harsh example of the grammatical figure known in antiquity as zeugma.

4. The use of the logically superfluous -que to connect sentences and paragraphs is a stylistic peculiarity of Latin writers of the fifteenth century; see Perosa, Studi, 2:23.

5. Poliziano refers to his translation of the Iliad into Latin, still an ongoing project when this poem was composed, imitating the opening lines of the Sixth Eclogue, where Vergil refers to an imagined epic on "kings and battles" (Eclogue 6.3). Troy was also known as Pergamum, which properly refers to the citadel of the city, and the epithet derives from Dardanus, the founder of Troy's royal line. The Greeks are commonly identified by epithets that are strictly applicable only to regions of Greece, like Argolicus from the Argolid peninsula in the Peloponnese.

6. The phrase, which is modeled on Statius, Silvae 3.2.7–8, is reechoed from Font. 70 here and at 191 below; see Add. 25.10, addressed to Alessandro Braccesi.

7. An island in the Aegean Sea, known for its associations with the cult of Aphrodite. Poliziano borrowed the phrase from Ovid, Metamorphoses 4.311, which he read in a manuscript before the correct variant Cytoriaco (from Mt. Cytorus in Paphlagonia) in Ovid's text became known.

8. Poliziano uses a Grecizing form of her name with final long e as a metrical convenience; elsewhere he artificially lengthens the second syllable (Epigr. Lat. 41.1, 42.1, 44.1, 45.1) or treats the i as a consonant (Epigr. Lat. 46.1).

9. A promontory in Laconia in Greece, known for its black marble and as an entry to the Underworld.

10. The muse of light poetry; see Epigr. Lat. 6.6, III.87.

11. An epithet of Apollo from Mt. Cynthus on Delos, the birthplace of the god.

12. The patron saint of Florence, here designated by the epithet pellitus (dressed in skins). His feast day was June 24.

13. In June 1473, Eleanor of Aragon, the daughter of King Ferdinand I of Naples, passed through Florence en route to Ferrara to marry Duke Ercole I d'Este, leaving her native city, whose ancient name of Parthenope was thought to derive from one of the Sirens. According to Leonardo

Bruni in his *History of the Florentine People*, 1.1–4, 6, ed. James Hankins in this I Tatti Renaissance Library (Cambridge, MA: Harvard University Press, 2001), Florence had been a Roman colony settled by veterans of Sulla's army.

14. Near Santa Maria Novella. Poliziano designates it by a Greek coinage from πάντες (all) and ἅγιος (holy). For the Florentines as "Sullans," see note 13 above.

15. The Prato d'Ognissanti was an open area to the north of the Borgo Ognissanti where jousts and horse races were held.

16. A town in Attica in Greece, known for its association with Nemesis, a goddess identified with envy.

17. The constellation Canis Major, which rises from July 24 to August 26, the hottest part of the summer, associated in Greek mythology with Maera, the dog of Icarius, which was translated to the sky.

18. The genealogy of Febris as a daughter of Night, and Erebus, a god of the Underworld, is modeled on Cicero, *On the Nature of the Gods* 3.44.

19. A region of North Africa west of Egypt.

20. Located in Thrace, the cold and mountainous region northeast of Greece. The imagery suggests the alternation of hot and cold accompanying a fever.

21. Temples to Febris were located on the Palatine (Pliny the Elder, *Natural History* 2.16; Cicero, *De natura deorum* 3.63; Aelian, *Varia Historia* 12.11), where Augustus erected a temple of Apollo following his victory at Actium; on the Quirinal, where the street known as the *Vicus Longus* ran (Valerius Maximus 2.5.6); and on the Esquiline, where there was a temple built by Marius to celebrate his victory over the Cimbri and the Teutons (Valerius Maximus 2.5.6).

22. The planet Venus, the Evening Star.

23. Modeled closely on Ovid, *Amores* 2.6.46: "Fate stands over you now, her distaff empty."

24. Personified Fame as a messenger is a common conceit in classical Latin poetry, but Vergil (*Aeneid* 9.474) is probably uppermost in Poliziano's mind here.

25. For the epithet of Apollo, see note 11 above. The number ten is not precise: Albiera died on July 14, about twenty days after she contracted the disease.

26. Sigismondo had been elected to the Priorate, the highest office in the government of Florence, in which he served for the two months of May and June earlier in that same year, 1473.

27. Albiera had a half brother, Luca degli Albizzi (1454–1530), the son of Maso's first wife, Albiera de' Medici, and an older sister, Giovanna, who died in 1488 and was commemorated by Poliziano in *Epigr. Lat.* 121.

28. Agnolo di Lorenzo della Stufa (1407–81), a leading figure in Florence, allied with the Medici, a Prior in 1446 and Gonfaloniere di Giustizia in 1471.

29. Poliziano wrote seven other epitaphs for Albiera (*Epigr. Lat.* 41–47); and others were composed by Alessandro Braccesi, Ugolino Verino, and Naldo Naldi.

THE BOOK OF EPIGRAMS

1. Son of Piero de' Medici and grandson of Cosimo, Lorenzo (1449–92) became the unofficial but unmistakable ruler of Florence upon his father's death in 1469. Poliziano, who was his junior by only five years, actively pursued his patronage and by the end of 1473 had a place in the Medici palace on the Via Larga.

2. The chief of the Muses, usually associated with epic poetry, invoked here, presumably because Poliziano was engaged in translating Homer.

3. Tyre in Phoenicia was famous for its luxurious purple dyes.

4. The reference is to the excesses of *Carnevale* in Florence. The epithet "Ogygian" refers to Thebes, although its etymology is obscure, while "Lyaeus" is a cult title of Dionysus. Apparently, the tree had been accidentally set on fire by inebriated revelers.

5. Possibly an oblique reference to Ercole d'Este (1431–1505), who became Duke of Ferrara in 1471, having served his predecessors as captain of the city's troops. His name gives rise to the play on Hercules (here called the "Tirynthian," because he came from Tiryns), who was associ-

ated with the poplar (Theocritus 2.121; Vergil, *Eclogues* 7.61; Propertius 4.9.29). "Ausonian," which originally referred to south Italy, was treated as a generalized epithet for Italy by ancient Roman poets.

6. The shade of the laurel tree was a frequent metaphor for Lorenzo's patronage in the circle of Medici poets and scholars.

7. In antiquity the Spanish river Ebro was called the *Hiberus*; Poliziano uses the epithet *Hesperius* with the contemporary Latin name to distinguish it from the river in Thrace known to ancient Romans as the *Hebrus*.

8. The example of a dog that is trained to attack enemies but protect friends recalls Plato's *Republic* 2.375e1, where the analogy is used to describe the class of guardians. The analogy was frequently cited in humanist literature.

9. The dates given in the heading to this poem in the Aldine cannot both be correct — Poliziano was fifteen, not thirteen years old in 1469 — although the specificity is curious. It is more likely that the year given is wrong, and the poem dates from 1473, when Fonzio had returned to Florence and Poliziano composed a lengthy elegy for him, the *Elegia ad Fontium*. Their eventual bitter falling out in 1483 is the subject of a long letter by Fonzio (*Letters to Friends*, 1.25) addressed to Poliziano. On Bartolomeo Fonzio, see the note on *Font.* 1.

10. Carlo Marsuppini (1449–ca. 1500) was the son of the famous Chancellor of Florence of the same name, whose translation of the first book of the *Iliad* inspired Poliziano to begin his version with Book 2. The younger Carlo was a pupil and admirer of Marsilio Ficino and, together with his brother Cristoforo, appears as an interlocutor in his *De Amore*, a commentary on the *Symposium* in the form of a dialogue. That is the backdrop for Poliziano's lighthearted exhortation to Marsuppini to turn to lighter pursuits, such as poetry. A number of Latin poems by the elder Marsuppini survive, for which see *Carlo Marsuppini: Carmi latini*, ed. Ilaria Pierini (Florence, 2014).

11. The phrasing draws on Propertius 3.1.8, and the metaphor reflects the ancients' use of pumice to smooth over a papyrus book roll.

12. Philetas of Cos (ca. 340–285 BCE) was a Greek scholar and poet of the Hellenistic period. Although his works have been lost, apart from a few fragments, he would have been known to Poliziano from references to him by Roman writers. And Poliziano would also have known from Stobaeus of one of Philetas' lost works, known as *Paignia* (Lat. *Lusus*).

13. The epithet *purpureus* conveys the idea of radiance, not color alone. It is not directly applied to Venus in classical poetry, but Poliziano was surely thinking of passages in Ovid where it describes Cupid, e.g., *Amores* 2.1.38, 2.9.34; *Ars amatoria* 1.232; and *Remedia Amoris* 701. In Horace (*Odes* 4.10.10) Venus is said to ride "on the wings of gleaming (*purpureis*) swans."

14. Del Lungo's identification of this person as Ponticus Virunius (Ludovico da Ponte) seems unlikely in the extreme, since there is no evidence that he ever came to Florence or had any connection with Poliziano. If the date given in *Ald.* is correct, it further militates against this identification, since the most likely date for da Ponte's birth is in the late 1460s. It is more likely that the date is incorrect and the addressee is Galeazzo Facino (b. ca. 1458–1506), called *il Pontico*, an associate of Ermolao Barbaro, who was at Padua when Poliziano visited in 1480. See *DBI* 44 (1994), s.v. Facino had recently completed a collection of verse, mostly in elegiacs.

15. A proverbial expression in classical Latin; cf. Vergil, *Eclogue* 7.42; Horace *Sermones* 2.5.8.

16. An unidentified poet, perhaps a fiction.

17. Antonio Benivieni (1443–1502), born into a prominent Florentine family, contemplated a literary career while a young man, but by at least 1470 he had turned to medicine, a field in which he became a pioneer in the use of autopsies. See *DBI* 8 (1955), 543–45. He was a close adherent of the Medici and treated Lorenzo de' Medici's daughter; he also belonged to the circle of Marsilio Ficino. In this tribute to the family, Poliziano mentions his brothers, Girolamo (1453–1542), a noted poet (ll. 19–20), and Domenico (1460–1507), a theologian and philosopher (ll. 21–26), as well as an unnamed third brother, also a physician (ll. 17–18).

18. *Scomma* is a later Latin Grecism (= σκῶμμα), which Poliziano probably came across in Macrobius (*Saturnalia* 7.3.1).

19. Charon was the ferryman of the Underworld; Parca, the name of one of the Fates.

20. Apollo (or Phoebus) was called "Lycian" because of his oracle at Patara in Lycia. His son by Coronis was Aesculapius, the mythical physician; the nymph Philyra had a son by him, Chiron, a Centaur distinguished for his great knowledge of medicine. Roman poets adopted the spelling "Phillyrides" in the matronymic as a metrical convenience; the scansion of *Coronidem* is likewise sanctioned by the practice of Ovid (*Metamorphoses* 15.624; *Fasti* 6.746).

21. Thamyras was a Thracian poet who was punished with blindness after losing a contest with the Muses, chief among whom was Calliope. His story is told in the second book of the *Iliad* (594–600), which Poliziano had translated.

22. Nestor, the ruler of Pylos, is represented in the *Iliad* as an old man. Cumae on the Bay of Naples was colonized from Chalcis in Euboea; hence the epithet "Euboean" was used by Roman poets to refer to the Cumaean Sibyl. Here Poliziano recasts the riddling phrase at Statius, *Silvae* 1.4.126, "to transcend the years of Euboean dust," in referring to her great age.

23. Pietro Riario (1445–74), nephew of Pope Sixtus IV on his mother's side, who appointed him as cardinal of San Sisto in 1471. See *DBI* (2016). He was a cultivated man, well known for his taste for pomp and luxury. In 1473 he was made archbishop of Florence, and in the same year he conducted a tour of northern Italian cities in support of the pope's political aims. When he died the following year in Rome, some suspected poison.

24. The lion (*il marzocco*) was the heraldic symbol of Florence.

25. The tradition that the Etruscans, the pre-Roman inhabitants of Tuscany, originally came from Lydia in Asia Minor, goes back to antiquity (e.g., Vergil, *Aeneid* 9.11).

26. Poliziano calls the rain after a drought *nectar*, the drink of the gods, extending a practice common among ancient poets, who used the term for sweet liquids, such as wine or honey.

27. Poliziano plays on the literal meaning of *verba dare* in Latin (to give words) and the figurative meaning (to cheat).

28. Cf. *Epigr. Lat.* II.13–14.

29. A member of the Riario family, he was appointed archbishop of Pisa by Pope Sixtus IV in 1474, a year after the date assigned to this epigram. He was a leading figure in the Pazzi conspiracy in 1478, but he was swiftly apprehended after the failed attempt on Lorenzo de' Medici's life and hanged from a window in the Palazzo Vecchio.

30. Celebrated humanist, who spent most of his career in Rome and enjoyed the patronage of powerful men such as Cardinal Bessarion and Pietro Riario, cardinal of San Sisto (see note 23). He was in Florence in 1473 to present Lorenzo de' Medici with a copy of his commentary on Martial. He enjoyed good relations with Poliziano before his death in 1478 at the early age of thirty-two, but his scholarship came in for withering criticism in the *Miscellanea*.

31. Extraordinarily influential Christian Platonist (1433–99), who first enjoyed patronage of the Medici family under Cosimo, although his influence waned in the years following the Pazzi conspiracy in 1478. He translated the complete works of Plato and Plotinus and other Neoplatonic philosophers.

32. The point of the epigram turns on a wordplay between *audire missam* (to hear mass) and *missum facere* (to pass over).

33. The name of the addressee is fictitious, drawn from literature such as Boccaccio's *Elegia di Madonna Fiammetta*. A Greek version appears as *Epigr. Gr.* 4.

34. The fictitious addressee gets his name from the pastoral tradition, in which it occurs as early as Theocritus.

35. The first of several poems directed against the itinerant poet Mabilio da Novate (d. 1479), who, after failures in Milan, Venice, and Urbino,

was in Florence from 1472 to 1475. Mabilio was also targeted in verse by Naldo Naldi and Alessandro Braccesi.

36. Perhaps Fabiano Benci (1423–81), a native of Montepulciano, who was a cleric active in the Apostolic Camera, the financial board of the papal administration.

37. A popular poet, Antonio di Guido (d. 1484), also known as Antonio "who sings on the bench," celebrated for his extemporizations in the vernacular. See Blake Wilson, "Canterino and Improvvisatore: Oral Poetry and Performance," in The Cambridge History of Fifteenth Century Music, ed. Anna Maria Busse-Berger and Jesse Rodin (Cambridge, 2015), 296–97.

38. Poliziano found this epithet, formed upon the name of a mountain range in Thessaly, in his text of Martial (7.8.2, 10.7.2), but modern editors rightly reject the reading there in favor of the epithet Odrysius.

39. This imaginary name for Florence, which was accepted by Bruni (History of the Florentine People, ed. James Hankins, 1.3), is owed to a textual corruption in the manuscripts of Pliny the Elder, Natural History 3.52.

40. A reference to Dante, Inferno 15.67, where Brunetto Latini reports that "ancient fame in the world called them blind," referring to the people of Florence.

41. Perhaps in reference to the refoundation of the University of Florence in 1473.

42. Probably a reference to Lorenzo's intervention during the severe drought of 1473.

43. The sack and capture of Volterra was orchestrated by Lorenzo in 1472.

44. A reference to the conspiracy of 1466 against Piero de' Medici, which his young son Lorenzo helped to thwart.

45. The great Athenian lawgiver of the sixth century BCE.

46. A reference to great building projects, such as the Basilica of San Lorenzo and the Palazzo Medici, most of which were in fact begun un-

der his grandfather Cosimo. For building projects in Florence in the time of Lorenzo, see *L'architettura di Lorenzo de' Medici*, ed. Gabriele Morolli et al. (exhibition catalog, Florence, 1992).

47. Fra Filippo Lippi (1406–69), a protégé of Cosimo and Piero de' Medici, who was born in Florence but was buried in the cathedral of Spoleto. In his "Life of Fra Filippo," Vasari tells the story of how Lorenzo de' Medici journeyed to Spoleto to request the return of his body to Florence. When this request was denied, Lorenzo contributed one hundred ducats toward the cost of Lippi's tomb and commissioned this epitaph from Poliziano to be inscribed on it.

48. The situation described in this epigram is entirely fictitious. On December 6, 1479, Lorenzo departed on a dangerous mission to Naples to conclude a peace with King Ferrante of Aragon, to bring to an end the bloody war following the suppression of the Pazzi conspiracy. Poliziano did not accompany him on this mission, and instead traveled to Venice, Padua, Mantua, and Verona. Lorenzo returned in triumph to Florence in March 1480, whereupon Poliziano wrote to him, excusing his conduct and begging leave to return. By August Poliziano was back in Florence, but no longer a member of the Medici household, although he was appointed Professor of Rhetoric and Poetry in the Studio in compensation.

49. Members of the Signoria, the governing council.

50. In 1473 Lorenzo transferred the law and medical faculties of the Florentine Studio to Pisa, retaining the lecturers in humanistic subjects in Florence. But the epigram may refer more generally to Lorenzo's large land-purchases in the Pisan contado and his wider attempts to establish himself there as a patron of the port city.

51. In Roman antiquity a garland of oak leaves, the *corona civica*, was awarded for saving the life of a citizen. The occasion of this epigram is unclear: it might refer to Lorenzo's activities during the drought of 1473, but the rhetoric better suits the aftermath of the Pazzi conspiracy.

52. The proverbially wise and aged king of Pylos, who accompanied the Greeks to Troy.

53. There was a severe famine in the latter part of 1473, which Lorenzo helped to alleviate.

54. Giuliano de' Medici (1453–78), son of Piero de' Medici and younger brother of Lorenzo, who was assassinated in the cathedral of Florence during the Pazzi conspiracy.

55. Castor and Pollux, celebrated in myth for fraternal love, sons of Tyndareos, who was in turn the son of Oebalus in Sparta.

56. Agamemnon and Menelaus.

57. A coastal town in Boeotia in Greece, in myth the home of Glaucus, who was transformed into a prophetic sea demon when he consumed a magical herb.

58. Marsilio Ficino (see note 31).

59. That is, the sun.

60. The epigram probably dates to 1473 when Poliziano was seeking Lorenzo's patronage but had not yet been taken into the Medici household, as demonstrated by the contemporary translation of this poem into Greek by Andronicus Callistus, who was active in Florence from 1471 to 1475.

61. A river in Lydia famous for its swans. The adjectival form of the name used by Poliziano is unattested in Latin or Greek and is tacitly corrected by Andronicus in his translation.

62. Lorenzo was frequently absent in Pisa in 1474.

63. Francesco Gaddi (1441–1504), a loyal adherent of the Medici, returned to Florence in 1475 after many years spent in Rome tending to his family's business interests. This epigram clearly predates his later diplomatic activity on behalf of Lorenzo de' Medici, which began with the crisis of 1478 and the Pazzi conspiracy.

64. Naldo Naldi (1436–ca. 1513) dedicated a book of Latin elegies to Lorenzo in 1474.

65. The Otto di Guardia e Balìa, housed in the Palazzo del Podestà (also known as the Bargello), was a police magistracy in charge of criminal affairs.

66. The goddess of justice.

67. Albiera degli Albizzi (1457–73); see the note on *Alb.* 1.

68. The line is repeated at *Alb.* 160.

69. This epigram celebrates the publication of the first book printed in Greek, an edition of the Greek grammar by Constantine Lascaris, published in Milan in 1476, the result of a relatively brief collaboration between Demetrius Damilas, an immigrant from Crete, and the printer, Dionigi Parravicino.

70. Called *Aonides*, from the region of Boeotia where Mt. Helicon is located.

71. Bernardo Bembo (1433–1519), Venetian nobleman and humanist, father of the more famous Pietro, served the Venetian senate on multiple diplomatic missions over the course of his career, including one to Florence in early 1475 to attend the celebration of an alliance among Venice, Milan, and Florence. Bembo took advantage of the occasion to cement his relations with Lorenzo de' Medici and other notables in Florence, including Ficino and his circle, and presumably also Poliziano. This poem was probably composed during this time, since there is no allusion to the complications that attended Bembo's next mission to Florence following the Pazzi conspiracy. Cristoforo Landino also wrote poetry on Bembo and his Platonic love for Ginevra de'Benci, subject of a portrait by Leonardo da Vinci. See Landino's *Poems*, translated by Mary P. Chatfield (Cambridge, MA, 2008) in this I Tatti Renaissance Library, 276–303. On Bembo see Nella Giannetto, *Bernardo Bembo, umanista e politico veneziano* (Florence, 1985).

72. In most accounts from antiquity, the Sirens who lured sailors to their doom were the daughters of the river-god Achelous.

73. The Latinized spelling of the Greek for "persuasion," who appeared in Greek literature as a goddess as early as Hesiod.

74. Hermes, who was born on Mt. Cyllene in Arcadia, supplied Odysseus with the magic herb *moly* to protect him from the magic of Circe (Homer, *Odyssey* 10.302–6).

75. Panezio Pandozzi of Cortona, of whom little is known except that he was taken on as a student by Marsilio Ficino on Poliziano's recommendation.

76. Pylades, in Greek myth the great friend of Orestes (son of Agamemnon), who was exiled to Phocis.

77. An oblique reference to Phintias, who was the companion of the Pythagorean hero Damon and whose name cannot scan in hexameters.

78. Pollux, devoted brother of Castor.

79. In Greek myth Sisyphus was condemned forever to roll the same rock up a hill, only to see it roll back.

80. All that we know of this humanist from the town of Monopoli in Bari we learn from Poliziano's references to him. In a letter to Lorenzo de'Medici, recommending Gioviano for a benefice, Poliziano describes him as tutor to Leonardo Tornabuoni. He is also the recipient of *Epigr. Gr.* 10, which Poliziano wrote in reply to a Latin poem by Crasso.

81. The form transmitted in *Ald.* must meant "Attic," but it is a peculiar and otherwise unattested formation.

82. Simonetta Cattaneo (1453–76), a famous beauty, the wife of Marco Vespucci, with whom Giuliano de' Medici was infatuated. Poliziano depicted her in mythologized tones in the *Stanze*, and her death was memorialized by several poets, including Lorenzo de' Medici. Botticelli is said to have used her as a model for a number of his idealized females, including Venus in *The Birth of Venus*.

83. The original is attributed to Asclepiades in the *Planudean Anthology* (3.12.43) and the *Palatine Anthology* (7.217), and the speaker is thus the tomb where Archeanassa, a courtesan, is buried, which is surely correct. Poliziano here follows the text and attribution to Plato found in Diogenes Laertius, making the philosopher the speaker.

84. The original, on the theme of a girl dying before marriage, is attributed to Sappho in both the *Planudean Anthology* (3.12.24) and the *Palatine Anthology* (7.489), but it is surely of Hellenistic date. The name "Timas" is not attested elsewhere as a woman's name.

85. This epigram in iambics is anonymous in the *Planudean Anthology* (4.26.13), but Poliziano may have thought it by Antipater, since it follows another epigram on Homer by him.

86. Galeotto Manfredi (1440–88), who became ruler of Faenza in 1477 with the support of Lorenzo, at whose urging also he married Francesca Bentivoglio. She later participated in the plot that led to his assassination.

87. This rare text was recovered circa 1295 by Maximus Planudes, who wrote some hexameter poems to celebrate it, including this one on Ptolemy's map translated by Poliziano (*Test. de Ptolemaeo* VII Nobbe): Εἰς πόλον εἰ γαίηθεν ἴδῃς, ἄμα πάντα δοκεύεις, | Εἰς χθόνα δ' οὐρανὸν εἰσαναβὰς ἄμα πᾶσαν ἂν εἶδες, | Νῦν οὖν πᾶσαν ὁρῶν ἄμα γῆν ἔμεν ἐς πόλον οἴου.

88. In the *Planudean Anthology* (1.1.2), this epigram on a painting or sculpture of Hercules wrestling the Libyan giant Antaeus is attributed to Diotimus, who was included in the *Garland of Meleager* (*Anth. Pal.* 9.391), and is entitled Διοτίμου εἰς Ἡρακλέα καὶ Ἀνταῖον:

Τὰν ἥβαν ἐς ἄεθλα πάλας ἤσκησε κραταιᾶς
    ἄδε Ποσειδῶνος καὶ Διὸς ἀ γενεά·
κεῖται δέ σφιν ἀγὼν οὐ χαλκέου ἀμφὶ λέβητος
    ἀλλ' ὅστις ζωὰν οἴσεται ἠθάνατον.
Ἀνταίου τὸ πτῶμα, πρέπει δ' Ἡρακλέα νικᾶν
    τὸν Διός. Ἀργείων ἀ πάλα, οὐ Λιβύων.

89. In mythology Antaeus, a son of Poseidon, was a giant living in Libya, who was slain by Hercules, the son of Jupiter. Their struggle is described in Lucan, *Bellum Civile* 4.621–29. Antonio del Pollaiuolo, an artist closely associated with Lorenzo de'Medici, made a painting of their combat, now in the Uffizi, as well as a small bronze, now in the Bargello; both date from the 1470s. See Alison Wright, *The Pollaiuolo Brothers: The Arts of Florence and Rome* (New Haven, 2005).

90. In the *Planudean Anthology* (3.7.3), this epigram in iambics is entitled Εἰς Νιόβην, but in the *Palatine Anthology* (7.311) it is attributed to Agathias, with the title "On Lot's wife":

Ὁ τύμβος οὗτος ἔνδον οὐκ ἔχει νεκρόν·
ὁ νεκρὸς οὗτος ἐκτὸς οὐκ ἔχει τάφον,
ἀλλ' αὐτὸς αὐτοῦ νεκρός ἐστι καὶ τάφος.

91. On Mabilio, see note 35. Novate was in the Duchy of Milan, which also went by the name of its ancient Gaulish inhabitants, the Insubres. The choice of meter (hendecasyllabic, a favorite of Catullus) is appropriate to the tone.

92. Poliziano imported the form *ploxonio* from Catullus 97.6, a savage depiction of a man called Aemilius, as it is attested in the manuscript Vatican City, Biblioteca Apostolica Vaticana, Ottob. lat. 1829 (R), and manuscripts and editions derived from it. Quintilian (1.5.8) reports that Catullus knew the word from a northern Italian dialect, which would make it appropriate in a description of Mabilio. It apparently means a wagon box.

93. These were early Roman dramatic poets of the third to second century BCE, whose audience was the average Roman citizen (Curius) straight from the farm.

94. Poliziano has either erred in scanning Euripides' name, or arbitrarily altered its vowel quantities.

95. Ancient biographies report this as a slander against Vergil.

96. Poliziano will have come across this information about the sixth-century BCE lyric poet Anacreon in Horace, *Epode* 14.9.

97. Presumably Xenophanes (ca. 570–467 BCE), a Presocratic philosopher who wrote in verse about theology and cosmology.

98. Poliziano found this tidbit about an otherwise unknown tragedian in the *Liber medicinalis* (59–61), a medical handbook by Quintus Serenus, which can be dated between the second and the fourth centuries CE.

99. Poliziano plays on the literal and metaphorical senses of *nasutus* (long-nosed/witty) and *sagax* (keen-scented/shrewd).

100. The "Molossian" was a breed of hunting dog from the coastal region in northwest Greece, famous in antiquity.

101. Perhaps referring to a district in the Oltrarno, modern Via del Ronco, where there was an installation for drying wool known as *del Cavallo*.

102. King of the winds.

103. In mythology, the Lydian king Tantalus was punished in the Underworld (*Dis* is the Latin name for its god) by being made to stand in the river Styx without being able to quench his thirst from it.

104. Enceladus, one of the Giants who fought against Zeus and was pinned under Mt. Etna in Sicily.

105. Acidalia in Thrace and Idalium in Cyprus were both associated with Venus.

106. A river in Boeotia, sacred to the Muses.

107. The wife of Quirinus, worshipped as a goddess.

108. A Greek name associated by Ovid (in *Fasti* 5.183–206) with Flora, the Roman goddess of flowers. In Botticelli's famous *Primavera*, Chloris, dwelling in Venus' realm, is impregnated by Zephyrus and is turned into Flora, who casts flowers (white roses rather than violets) on the ground. See Charles Dempsey, *The Portrayal of Love: Botticelli's Primavera and Humanist Culture at the Time of Lorenzo the Magnificent* (Princeton, 1992).

109. Alternating glyconics and asclepiads, known as the Fourth Asclepiad, a rhythm used twelve times by Horace in his *Odes*.

110. Alessandro Cortesi (ca. 1460–90) was born at San Gimignano but was in Florence at some point in the seventies. See *DBI* 29 (1983), 750–54. He studied with Gioviano Crasso (n. 80) and remained an adherent of the Medici during his subsequent career, which was prosecuted mostly in Rome until his untimely death at the age of thirty. His brother, Paolo Cortesi, later engaged in a famous literary controversy with Poliziano.

111. The nightingale. Daulis, a city of Phocis in central Greece, was the scene of the rape of Philomela by Tereus, who was married to her sister, Procne. The sisters were turned into birds, one of them into a nightingale, which is therefore referred to as the "Daulian" by poets.

112. Giuliano Salviati (1449–1512), married to Lorenzo's niece in 1476.

113. Theocritus, *Idyll* 13.3: οὐχ ἁμῖν τὰ καλὰ πράτοις καλὰ φαίνεται ἦμεν.

114. Theocritus, *Idyll* 3.20 (= ps. Theocritus, *Idyll* 27.4): ἔστι καὶ ἐν κενεοῖσι φιλήμασιν ἁδέα τέρψις.

115. Hesiod, *Opera* 825: ἄλλοτε μητρυιὴ πέλει ἡμέρη, ἄλλοτε μήτηρ.

116. Hesiod, *Opera* 266: ἡ δὲ κακὴ βουλὴ τῷ βουλεύσαντι κακίστη.

117. A pun on the name of the legendary Athenian lawgiver Dracon, whose name means "serpent."

118. Theodore Gaza (ca. 1400–1475), a Byzantine immigrant who reached Italy around 1440 and was active in Mantua, Ferrara, and Rome. His Greek grammar circulated widely in manuscript and was used by Poliziano in tutoring the children of Lorenzo de' Medici. In addition to the following epigram, Poliziano wrote three Greek epigrams on him (*Epigr. Gr.* 13, 15, 16). Two Latin epigrams on Theodore by Manilio Ralle Spartano were incorrectly attributed to Poliziano by Del Lungo, 148 (= *Epigr. Lat.* 73 and 74 in his edition); see Perosa, *Studi*, 1:33.

119. That is, Greek and Latin.

120. Endymion, with whom the moon goddess fell in love, was a handsome mortal, who now sleeps eternally in a cave on Mt. Latmos in Asia Minor.

121. Chronological considerations, among others, make the identification of "Bassus" as Angelo Colozzi da Iesi, proposed by Del Lungo, implausible. There is much merit in the hypothesis that this and the following epigram were actually addressed by someone else to Poliziano, employing the name he used in his youth, and mistakenly included in the collection by Sarti.

122. Mythical king of Praeneste, endowed with three lives and three bodies, who was defeated by Evander, as recounted by Vergil (*Aeneid* 8.561–67).

123. That is, the Tuscans, referring to the ancient tradition that the Etruscans immigrated to Tuscany from Lydia.

124. A reference to Horace, who was born in Venosa (anc. Venusia).

125. A reference to pastoral poetry, which was particularly associated with Theocritus and Sicily. Tityrus is the name of a shepherd in Vergil's *Eclogues*.

126. A Greek colony on the coast southeast of Naples, famous for its roses. Poliziano has borrowed a phrase from Vergil, *Georgics* 4.119.

127. The nightingale; see note 111.

128. This uneven exchange of armor between Glaucus and Diomedes, the son of Tydeus, is described by Homer, *Iliad* 6.119–236.

129. The setting is fictitious, as is the name, taken from the mythical, hundred-eyed guardian of Io.

130. A spring at Nemea where the parched Argive army found water on its march against Thebes, described in Book 4 of Statius' *Thebaid*.

131. A reference to the story of the Lycian peasants who refused water to Leto, told by Ovid in *Metamorphoses* 6.317–81.

132. See note 103.

133. The name is Greek, meaning "chatter," taken from Horace, *Odes* 1.22.

134. For this bizarre opening simile, Poliziano draws on the collection of extraordinary facts about animals by Aelian (ca. 165–230 CE), his *De natura animalium*, in which he describes how a deer can lure a snake to its death by breathing heavily into its den (2.9) and replaces its older horns (12.18).

135. Venus; see note 105.

136. In 1477 Poliziano received the priorate of San Paolo Apostolo (San Paolino) in Florence as a benefice thanks to Lorenzo de' Medici's influence. See Picotti, "Tra il poeta ed il lauro," 269–70, 290, 297.

137. The point depends on the wordplay in Latin with *Paulus* (Paul) and *paulus* (little).

138. The name and the situation are surely fictitious.

139. Of these two lovers of Aphrodite, Anchises was struck by Zeus' thunderbolt at her behest, while Adonis, whom she loved passionately, died young.

140. In myth, Pegasus was the winged horse of Perseus, and Cyllarus was the horse of Castor, who came from Sparta, once ruled by Oebalus.

141. Domizio Calderini (1446–78), a humanist scholar and commentator on Statius, Martial, and Ovid, whom Poliziano at first admired but whose errors later came in for scathing exposure in the *Miscellanea*.

142. Donato Acciaiuoli (1429–78), man of letters and public servant, who served the Medici in many capacities. This epitaph is inscribed on his tomb in the Certosa di Firenze.

143. A serpent appears in the coat of arms of the Sforza, dukes of Milan.

144. Giovanni Antonio Campano (1429–77), whose speeches, histories, letters, and poetry achieved wide recognition during his life, served several popes but died in disgrace after opposing the policy of Sixtus IV.

145. The references are to Campano's occasional verse. Momus was the personification of criticism, characterized by a phrase taken from Horace, *Epistles* 2.2.60: *nigro sale* (lit., "black salt") is a metaphor for coarseness, for which Poliziano creates a new metaphor for refined wit ("snow-white"), which he associates with Mercury.

146. Gentile Becchi (ca. 1425–97), tutor to Lorenzo and Giuliano de' Medici, and a lifelong supporter of the Medici family. He became bishop of Arezzo in 1473. This ode was composed in the aftermath of the Pazzi conspiracy.

147. So called because each stanza consists of two rhythms — three lines of the second asclepiad, followed by a glyconic, a pattern Poliziano found in, e.g., Horace, *Carmina* 1.6.

148. In Greek mythology Zeus was sometimes depicted as bearing a shield (the *aegis*) with the head of a Gorgon on it.

149. The allied states of Florence, Venice, and Milan are symbolized by the Marzocco (see note 24), the lion of St. Mark, and the serpent.

150. Hercules here is Ercole d'Este, Duke of Ferrara, who commanded the forces of the League against the papal forces in the war of 1478–80. France's Louis XI also backed the League.

151. In Florence, Biblioteca Medicea Laurenziana, MS Plut. 90.37, this poem follows *Add.* 5 and 6 and is entitled *In Chrysocumum*, with the grammatical forms referring to the addressee in the masculine gender. The most plausible scenario is that the poem was bowdlerized to be included in the Aldine edition, while the other two poems, which did not lend themselves to such adjustments, were simply omitted.

152. See note 103.

153. In 1479 this epigram was inscribed on the reverse of a memorial stele to Domizio in his birthplace of Torri del Benaco.

154. A spring on Mt. Helicon.

155. Peirene, a spring associated with the Muses at Corinth, where Sisyphus was king.

156. A stream on Mt. Helicon.

157. A pastoral poet of the mid-second century BCE. Poliziano read this epigram in the *Planudean Anthology* (4.200).

158. Pope Innocent VIII, born Giovanni Battista Cibo (1432–92), succeeded Sixtus IV in 1484, a change that was especially welcome to the Medici and their supporters. The ode is in the Sapphic meter.

159. The three Sirens, daughters of the river Achelous, and Orpheus, the son of Apollo, who lived in Thrace, the land of a people known as the Cicones.

160. The city by the Hellespont, here designated by reference to the myth of Phrixus and Helle who crossed it on the golden ram, is Constantinople. Ever since its capture by the Ottoman Turks in 1453, there had been crusading projects to retake it, as there had been plans to recapture Palestine, here designated by the region of Idumea.

161. A reference to the death of Sixtus IV at the age of seventy.

162. Matthias Corvinus (1443–90), an enthusiastic patron of Italian artists and humanists.

163. Above, note 39.

164. Perhaps to be identified with Francesca Scotti (d. 1509); no trace of her poetry survives.

165. At the Medici villa at Poggio a Caiano, near Prato. *Ambra* is also the title of a poem by Lorenzo, as well as one of Poliziano's *Silvae*.

166. Punning on the name of Lorenzo.

167. Lorenzo di Pierfrancesco de' Medici (1463–1507), known as *il Popolano*, second cousin of Lorenzo, from the cadet branch of the family, dedicatee of the *Manto* and *Add.* 2. He was adopted by Lorenzo il Magnifico after the death of his father in 1476, but eventually sided against

Piero in 1494. He and his brother, Giovanni, adopted the name *Popolano* after the expulsion of Piero, to distinguish their politics from those of the main branch of the family.

168. The spring (note 165) gives its name to the villa at Poggio a Caiano.

169. Piero de' Medici (1472–1503), the oldest son of Lorenzo, whom Poliziano tutored until 1480. Piero, known as *il Fatuo*, to distinguish him from his grandfather Piero *il Gottoso* or "the Gouty," succeeded Lorenzo in 1492 as unofficial head of state. But he fell far short of his father's considerable talents and was forced into exile just two years later in the aftermath of the invasion of Italy by Charles VIII of France. He died while fighting the French in 1503, when his boat capsized in the river Garigliano near Cassino.

170. Il Magnifico adopted his namesake in 1476 upon the death of the younger man's father.

171. The College of the Cardinals is designated by the periphrasis "the fathers wearing caps."

172. He was sent to France, together with Gentile Becchi and Antonio Canigiani, to congratulate the new king, Charles VIII, in 1483.

173. Thalia, a Muse associated with comedy and lyric poetry.

174. *Stilus* can also refer to the writing instrument or the writing: Poliziano may be referring to effects on his penmanship of writing while on horseback.

175. The meter is the so-called Third Asclepiadean, in which each stanza is composed of three lesser Asclepiadeans followed by a glyconic, used by Horace in nine of his *Odes*.

176. A mountain in the region of Phocis in Greece with two peaks, sacred to Apollo and the Muses.

177. Identified in Florence, Biblioteca Medicea Laurenziana, MS Plut. 90.37 as Bartolomeo Scala (1428–97), a man of humble origins, the son of a miller, who enjoyed a spectacular rise to power and held several public offices under the Medici. He feuded openly with Poliziano in 1493–94 over matters of literary style, but Poliziano did not let his dislike for Scala affect his admiration for his accomplished daughter, Alessandra,

whom he celebrated in several poems. Poliziano's editors suppressed the identity of the poem's target out of tact, but it is not difficult to identify Scala as its subject. Its composition probably dates to circa 1486 (see Brown, *Bartolomeo Scala*, 211–13), after Scala's election as Gonfalonier of Justice. The meter, appropriately enough, is that of Horace's first ten *Epodes*, alternating iambic trimeters and dimeters.

178. Scala owned considerable property within Florence, parts of which had been left undeveloped after the population had been halved by plague in the previous century. Between 1473 and 1480, on land that he owned in Borgo Pinti, he built a classically inspired home, now known as the Palazzo della Gherardesca.

179. Scala had this motto (*gradatim*) inscribed on the façade of his house; a pun on his own name, it implied that he had risen by merit.

180. The target is perhaps Michael Marullus, on whom see *Add.*, note 3, below.

181. The Phrygian king who was given ass's ears by Apollo as punishment for his bad taste.

182. Unknown. The meter, iambic dimeter, is not common in classical Latin verse. On this poem and 126, see now Silvia Rizzo, "Poliziano, *Puella e Anus*," in *Italia medievale e umanistica* 57 (2016): 118–227, which appeared too late to be taken into account in this edition.

183. Cos was known in antiquity for the manufacture of fine, light dresses.

184. A mountain in Sicily known for its honey.

185. An epithet of Dionysus.

186. Apollo, who tended the flocks of Admetus on the banks of the river Amphrysus in Thrace.

187. That is, he is thirty-three years old, which would date the epigram to circa 1487

188. This garment, which inspires sexual desire, makes its first appearance in Homer's *Iliad* 14.214–15.

189. The epigram (*Anth. Pal.* 6.331), which is untitled in the *Planudean Anthology* (6.11.3), is attributed to Gaetulicus:

παῖδα πατὴρ Ἄλκων ὀλοῷ σφιγχθέντα δράκοντι
    ἀθρήσας δειλῇ τόξον ἔκαμψε χερί·
θηρὸς δ' οὐκ ἀφάμαρτε, διὰ στόματος γὰρ ὀιστός
    ἤιξεν τυτθοῦ βαιὸν ὕπερθε βρέφους.
παυσάμενος δὲ φόβοιο παρὰ δρυὶ τῆδε φαρέτρην
    σῆμα καὶ εὐτυχίης θῆκε καὶ εὐστοχίης.

190. Lines 5 and 6 are interpolated by Poliziano; they are absent from the Greek original.

191. The epigram has the title Εἰς ἀφύλακτον οἶκον in the *Planudean Anthology* (4.22.6) and is attributed to Julian the Egyptian in the *Palatine Anthology* (9.654):

Κερδαλέους δίζεσθε δόμους, λῄστορες, ἄλλους·
    τοῖσδε γάρ ἐστι φύλαξ ἔμπεδος ἡ πενίη.

192. This is not a free translation of *Anth. Plan.* 1.77.4 (= *Anth. Pal.* 9.346), as Del Lungo puts it; rather, in these hendecasyllabics Poliziano has merged the theme of the closely related poem *Anth. Plan.* 4.9.14 (= *Anth. Pal.* 16.141), on a swallow that built its nest near a painting of Medea, with the adjacent epigram *Anth. Plan* 4.9.15 (= *Anth. Pal.* 16.142), on a statue of Medea.

193. From the anonymous *Anth. Plan.* 1.20.11 (= *Anth. Pal.* 9.529), a monostich redone into a couplet in iambic dimeters:

Λέκτρον ἑνὸς φεύγουσα λέχος πολλοῖσιν ἐτύχθην.

194. From the anonymous *Anth. Plan.* 1.20.10 (= *Anth. Pal.* 9.124), a monostich remade as a couplet in iambic dimeters:

Ποῖ Φοῖβος πεπόρευτο Ἄρης ὅτ' ἐμίγνυτο Δάφνῃ;

195. The dative in -*e* in Greek names is sporadically attested in manuscripts and more widely found in inscriptions.

196. From the anonymous *Anth. Plan.* 1.25.3 (= *Anth. Pal.* 9.146):

Ἐλπίδα καὶ Νέμεσιν Εὔνους παρὰ βωμὸν ἔτευξα,
    τὴν μέν, ἵν' ἐλπίζῃς· τὴν δ', ἵνα μηδὲν ἔχῃς.

197. The epigram is ironic: Eunus means "kindly," while Nemesis is the Greek goddess of retribution.

198. From the anonymous *Anth. Plan.* 1.20.8 (= *Anth. Pal.* 9.130), an elegiac couplet redone into iambic dimeters:

Παλλάδος εἰμὶ φυτόν· Βρομίου τί με θλίβετε κλῶνες;
αἴρετε τοὺς βότρυας· παρθένος οὐ μεθύω.

199. A cult name of Bacchus.

200. Giovanna degli Albizzi (1468–88), the older sister of Albiera degli Albizzi, married Lorenzo Tornabuoni in 1486 and gave birth to one son, but she died in childbirth during her second pregnancy.

201. Michele Verino (or, di Vieri, 1469–87) was the son of the poet Ugolino Verino. His premature death was caused by a blow to the groin. In the year of his death his only poetical work was published, *De puerorum moribus disticha*, a collection of moral maxims in couplets.

202. Poliziano included the *Preface* in a letter (*Letters* 7.15) to Paolo Comparini, canon of the basilica of San Lorenzo. In May 1488, Lorenzo de' Medici commissioned a production of Plautus' *Menaechmi* from Comparini, who asked Poliziano to compose the prologue.

203. Poliziano found *mōlǐtor* in an obscene sense in Ausonius, *Epigrammata* = 101.3 in R. P. H. Green's edition (Oxford, 1999).

204. Poliziano had read in Quintilian (*Institutes* 10.1.99) the attribution of this assessment of Plautus' Latinity to L. Aelius Praeconinus, also known as Aelius Stilo, a grammarian of the late second century BCE.

205. Literally, "members of the *gens Curia*," a family noted for its severe morals; the "Curii" was a byword for virtue in Silver Latin.

206. That is, they wear the costume of members of religious orders such as the Dominicans or Franciscans.

207. The rhythm is iambic dimeters, a common meter in early Christian hymns.

208. The first line is taken from the Vulgate of the first chapter of the Gospel of St. Luke and accommodated to the meter, which is iambic

dimeter, a common form in early Christian hymns, in which classical norms in quantity or elision are not strictly observed.

209. According to Luke 2:22–35, Mary and Joseph brought the infant Jesus to the temple in Jerusalem to offer a sacrifice, where they encountered Simeon, who had been told by the Holy Spirit that he would not see death until he had seen the Lord's Christ. He took Jesus in his arms and spoke a prayer (the *Nunc dimittis*) and a prophecy of the crucifixion.

210. A Roman official of the third century CE, perhaps of eastern origin, who wrote a *History of the Empire after Marcus* in Greek, which Poliziano translated into Latin in 1487.

211. Lorenzo de' Medici commissioned a bust of the famous Florentine artist Giotto (1266–1337) with this epitaph in the cathedral of Santa Maria del Fiore, which was still sometimes known as Santa Reparata, after the church that had stood on that site previously.

212. The campanile of the cathedral, designed by Giotto.

213. Heinrich Isaac (1450–1517), a Flemish composer who was in the service of the Medici at the time of Lorenzo's death, which is commemorated in this ode, the predominant rhythm of which is a combination of glyconic and dochmiac, apparently an attempt to evoke the mood of a Greek tragic ode. But Poliziano's treatment of these meters is quite free; see Paoli, "La trenodia di Poliziano."

214. The first three lines are adapted from the Vulgate version of Jeremiah 9:1, "O that my head were waters, and my eyes a fountain of tears."

215. The "laurel" is Lorenzo de' Medici.

216. In the manuscripts the poem is followed by a performance note: "Who will give water for my *etc. And it is repeated up to the verse* O dolor, dolor! *etc.*"

217. See note 157 above. In a letter (*Letters* 7.14) to Antonio Zeno, Poliziano relates that he composed this translation while still quite young (*paene puer adhuc*).

218. Francesco Gonzaga (1444–83), who became a cardinal in 1461, bishop of Mantua in 1466. This ode in Sapphic stanzas was inserted into

Poliziano's *Orfeo* after line 140 for a performance in which Baccio Ugolini played the role of Orpheus, and they appear in this position in early editions of the *Orfeo*.

219. A reference to the red cap of a cardinal and the papal miter, an office predicted for Gonzaga by Poliziano.

220. Thalia, the Muse of comedy, representing here all the Muses.

221. A river on the west coast of Asia Minor (mod. Gediz Çayi), of which the gold-bearing Pactolus is a tributary.

222. Aphrodite, to whom the island of Cythera was sacred.

223. The dragon that guarded the Golden Fleece in Aea.

224. The river Mincio runs through Mantua, Vergil's home. The reference to Vergil's patron Maecenas points to Mantua's other great denizen, Cardinal Gonzaga, also a patron of poets.

225. According to most versions of the myth, the sisters of Phaethon were transformed into poplars on the banks of the Po, where they mourned their brother, but in Vergil's *Eclogues* (6.62–63) they became alders. The river itself, where Phaethon fell to his death, became a constellation.

226. According to Vergil, *Aen*eid 10.198, Mantua was founded by Ocnus, a son of the river-god Tiber and a prophetess, Manto, whose name he gave to the city.

THE BOOK OF GREEK EPIGRAMS

1. Zanobi Acciaiuoli (1461–1519), who had been a student of Poliziano, was attracted by the preaching of Savonarola and entered the Dominican order in the convent of San Marco one week after the date of this preface. See *DBI* 1 (1960), s.v.

2. Acciaiuoli's praise of Poliziano's Greek compositions is not misplaced. They compare very creditably with the work of earlier contemporaries such as Filelfo, but the epigrams, especially those from his youth, also exhibit a number of defects in language, style, and meter, which are cataloged in the introduction to Pontani's edition (2002): cv–cxxxviii.

3. The point of the epigram turns on Poliziano's apparent misunderstanding that the imperative of the Greek verb χαίρειν could be used interchangeably as a form of both greeting and malediction, when the latter usage in fact is only found in a different construction.

4. Poliziano's *Epigr. Lat.* 19 is reprinted here and translated into Greek. We cannot know if he intended it also to appear in his eventual publication of Latin epigrams.

5. The humanist Carlo Valgulio da Brescia (ca. 1450–1517), translator of Aelius Aristides, Plutarch, and Dio Chrysostom among others, corresponded with Poliziano from Arezzo in 1475. It is possible that he had addressed Greek verses earlier to Poliziano, to which this epigram may be a response.

6. From the cave on Parnassus.

7. A city in the Peloponnese, called "breeder of horses" by Homer.

8. The sense of the final couplet is obscure, but the "burden" is probably a reference to Poliziano's translation of Homer.

9. *Epigr. Lat.* 18.

10. The humanist Buoninsegni (1453–post 1512) was a friend of Poliziano and Ficino, author of epigrams in Greek, and a translator of Plutarch.

11. The cypress.

12. The olive, sacred to Athena, the goddess of wisdom, is here symbolically linked to the laurel, sacred to Apollo, the god of poetry.

13. Poliziano had seen several references in Latin poets to the ancient practice of marking a propitious day on the calendar with a white pebble.

14. Gioviano Crasso, the addressee of *Epigr. Lat.* 52. Poliziano is responding to a Latin epigram addressed to him by Crasso, preserved in Florence, Biblioteca Medicea Laurenziana, Plut. 90 sup. 37, f. 124v (reproduced here from Pontani's edition [2000], 49, with modernized spelling):

> *Ad Angelum, Hetrusci generis decus ac delitias, Jovianus Crassus.*
> Qui potes extemplo sublimis edere versus,
>   Ingenii partem da mihi, quaeso, tui,

Quod tibi felicis gravido iam matris in alvo
  Regnator superum Iuppiter ipse dedit.
Hoc superare vales ardentia sidera, magnos
  Aetheris hoc summi laetus adire deos.
Te genitus pulchra velox Atlantide Maia
  Nomen ab officio iussit habere suo,
Interpres Latiae fidus Graiaeque Camenae,
  Sospite quo magnus noster Homerus erit.

You who can produce such sublime poetry off the top of your head, please give me a bit of your genius, which Jupiter himself, the ruler of the gods, had already given to you while you were in your fortunate mother's pregnant womb. With it you are able to surpass the blazing stars, with it you can joyfully approach the great gods of heaven's summit. The swift son of lovely Maia, Atlas' daughter [sc. Mercury, messenger of the gods], gave orders that you take your name from his job [a play on Greek ἄγγελλος (messenger) and Poliziano's name], our trustworthy interpreter of the Greek and Latin Muse, whose well-being assures us of Homer's greatness.

15. Νυκτέλιος (nightly) was an epithet of Dionysus.

16. Sc. of Orpheus.

17. Ἐριούνιος was an epithet of uncertain meaning for Hermes, the messenger god. Poliziano is playing on the association of his name "Angelo" with Greek ἄγγελος for "messenger."

18. That is, the Muses.

19. John Argyropoulos (ca. 1415–87), a Byzantine scholar who first came to Italy in 1438 for the council held at Ferrara and Florence, then settled in Padua in 1441. He taught Greek at the Studio in Florence from 1456 to 1471, before relocating to Rome. He returned to Florence in 1477, where he taught again, before finally returning to Rome in 1481, where he spent the final years of his life. In Florence he was chiefly known as an exponent of Aristotelian philosophy, and he published a popular translation of the *Nicomachean Ethics*, among other translations of Aristotle.

20. This epigram is the earliest attempt at composition in the Doric dialect in Renaissance Italy.

21. The blind seer who foretells the future of the Argonauts' expedition on the condition that Calais and Zetes, the sons of Boreas, free him from the Harpies, winged female monsters who were stealing his food.

22. Goddess of youth, given to Heracles as his wife after his death and deification.

23. The addressee of *Epigr. Lat.* 81 and 82.

24. Greek for Italy, from the name of the inhabitants that early colonists encountered in southern Italy.

25. Theodore died in 1475 or 1476 in Calabria, in the part of Italy known as "Greater Greece."

26. Referring to the still recent fall of Constantinople in 1453.

27. The Byzantine scholar Demetrius Chalcondyles (1423–1511) arrived in Italy in 1449 and taught Greek in Perugia and Padua before becoming a professor in the Florentine Studio (1475–91). He was responsible for the first editions of Homer, Isocrates, and the Suda. In his last years he taught in Milan, where he died.

28. This epigram resembles *Epigr. Lat.* 91 and 110, both addressed to an unnamed Greek poet, but if their target is the same person, it does not help with the identification of this otherwise unknown Cornelius.

29. Sc. Demetrius Chalcondyles; see note 27.

30. Paul II, who was pope from 1464 to 1471, and his successor, Sixtus IV.

31. The celebrated Florentine polymath Paolo dal Pozzo Toscanelli (1397–1482), who collaborated with Brunelleschi on the construction of the dome of Santa Maria del Fiore. He was best known as an astronomer and geographer, whose project of crossing the Atlantic to reach India was conceived in 1441 and later inspired Columbus.

32. Aphrodite, so called because of her association with the island of Cyprus.

33. Poliziano probably met the humanist Giampietro Arrivabene (1440–1504) during his visit to Mantua in 1480.

34. This legend was known to Poliziano from a number of ancient sources, including Pliny the Elder, Aelian, and Olympiodorus. Mopsopia was an ancient name for Attica, which was famous for its honey.

35. A Greek lyric poet of the early sixth century BCE. Poliziano alludes to a description of Stesichorus at *Anth. Pal.* 2.128–30.

36. Presumably identical with the subject of *Epigr. Lat.* 97 before it was bowdlerized, and *Add.* 5 and 6.

37. Giovanni Ciampolini (1446–ca. 1505), a merchant and collector of Roman antiquities, which were kept in his house at 37 via de' Balestrari.

38. The sense of the Latin original is obscure, Poliziano's translation even more so.

39. Alessandra Scala (1475–1506) was a love interest of Poliziano's last years, celebrated for her beauty and learning. His rival for her affections was Janus Lascaris, who also wrote epigrams in her honor, but ultimately she married the poet Michael Marullus Tarchaniota, another Greek exile, sometime after Poliziano's death.

40. A production of the play in the original Greek at her father's villa in 1493, in which she gave a riveting performance in the lead role at the age of eighteen.

41. Poliziano includes an epigram penned by Alessandra in response to his.

42. Repeats verbatim an ancient Greek proverb.

43. Greek ζόφος (darkness) was a poeticism for "the West," but Alessandra shows her learning by following Strabo's interpretation (10.2.12) of the word as "north."

44. There is little to suggest that Poliziano ever mastered Hebrew beyond the passing acquaintance demonstrated in *Miscellanea* 1.14 and 83.

45. That is, they compete over Poliziano as did Virtue and Vice over Heracles in the anecdote recounted by Xenophon (*Memorabilia* 2.1.21–33).

46. An Egyptian king of the eighth century BCE, known to Alessandra, from the Greek historian Diodorus Siculus, as a great lawgiver.

47. Two proverbial expressions drawn from rather obscure Greek texts, in the first of which Alessandra ironically likens herself to a fly in comparison to the great Poliziano, while in the second she suggests that Poliziano's judgment of her is as clouded as those who would compare Athena's gray eyes to a kitten's.

48. That is, Santa Maria del Fiore, the cathedral of Florence, often called by the name of the church that had earlier stood on its site.

49. Poliziano knew this anecdote about Simonides, the Greek lyric poet of the late sixth to early fifth century BCE, from several sources, including the *Suda* and Plutarch. Just how Poliziano understood this anecdote is not made clear by the final line, which is apparently addressed to a mendicant he encountered at the entrance.

50. A cothurnus was a boot that could fit on either foot. The anecdote is recounted by Xenophon (*Hellenica* 2.3.30), referring to Theramenes, who was put to death by Critias, one of the so-called Thirty Tyrants at Athens, in 403 BCE.

51. The plural in the title probably refers to the following three epigrams as well.

52. Perhaps identical with the subject of the next epigram, or a self-address of the poet; but the name Angelo is very common.

53. The proverb is biblical: Proverbs 27:17, "iron sharpens iron."

54. The Spartan mother who kills her cowardly son was a popular topic in Greek epigram. Poliziano's model is an anonymous epigram from the *Planudean Anthology* (1.5.1 = *Anth. Pal.* 9.61), which was followed by two further epigrams on the same theme by Palladas (*Anth. Pal.* 9.397) and Julianus (*Anth. Pal.* 9.447).

55. Poliziano draws upon four epigrams from the *Planudean Anthology* (1.4.1–4 = *Anth. Pal.* 9.11–13b).

56. A variation on the first epigram in the *Planudean Anthology* (*Anth. Pal.* 9.357), where it is attributed to Archias.

57. The phrasing imitates a verse of Parthenius, cited by Aulus Gellius (13.27.1) and Macrobius (5.17.18) as the model of Vergil, *Georgics* 1.437. Ino, driven mad, jumped with Melicertes into the sea. She became the sea nymph Leucothea, he the marine divinity Palaemon. When his body was found near Corinth, the Isthmian Games were instituted in his honor.

58. Son of Lycurgus, the king of Nemea, who was killed by a snake and in whose honor the Nemean Games were instituted.

59. It is not clear where Poliziano found the text of this Latin epigram (*Anthologia Latina* 1.709, ed. A. Riese [Leipzig, 1869], 1:159–60), nor on what basis it is attributed to Germanicus in *Ald.* In a letter to Urceo, written a few months before his death (*Epist.* 5.7), he thought it by Augustus. In the same letter Poliziano characterizes his version as an imitation of two Greek epigrams in the *Planudean Anthology* (1.23.1 = *Anth. Pal.* 9.56, and 3.22.33 = *Anth. Pal.* 7.542).

60. This is the second distich of *Anth. Plan.* 1.4.5 (= *Anth. Pal.* 9.137), where it is presented as the emperor Hadrian's reply to the protests of a starving grammarian: "Half of me is dead, and hunger tests the other half. Sire, save a musical half-tone of me."

61. That is, the sun, from the Greek "the shining one."

62. A version of Ausonius, *Epigrammata* 25 Green, where the heading identifies it as a translation from Greek, but the original epigram does not survive. The anecdote was known to Poliziano (and Ausonius) from Plutarch, *Moralia* 241F, where the mother's words almost scan as a pentameter.

63. An allusion to the spear of Achilles, which neither Patroclus nor any of the other Greeks could lift, and the sight of which Hector could not bear (*Iliad* 22.131–37).

64. Guarino Favorino Camerte (ca. 1445–1537), Poliziano's student and tutor to Giovanni de' Medici, the future pope Leo X. This epigram was included in a letter written by Poliziano in 1493/4 to serve as a preface to the *Thesaurus Cornucopiae et Horti Adonidis* by Guarino and Carlo Antinori, which was later published by Aldus in 1496.

65. That is, Greece, an inspiration for Poliziano and his peers, whose cultural heritage was now being fostered by them.

66. Giovanni Pico della Mirandola (1463–94), brilliant philosopher and close friend of Poliziano. The epigram was sent to Pico with *Letter* 12.7, which concludes with the following notice: "I am also sending you this Greek epigram, which I recently babbled out because I was angry at your astrologers who are detaining you in the country while you quarrel with them longer than even I would wish." The work he refers to is the *Disputationes adversus astrologiam divinatricem*, which was published posthumously in Bologna in 1496.

67. A parody of a poem by Lascaris (*Epigrammata* 11) that accompanied a gift of a comb to Alessandra. Poliziano's epigram puns on the obscene sense of κτείς (comb) for a woman's pubes.

68. A variation on an epigram by Julian the Apostate (*Anth. Pal.* 9.365). Line 3 possibly refers to the great organist of Santa Maria del Fiore, Antonio Squarcialupi, a protégé of Lorenzo de' Medici.

69. Guidubaldo I da Montefeltro (1472–1508), the Duke of Urbino, who was about twenty-one years old when Poliziano composed this tribute.

70. In a letter to Pico (*Letters*, ed. Butler, 1.7), dating probably from 1493/4, Poliziano writes that he has heard that Pico has burned the amatory poetry that he had earlier composed under the title of *Amores* ("Loves" or "Cupids"). He includes this epigram in the letter as a playful commemoration of the event.

71. A variation on a theme found in five epigrams in the *Planudean Anthology* (4.12.26–30 = *Anth. Pal.* 16.178–82) on the famous painting, by the ancient Greek painter Apelles, of Aphrodite emerging from the sea. It was originally placed in the temple to Asclepius on Cos, but later brought to Rome by Augustus, who displayed it in the Temple of Julius Caesar.

72. A variation on a theme that Poliziano found in six epigrams in the *Planudean Anthology* (14.12.19, 21–25, and 104 = *Anth. Pal.* 16.171, 173–77, and 9.321).

73. Poliziano thought that this epigram on a hermaphrodite, which had commonly been ascribed to Antonio Beccadelli (1394–1471), was by the

obscure fourteenth-century Venetian poet Pulce da Custoza. It has since been securely attributed to Hildebert of Lavardin (ca. 1055–1133).

74. This epigram was included with a letter (12.8), written in 1493 to Bartolomeo Scala (1430–97), the chancellor of the Republic of Florence, with whom Poliziano had crossed swords over the grammatical gender of the Latin noun *culex* (mosquito). Poliziano's Greek epigram responds to one in Latin by Scala inspired by *Anth. Pal.* 5.151.

TO BARTOLOMEO FONZIO

1. Also known as Bartolomeo Della Fonte (1446–1513), one of the leading humanists in Florence during the second half of the fifteenth century. Like Poliziano, his early life was led under straitened financial circumstances, which eventually drove him to give up his studies in Florence and seek patronage in the court of Borso d'Este at Ferrara in 1469. By 1473, when Poliziano composed this elegy, he had returned to Florence; see note 9 on *Epigr. Lat.* 5.

2. One of the most successful condottieri of his era, Federico da Montefeltro (1422–82) was lord of Urbino from 1444 and ruled as duke from 1474 until his death. In 1472, the year before the composition of this poem, he led Florentine troops in the capture of Volterra (see ll. 31–32, below). He was also a patron of artists such as Piero della Francesca and scholars such as Cristoforo Landino.

3. The reference is to Federico's skill in siege warfare, utilizing heavy artillery and tunneling.

4. *Gradivus* is an epithet of Mars that remains unexplained. The god was associated with the Getae and the Bistonians, both warlike Thracian tribes.

5. Perhaps a reference to the dance of the three Graces, as depicted, for example, by Botticelli in his *Primavera*.

6. Ercole d' Este (above, note 150 on *Epigr. Lat.* 96), Duke of Ferrara, situated near the river Po (where myth locates the fall of Phaethon), Modena, and Reggio.

7. Ferrante of Aragon, king of Naples from 1458 to 1494, whose territory is identified by references to the Galaesus, a river near Taranto that was once a colony founded by Spartans (called "Oebalian," after a mythical king), and Parthenope, an ancient name for Naples derived from one of the Sirens.

8. In December 1472 Lorenzo ordered the transfer of the Studio (or University) of Florence to Pisa, which took place the following November. Law and medicine were henceforth taught in Pisa, while instruction in the humanities remained in Florence. Humanists friendly to the Medici celebrated these changes as a refoundation of the university.

9. Having just turned twenty, Lorenzo was victorious in a joust held on February 7, 1469. Nothing is known of the poem by Ugolino Verino (1438–1516) mentioned by Poliziano; Luigi Pulci's celebratory poem *La giostra* does survive; a joust won by Lorenzo's brother Giuliano in 1475 was celebrated by the poet Naldo Naldi in his *De ludicro hastatorum equitum certamine*.

10. In 1466 a conspiracy against Piero de' Medici, led by Luca Pitti, Dietisalvi Neroni, and Agnolo Acciaiuoli, was said to have been foiled by decisive action taken by the young Lorenzo. Dietisalvi, along with other conspirators, was condemned to twenty years in exile.

11. Cristoforo Landino (1424–98) reedited his earlier three-book collection of Latin verse called *Xandra* in 1458–59 and rededicated it to Piero de' Medici. It is published in this I Tatti Renaissance Library, trans. Mary P. Chatfield (Cambridge, MA, 2008). His philosophical treatise *De anima* was first dedicated to Borso d'Este, the Duke of Ferrara, and after his death in 1471 to his successor, Ercole I d'Este.

12. After the lost poem on Lorenzo's victory in the joust of 1469 (see note 9) and other poems dedicated to members of the Medici family, Ugolino turned to the composition of an epic poem on Charlemagne; the *Carlias* was begun about 1465 and finished by 1480. See the edition by Nikolaus Thurn (Munich, 1995), 16. Verino's *Fiametta* and *Paradisus* are published in this I Tatti Renaissance Library, ed. Allan M. Wilson (Cambridge, MA, 2016); the latter work presents Cosimo de' Medici as quite literally on the side of the angels.

13. Poliziano depicts Fonzio as free to turn his talents to topics not tied to the Medici and here refers to a lost or never completed work on the labors of Hercules, which presumably would have been dedicated to Ercole I d'Este. The catalog of Hercules' labors include the Nemean (from Cleonae, a city in the Argolid near Nemea) lion; Hercules, a descendant of Alceus, taking the burden of the sky from Atlas; the capture of the bulls of the monster Geryon on Erythea, a legendary island in the far west; the capture of the wild boar of Erymanthus; the capture of the enormous hind of Ceryneia; and the war against the Amazons near the river Thermodon of Pontus.

14. His translation of the *Iliad*, which he discontinued after reaching Book 5 in 1475.

15. This catalog of mythical tortures includes Phalaris, the tyrant of Syracuse, founded by colonists from Corinth (also called Ephyra), who was roasted alive in the bronze bull he had used to torture others; Tantalus, condemned to punishment in the afterlife, where his thirst and hunger could never be satisfied, although water and fruit were always close at hand; Ixion, king of the Lapiths by the river Atrax in Thessaly, who was tied to a wheel of serpents; Tityus, whose liver was perpetually reproduced as vultures fed on it; and Cerberus, the three-headed guard dog of the Underworld.

16. Pythagoras.

17. Propertius.

18. The constellations of Orion, the Kids (here singular for metrical convenience), and Aquarius (identified with Ganymede, the Trojan boy abducted by Zeus) are all associated with stormy weather. And in Solinus, a third-century CE grammarian and author of *On the Wonders of the World*, Poliziano found a reference to the "star of Helen" (identified as "the bride from Therapnae," a city near Sparta), which was "most dangerous to sailors."

19. Homer, who, according to some traditions, was born in Smyrna, a city in the region of Asia Minor known as Maeonia.

20. Franco (1448–94), a priest and a poet of light verse, became affiliated

with the Medici family in the early 1470s and remained so for the remainder of his life.

21. Marsilio Ficino (above, note 31 on *Epigr. Lat.* 17) is the subject of the following seventeen couplets, which refer to his expertise in natural philosophy (157–70); medicine (171–72); Neoplatonic philosophy, with polemics against Epicurus and Lucretius (173–80); and music (181–88). On Ficino's hostility to Epicureanism, see James Hankins, "Ficino's Critique of Lucretius," in *The Rebirth of Platonic Theology*, ed. James Hankins and Fabrizio Meroi (Florence, 2013), 137–54.

22. Homer refers to a chain of gold mentioned at *Iliad* 8.19–20, by which the other gods might try to pull Zeus down. The Neoplatonists read this as an allegorical reference to metaphysical hierarchy in Nature.

23. In lines 175 to 180, Poliziano gives a remarkably accurate, compressed account of Ficino's metaphysical theory of the five substances, for which see Michael J. B. Allen, "Ficino's Theory of the Five Substances and the Neoplatonists' *Parmenides*," *Journal of Medieval and Renaissance Studies* 12 (1982): 19–44.

24. Like Apollo's son Orpheus, who dwelt in Thrace, a land also inhabited by a people called the Odrysae, Ficino's music was said to have been able to charm beasts, such as the lions of Marmarica, a region of North Africa, or the tigers on Mt. Amano in Asia Minor, or inanimate stones of the Caucasus or Sicily. Ficino was well known for his performances of Orphic hymns and other Platonic texts to the lyre; see James Hankins, "Humanism and Music in Italy," in *The Cambridge History of Fifteenth Century Music* (Cambridge, 2015), 231–62, esp. 236–39 and 254–56.

25. Andronicus Callistus, itinerant Greek scholar, born in Constantinople early in the fifteenth century, was a kinsman of Theodore Gaza, who had taught or lectured in Padua, Bologna, and Rome before coming to Florence in 1471 to succeed John Argyropoulos in the Florentine Studio. There he inspired Poliziano with his lectures on Homer and Demosthenes (cf. *Font.* 193–98) and perhaps introduced him to the epigrams in the Greek Anthology. He was known as one of the first Greeks to teach Aristotle in Italy. In 1475 he moved to Milan and thence to London, where he died in poverty before 1487.

26. Ugolino Verino (above, notes 9 and 12); Carlo Marsuppini (1449–ca. 1500), son of the more famous Carlo Marsuppini, who was chancellor of Florence from 1444 to 1453 (above, note 10 on *Epigr. Lat.*); and Giovanni Battista Buoninsegni (above, note 10 on *Epigr. Gr.* 5) were all also students of Andronicus.

27. Vespasiano da Bisticci (1421–98), humanist and book dealer.

28. In myth, Asclepius of Epidaurus brought back to life Androgeos, the son of Minos, and became the god of medicine.

29. Venus, the Evening Star, associated with Cythera, an island sacred to the goddess.

30. The Hyantes inhabited Boeotia in Greece, a region sacred to the Muses.

31. Niccolò Michelozzi (1444–1526), a student of Ficino and friend of Poliziano, who became Lorenzo's personal secretary in 1471. No poetry survives under his name.

32. There is surprising imprecision in Poliziano's comparison of the epigrams of Alessandro Braccesi (note 27 on *Add.* 25) with the *Amazonis* (not *Amazonia*), an epic poem by epigrammatist Domitius Marsus, mentioned by Martial (*Epigrammata* 4.29.6).

33. Domitius Marsus, Valerius Catullus, the emperor Augustus, Lentulus Gaetulicus, and Albinovanus Pedo are all mentioned by Martial as predecessors in the genre of epigram, but, with the exception of Catullus, their works have been lost. Martial was known in the Middle Ages by the nickname *Cocus* (Cook).

34. Poliziano refers to the sun first as Phaethon, an ancient epithet of the sun itself, not here his son, and then as "the Cynthian," an epithet of Apollo derived from Mt. Cynthus on the island of Delos.

A SILVA ON SCABIES

1. A mythical, fire-breathing monster—part lion, part dragon, part goat—slain by Bellerophon.

2. A burning river in the Underworld.

3. In myth, Machaon, the son of Asclepius, was a physician in the Greek army at Troy; Chiron, the centaur and tutor of Achilles, was mentor to Asclepius; Melampus, the son of Amython, was a physician and seer; the celebrated physician Asclepius, son of Apollo, was venerated as a serpent at Epidaurus; Apollo, also identified as a healer, delivered prophecies at Delphi not far from the Corycian cave on Mt. Parnassus; and Paeon was the name of the healing god in Homer, which became an epithet of Apollo.

4. Ganymede, the Trojan boy from the vicinity of the river Sagaris in Phrygia, and Hebe, the daughter of Jupiter and Juno, served at the gods' table on Olympus.

5. That is, he cannot detect the sweetness of honey, whether from Attica (for which Mopsopia was an old name) or Mt. Hybla in Sicily; and sugar water from Messina (for which Zancle was an ancient name) tastes like the bitter herbs habrotonum and absinthe.

6. Sirius, the Dog Star, who belonged to Icarius before being transformed.

7. The Sabaeans (*Sabaeum* is a genitive) were a people of southwest Arabia, associated by Vergil (*Georgics* 1.57) with incense.

8. Female devotees of Dionysus, known as *Thyies*, were a byword for madness. She is here depicted in Thrace, a region associated with Bacchic cult, identified by Mt. Ismarus, Mt. Othrys, Mt. Pangaeus, and the river Strymon.

9. The pre-Socratic philosopher Democritus (460–370 BCE), referred to as the "laughing philosopher," was known to Poliziano as the author of the atomic theory of the universe from his readings in Lucretius, who attributed to him the theories of the origin of night and day outlined in the *De rerum natura* at 5.650–70.

10. This catalog of north African serpents derives from Lucan's description of the dangers of the Libyan desert in Book 9 of the *Pharsalia*.

11. The names in this catalog of combatants in the legion of vermin represent a bravura display of Poliziano's command of Greek and his famil-

iarity with relatively obscure texts such as the pseudo-Homeric *Battle of Frogs and Mice*, which is his model here.

12. Rhoeteum was a city and promontory in the Troas, thus a reference to Poliziano's translation of Homer's *Iliad*.

13. An allusion to Poliziano's *Stanze per la Giostra*, a poem in the vernacular about the victory of Giuliano de' Medici, grandson of Cosimo, in a joust held in the Piazza Santa Croce in 1475.

14. That is, Cerberus, the three-headed dog that guards the entrance to the Underworld.

15. Another reference to the interruption of Poliziano's translation of the *Iliad* into Latin.

16. The Euripus, the channel between the Greek island of Euboea and the mainland, the seas around the island of Carpathus between Crete and Rhodes, and the Aegean Sea were all bywords in ancient poetry for stormy waters.

17. Probably a reference to the hazardous relations between Florence and Rome in the aftermath of the Pazzi conspiracy.

18. That is, from south (Libya) to north (the Riphaean mountains in Scythia), and from Morocco in the west, where Tethys, the goddess of the sea, receives the Titan sun god, to the east, where the dawn-goddess Aurora, daughter of Pallas Athena, rises.

19. Poliziano figuratively calls Lorenzo his father and avers that the mere sight of him would give Poliziano the strength to endure the torments of celebrated victims in Greek myth, including Prometheus, the son of Iapetus; Tantalus; Sisyphus, who lived in Corinth, once called Ephyra; Alcyoneus, in some accounts a giant imprisoned beneath Vesuvius; and the Giants who were defeated by Zeus on the Phlegraean Fields.

20. Since December 1472 the Studio of Florence was situated in Pisa, and thus figuratively home to the Muses, which in myth was among the Boeotians, once known as the Hyantes. Lorenzo would attend the opening of each academic year in Pisa, which, as reported by Strabo (5.2.5) was founded by a tribe called the Pisatae, who had accompanied Nestor,

the son of Neleus, to Troy. In 1472 Volterra capitulated to Lorenzo, who constructed a new citadel on the site.

21. Poliziano imagines Lorenzo at the Medici villa of Cafaggiolo in Mugello, north of Florence, where the rivers Sieve and Carza flow.

22. Piero de' Medici, son of Lorenzo, whom Poliziano tutored from 1475 to 1479.

ADDITIONAL POEMS

1. Opinions vary on the identification of the lions. Recent critics see a reference to Coluccio Salutati's *De laboribus Herculis* 3.8, with the lions representing two types of anger, which would seem to fit the circumstances of 1478 to 1480, when Poliziano's relations with Lorenzo were troubled, unless the epigram is merely ironic and playful.

2. On Lorenzo di Pierfrancesco de' Medici, see note 167 on *Epigr. Lat.* 107. In the latter part of the decade of the 1480s, he championed both Marullus and Bartolomeo Scala, which could not have pleased Poliziano.

3. Michael Marullus Tarchaniota, born in Constantinople in 1453, shortly before the fall of the city to the Ottoman Turks. Soldier, poet, and adventurer, he married Alessandra Scala in 1496, only to drown while crossing a river in 1500. He had arrived in Florence by 1489, where he was protected by the patronage of Lorenzo di Pierfrancesco, which is probably the approximate date of this and the following epigram, because very soon afterward he earned the lasting ire of Poliziano for his criticisms of the *Miscellanea*, which were published in the same year. Marullus' *Poems*, published in this I Tatti Renaissance Library, ed. Charles Fantazzi (2012), contain a series of venomous epigrams against "Ecnomus," his name for Poliziano.

4. The younger brother of Lorenzo, who at the age of twenty-four was assassinated in the cathedral of Florence on the morning of April 26, 1478, a victim of the failed Pazzi conspiracy.

5. See *Epigr. Gr.* 26.

6. A literary spoof, playing on the ancient interpretative tradition that the shepherd lovers Corydon and Alexis, who figure in Vergil's *Eclogue* 2, are masks for the poet and his male lover.

7. Poliziano's tribute was included in a volume of songs and poetry set to music by Antonio Squarcialupi (1416–80), also known as Antonio degli Organi. He was organist in the cathedral of Florence for over twenty years. After his death, Lorenzo had a bust erected in his honor in the cathedral.

8. Like the four following poems, an alternative version of the epitaph eventually chosen for Giotto's monument (*Epigr. Lat.* 130).

9. The famous painter of ancient Greece (above, note 71 on *Epigr. Gr.* 54) who was the only artist Alexander the Great allowed to paint his portrait.

10. Greek sculptor of the fourth century BCE.

11. Famous artist and craftsman of Greek myth.

12. An allusion perhaps to the famous epitaph of Ennius, known to Poliziano from Cicero's *Tusculan Disputations* 1.34.8.

13. Greek sculptor and architect of the fifth century BCE, who designed the statue of Athena for the Parthenon on the Acropolis of Athens.

14. The "navicella," a mosaic by Giotto, now heavily restored, originally located in the eastern porch of the old basilica of St. Peter.

15. Poliziano puns on two senses of *carpere*, "to criticize" and "to pluck," as in surreptitiously stealing amatory favors.

16. Cf. *Epigr. Gr.* 57.

17. Francesco Salviati (1443–78): see note 29 on *Epigr. Lat.* 16.

18. Andronicus Callistus: note 25 on *Font.* 193.

19. A reference to his lectures on Homer, to which Poliziano alludes also in *Font.* 195–96.

20. Andronicus' translation into Latin of Aristotle's treatise *On Generation and Corruption*, still unedited, was dedicated to Lorenzo. It is preserved in Florence, Biblioteca Medicea Laurenziana, Plut 58.33. The

preface has been edited by James Hankins in his *Humanism and Platonism in the Italian Renaissance* (Rome, 2004), 2:297–303.

21. The friend, who is addressed as Iohannes (l. 13) and described as a resident of San Gimignano (l. 29), has been identified as Giambattista Catalicio (ca. 1450–1515), who taught at San Gimignano from 1471 to 1476. But the identification has been rightly called into question, since he is referred to in lines 13 and 14 without irony as a *doctus senex*, though he was roughly contemporary with Poliziano.

22. The constellation Leo, identified with summer by ancient astronomers, since the sun passed through it during the summer solstice.

23. Apollo (note 11 on *Alb.* 60).

24. That is, Castor and Pollux, the sons of Tyndarus' wife, Leda, by Zeus, here representing the constellation Gemini. The sun begins its transit in Gemini in late May.

25. Calliope.

26. The Hippocrene, the spring on Mt. Helicon created by the hoof of the winged horse Pegasus, born from the severed neck of the Gorgon Medusa.

27. Alessandro Braccesi (1445–1503) was a poet and a civil servant, secretary of the Florentine Republic from 1483 to 1487. His *Epigrammatum libellus* (1477), dedicated to Lorenzo, contains two poems addressed to Poliziano as "Bassus."

28. The poets referred to here were all elegists: the Greek poets Mimnermus (seventh century BCE), Antimachus of Colophon (fourth century BCE), and Callimachus of Cyrene (third century BCE); and the first-century BCE Roman elegists, Propertius from Assisi in Umbria; Tibullus, who wrote of his love for Delia; Cornelius Gallus, who committed suicide; and Ovid, who ended his life in exile among the Getae.

29. That is, the Muses.

30. From a noble family of Pistoia, Baldinotti was born in 1450 and entered the orbit of Lorenzo de' Medici in Florence by 1473, when he presumably came under the influence of Poliziano. He wrote poetry on light

subjects in Italian and Latin. The unsuccessful conspiracy of his father and his brother against Lorenzo in 1485 compelled him to leave Florence and spend the rest of his life in Rimini, where he died in 1511.

31. Hyantes was an ancient name for the Boeotians, who inhabited the region of Helicon, hence supplying an epithet for the Muses.

32. Aeolus, descendant of Hippotes, was the ruler of the winds, whom Odysseus entertained for a month with stories of the Trojan War and the return of the Achaeans, as Homer relates (*Odyssey* 10.14–16); but Odysseus did not sing to him. Post-Homeric traditions situated the Cyclopes in Sicily, where Mt. Hybla is located, and the Sirens in the sea to the north, but they were not associated in myth. Poliziano, it would seem, is having fun.

33. Atlas was turned into a mountain, and the Ethiopian companions of Andromeda's suitor Phineas (here referred to as the people of Cepheus, their king) was turned to stone by Perseus, who carried the Medusa's head.

34. Zetes and Calais were the sons of Boreas, the North Wind; Hermes, the gods' winged messenger, killed Argus, who kept watch over Io; Perseus, the son of Danae, was conceived by Zeus in a shower of gold.

35. The Getae, together with the Bessi, Sarmatians, and Coralli, inhabited the region of Tomi, where Ovid had been banished.

36. A reference to Horace's *Epodes*, composed in the tradition of Greek iambics.

DUBIA

1. An epigram beneath a clock painted in the transept of Santa Maria Novella, attributed to Poliziano by Del Lungo, 163.

2. Commonly attributed to Poliziano, this palindrome couplet accompanies a painting of Cain and Abel in the cloisters of Santa Maria Novella. See Del Lungo, 163.

3. A motto used by Piero di Lorenzo de' Medici, to accompany an emblem showing interwoven green branches in the midst of flames. See Del

Lungo, 164. The second half of the hexameter is taken from Petronius, *Satyricon* 121.106.

4. Francesco d'Angelo (1446–88), also known as "il Cecca," engineer and military architect. He was killed during the Florentines' siege of the fortress at Piancaldoli. The rest of the epitaph as given by Vasari is: *Vixit annos XXXXI, menses IV, dies XIII. Obiit pro patria telo ictus. Piae sorores monimentum fecerunt MCCCCLXXXVIII* (He lived forty-one years, four months, and thirteen days. He died for his country, struck down by a spear. His devoted sisters constructed the monument in 1488.)

Concordances
to the Book of Epigrams

❧❧❧

a. Between this Edition and that of Isidoro Del Lungo (1867)

This edition	Del Lungo (1867)
1	2
2	3
3	11
4	12
5	1
6	*Elegiae* 9
7	4
8	105
9	*Elegiae* 6
10	5
11	6
12	7
13	9
14	10
15	55
16	8
17	20
18	106
19	107
20	43
21	23
22	17
23	40
24	92
25	34

This edition	Del Lungo (1867)
26	13
27	16
28	42
29	14
30	27
31	41
32	36
33	21
34	35
35	28
36	15
37	25
38	24
39	93
40	94
41	65
42	66.1–2
43	66.3–4
44	67
45	68
46	69
47	70
48	22
49	57
50	*Elegiae* 11
51	18
52	19
53	75
54	76
55	77
56	78
57	*Gr. Epigr.* 1
58	*Gr. Epigr.* 2
59	*Gr. Epigr.* 3

This edition	Del Lungo (1867)
60	33
61	Gr. Epigr. 13
62	Gr. Epigr. 4
63	Gr. Epigr. 5
64	44
65	45
66	46
67	47
68	48
69	49
70	50
71	51
72	Elegiae 5
73	Odae 7
74	95
75	96
76	Gr. Monost. 1
77	Gr. Monost. 2
78	Gr. Monost. 3
79	Gr. Monost. 4
80	108
81	71
82	72
83	109
84	37
85	38
86	58
87	52
88	Elegiae 10
89	26
90	59
91	54
92	39
93	80

This edition	Del Lungo (1867)
94	81
95	79
96	*Odae* 2
97	64
98	82
99	110
100	Ex Moscho 2
101	*Odae* 4
102	97
103	98
104	32
105	99
106	100
107	*Elegiae* 12
108	*Odae* 6
109	*Odae* 10
110	53
111	*Odae* 8
112	61
113	*Gr. Epigr.* 6
114	60
115	*Gr. Epigr.* 7
116	*Gr. Epigr.* 8
117	*Gr. Epigr.* 9
118	*Gr. Epigr.* 10
119	*Gr. Epigr.* 11
120	*Gr. Epigr.* 12
121	84
122	122 (101)
123	83
124	*Gr. Epigr.* 14
125	Praefatio in *Menaechmos*
126	*Odes* 9

This edition	Del Lungo (1867)
127	*Hymni* 1
128	*Hymni* 2
129	*Odae* 5
130	86
131	*Odae* 11
132	Ex Moscho 1
133	*Odae* 1

b. Between the Edition of Del Lungo (1867) and this Edition

Del Lungo (1867)	This edition
Epigrammata Latina	
Ad amicos et proceres	
1	5
2	1
3	2
4	7
5	10
6	11
7	12
8	16
9	13
10	14
11	3
12	4
13	26
14	29
15	36
16	27
17	22
18	51
19	52
20	17
21	33

Del Lungo (1867)	This edition
22	48
23	21
24	38
25	37
26	89
27	30
28	35
29	Add. 1
30	Add. 2
31	Add. 3
32	104
33	60
34	25
35	34
36	32
37	84
38	24
39	92
40	23
41	31
42	28
Invectiva	
43	20
44	64
45	65
46	66
47	67
48	68
49	69
50	70
51	71
52	87
53	110
54	91

Del Lungo (1867)	This edition
Amatoria	
55	15
56	Add. 4
57	49
58	86
59	90
60	114
61	112
62	Add. 5
63	Add. 6
64	97
Epitaphia	
65	41
66	42, 43
67	44
68	45
69	46
70	47
71	81
72	82
73	omitted[1]
74	omitted[2]
75	53
76	54
77	55
78	56
79	95
80	93
81	94
82	98
83	123
84	121
85	38
86	130

Del Lungo (1867)	This edition
87	Add. 10
88	Add. 11
89	Add. 12
90	Add. 13
91	Add. 14
92	24
Inscriptiones Variae	
93	39
94	40
95	74
96	75
97	102
98	103
99	105
100	106
101	122
102	Dubia 1
103	Dubia 2
104	Dubia 3
Miscellanea	
105	8
106	18
107	19
108	80
109	83
110	99
111	Add. 7
Elegiae	
1	24
2	25
3	26
4	27
5	72

Del Lungo (1867)	This edition
6	9
7	*Alb.*
8	See *Font.*, n. 1
9	6
10	88
11	50
12	107
13	Add. 27
Odae	
1	133
2	96
3	Add. 28
4	101
5	129
6	108
7	73
8	111
9	126
10	109
11	131
Hymni in divam Virginem	
1	127
2	128
Prologus in Plauti comoediam Menoechmos	
pp. 281–84	125
Silvae[3]	
Graecorum poetarum quae latine vertit	
Iliadis libri II–V	omitted
Ex Moscho.	
1	132
2	100
Ex Callimacho	
Hymni 5, In Palladis lavacra[4]	omitted

Del Lungo (1867)	This edition
Ex Sibyllinis	
De ludis saecularibus[5]	omitted
Epigrammata	
1	57
2	58
3	59
4	62
5	63
6	113
7	115
8	116
9	117
10	118
11	119
12	120
13	61
14	124
Monosticha	
1	76
2	77
3	78
4	79
Addenda	
Epigrammatis latinis	
54b	19
60b	Add. 15

NOTES

1. Now attributed to Manilio Rullo.

2. Ibid.

3. Published in *Silvae*, ed. Fantazzi, in this I Tatti Renaissance Library series (2004).

4. Published in Poliziano's *Miscellaneorum centuria prima*, cap. 80, but not included in the *Liber Epigrammatum*.

5. Ibid., cap. 58.

Bibliography

ॐ१ॐ

EDITIONS OF POLIZIANO'S WORKS

[Opera.] Venice: Aldus Manutius, July 1498. Edited by Alessandro Sarti. Available online via the Münchener DigitalisierungsZentrum's Digitale Bibliothek (Munich Staatsbibliothek) and via the Digital Vatican Library. The Vatican copy has notes by Scipione Forteguerri, known as Carteromachus.

Opera quae quidem extitere hactenus omnia. Basel: Episcopius, 1553. Available online via eRara (Universitätsbibliothek, Basel).

Prose volgari inedite e poesie latine e greche edite e inedite di Angelo Ambrogini Poliziano. Edited by Isidoro Del Lungo. Florence: G. Barbèra, 1867. Available online via HathiTrust.

Epigrammi greci. Edited by Anthos Ardizzoni. Florence: La Nuova Italia, 1951.

Sylva in scabiem. Edited by Alessandro Perosa. Rome: Edizione di Storia e Letteratura, 1954.

Della congiura dei Pazzi (Coniurationis commentarium). Edited by Alessandro Perosa. Padua: Antenore, 1958. Contains an edition of three epigrams against Francesco Salviati (*Add.* 20–22).

Opera omnia. Edited by Ida Maïer. 3 vols. Turin: Bottega d'Erasmo, 1970–1971. Photo-reprint of the 1553 edition as well as Del Lungo (1867) and additional materials.

Miscellaneorum centuria secunda. Edited by Vittore Branca and Manlio Pastore Stocchi. Florence: Alinari, 1972. Reprint, Florence: Olschki, 1978.

Sylva in Scabiem. Edited by Paolo Orvieto. Rome: Salerno, 1989.

Silvae. Edited by Francesco Bausi. Florence: Olschki, 1996.

Poesie volgari. Edited by Francesco Bausi. 2 vols. Manziana (Rome): Vecchiarelli, 1997.

Liber Epigrammatum graecorum. Edited by Filippomaria Pontani. Edizione Nazionale dei Testi Umanistici 5. Rome: Edizioni di Storia e Letteratura, 2002. With commentary and Italian translation.

Due poemetti Latini. Edited by Francesco Bausi. Rome: Salerno, 2003.

Silvae. Edited and translated by Charles Fantazzi. I Tatti Renaissance Library 14. Cambridge, MA: Harvard University Press, 2004.

Poesie. Edited by Francesco Bausi. Turin: UTET, 2006.

Letters. Volume 1: Books I–IV. Edited and translated by Shane Butler. I Tatti Renaissance Library 21. Cambridge, MA: Harvard University Press, 2006.

Coniurationis commentarium. Edited with an introduction and translation by Marta Celalti. Alessandria: Edizioni dell'Orso, 2015.

OTHER EDITIONS

Ianus Pannonius. *Opera quae reperiri potuerunt omnia*. Edited by Janus Sambucus. Vienna: Caspar Stainhofer, 1569. Reprint, Budapest, 1972.

Bartolomeo Fonzio. *Letters to Friends*. Edited by Alessandro Daneloni and translated by Martin Davies. I Tatti Renaissance Library 47. Cambridge, MA: Harvard University Press, 2011.

Michael Marullus. *Poems*. Translated by Charles Fantazzi. I Tatti Renaissance Library 54. Cambridge, MA: Harvard University Press, 2012.

Aldus Manutius. *Humanism and the Latin Classics*. Edited and translated by John N. Grant. I Tatti Renaissance Library 78. Cambridge, MA: Harvard University Press, 2017.

STUDIES

Bigi, Emilio. "Angelo Ambrogini." *Dizionario biografico degli italiani* 2 (1960): 691–702.

———. *La cultura del Poliziano e altri studi umanistici*. Pisa: Nistri-Lischi, 1967.

Branca, Vittore. *Poliziano e l'umanesimo della parola*. Turin: Einaudi, 1983.

Brown, Alison. *Bartolomeo Scala (1430–1497), Chancellor of Florence: The Humanist as Bureaucrat*. Princeton: Princeton University Press, 1979.

_____. *The Medici in Florence: The Exercise of Language and Power.* Florence: Olschki, 1992.

Cameron, Alan. *The Greek Anthology from Meleager to Planudes.* Oxford: Oxford University Press, 1993.

Celati, Marta. "La seconda redazione del *Coniurationis commentarium* di Angelo Poliziano e l'edizione romana di Johannes Bulle." *Humanistica* 9, n.s. 5 (2017): 283–92.

Del Lungo, Isidoro. *Florentia: Uomini e cose del Quattrocento.* Florence: G. Barbèra, 1897.

Godman, Peter. *From Poliziano to Machiavelli: Florentine Humanism in the High Renaissance.* Princeton: Princeton University Press, 1998.

Grafton, Anthony. *Joseph Scaliger: A Study in the History of Classical Scholarship. I: Textual Criticism and Exegesis.* Oxford: Clarendon Press, 1983. Chapters 1–3 discuss Poliziano and his legacy as a textual critic.

_____. "On the Scholarship of Politian and Its Context." *Journal of the Warburg and Courtauld Institutes* 45 (1977): 150–88.

Hutton, John. *The Greek Anthology in Italy to the Year 1800.* Ithaca: Cornell University Press, 1935.

Maïer, Ida. *Ange Politien. La formation d'un poète humaniste (1469–1480).* Geneva: Droz: 1966.

_____. *Les manuscrits d'Ange Politien: Catalogue descriptif.* Geneva: Droz, 1965.

Martelli, Mario. *Angelo Poliziano: Storia e metastoria.* Lecce: Conte, 1995.

Martines, Lauro. *April Blood: Florence and the Plot against the Medici.* Oxford: Oxford University Press, 2003.

Mioni, Elpidio. "L' *Anthologia Planudea* di Angelo Poliziano." In *Medioevo e Rinascimento Veneto con altri studi in onore di Lino Lazzarini*, 1:541–55. 2 vols. Padua: Antenore, 1979.

Orvieto, Paolo. "Angelo Poliziano." In *Storia della letteratura italiana, Volume III: Il Quattrocento*, edited by Enrico Malato, 457–515. Rome: Salerno Editrice, 1996.

_____. *Poliziano e l'ambiente mediceo.* Rome: Salerno, 2009.

Paoli, Ugo Enrico. "La trenodia di Poliziano." *Studi italiani di filologia classica* 16 (1939): 165–76.

Patetta, Federico. "Una raccolta manoscritta di versi e prose in morte d'Albiera degli Albizzi." *Atti della Reale Accademia delle Scienze di Torino* 53 (1917–1918): 290–94, 310–28.

Perosa, Alessandro. "Contributi e proposte per la pubblicazione delle opere latine del Poliziano." In *Il Poliziano e il suo tempo: Atti del IV Convegno internazionale di studi sul Rinascimento, Firenze, Palazzo Strozzi, 23–26 settembre 1954*, 89–100. Florence: Sansoni, 1957. Reprinted in Perosa, *Studi* (2000).

_____. "Febris: A Poetic Myth Created by Poliziano." *Journal of the Warburg and Courtauld Institutes* 9 (1946): 74–95. Reprinted in Perosa, *Studi* (2000).

_____. *Studi di filologia umanistica.* Edited by Paolo Viti. 3 vols. Rome: Edizioni di Storia e Letteratura, 2000. Volume 1 contains Perosa's studies on Poliziano.

_____. "Studi sulla tradizione delle poesie latine del Polizianio." In *Studi in onore di Ugo Enrico Paoli*, 539–62. Florence: Le Monnier, 1956. Reprinted in Perosa, *Studi* (2000).

Picotti, Giovanni Battista. "Tra il poeta ed il lauro. Pagina della vita di Agnolo Poliziano." *Giornale storico della letteratura italiana* 65 (1915): 263–303, and 66 (1915): 52–104. Reprinted in his *Ricerche umanistiche*, 3–86. Florence: Nuova Italia, 1955.

Polizzotto, Lorenzo. *The Elect Nation: The Savonarolan Movement in Florence, 1494–1545.* Oxford: Oxford University Press, 1994.

Rubinstein, Alice Levine. "Imitation and Style in Angelo Poliziano's *Iliad* Translation." *Renaissance Quarterly* 36.1 (1983): 48–70.

Wilson, Nigel Guy. *From Byzantium to Italy: Greek Studies in the Italian Renaissance.* 1st ed. Baltimore: Johns Hopkins Univeristy Press, 1992. 2nd ed. London: Bloomsbury, 2017.

Index of First Lines

❧❧❧

A = Elegy for Albiera degli Albizzi, E = Book of Epigrams, G = Book of Greek Epigrams, F = To Bartolomeo Fonzio, S = Silva on Scabies, Add = Additional Poems, Dub = Dubia

LATIN POEMS

GREEK POEMS

General Index

ৡ৸৻৶

416

Publication of this volume has been made possible by

The Myron and Sheila Gilmore Publication Fund at I Tatti
The Robert Lehman Endowment Fund
The Jean-François Malle Scholarly Programs and Publications Fund
The Andrew W. Mellon Scholarly Publications Fund
The Craig and Barbara Smyth Fund
for Scholarly Programs and Publications
The Lila Wallace–Reader's Digest Endowment Fund
The Malcolm Wiener Fund for Scholarly Programs and Publications